**AMY KALTON**

# ATKINS DIET PLAN 2021:

A Comprehensive and Exhaustive Cookbook to Teach Beginners the Secrets of Healthy Weight Loss the Atkins Way (Including 500 Fast and Easy Recipes)

# © Copyright 2020 - All rights reserved.

The content contained within this book may not be reproduced, duplicated or transmitted without direct written permission from the author or the publisher.

Under no circumstances will any blame or legal responsibility be held against the publisher, or author, for any damages, reparation, or monetary loss due to the information contained within this book. Either directly or indirectly.

## Legal Notice:

This book is copyright protected. This book is only for personal use. You cannot amend, distribute, sell, use, quote or paraphrase any part, or the content within this book, without the consent of the author or publisher.

## Disclaimer Notice:

Please note the information contained within this document is for educational and entertainment purposes only. All effort has been executed to present accurate, up to date, and reliable, complete information. No warranties of any kind are declared or implied. Readers acknowledge that the author is not engaging in the rendering of legal, financial, medical or professional advice. The content within this book has been derived from various sources. Please consult a licensed professional before attempting any techniques outlined in this book.

By reading this document, the reader agrees that under no circumstances is the author responsible for any losses, direct or indirect, which are incurred as a result of the use of information contained within this document, including, but not limited to, errors, omissions, or inaccuracies.

# Table of Contents

**INTRODUCTION** .................................................. 12
    WHAT ARE CARBS? ........................................ 12
    SUGAR ............................................................... 12
    STARCH ............................................................. 12
    WHY DO WE NEED CARBS? ............................ 13

**CHAPTER 1: SHOPPING GUIDE FOR ATKINS DIET** . 14
    CHECK THE LABEL ........................................... 15
    WHAT SHOULD WE EAT? ................................ 15

**CHAPTER 2: CONVENIENCE FOODS** ..................... 19

**CHAPTER 3: KEYS TO SUCCESS ON ATKINS** ......... 20

**CHAPTER 4: ATKINS IN THE MODERN WORLD** .... 22
    BE PREPARED ................................................... 22
    FAST FOOD ESTABLISHMENTS ........................ 22
    RESTAURANTS .................................................. 22
    PARTIES ............................................................ 23
    ATKINS ON THE GO ......................................... 23
    EN ROUTE ........................................................ 23
    DINE-IN, DINE OUT ......................................... 23
    DINING MECCAS .............................................. 23
    STAY IN MOTION ............................................ 24

**CHAPTER 5: HOW TO STAY CONSISTENT ON THE ATKINS DIET** ......................................................... 25
    BE REALISTIC WITH YOUR GOALS .................. 25
    FOCUS ON YOUR GOAL'S PROCESS ............... 25
    KEEP A JOURNAL ............................................ 26
    FIND YOUR TRIBE ........................................... 26
    SHOW UP FOR YOURSELF .............................. 26
    BE KIND TO YOURSELF ................................... 27
    CELEBRATE YOUR SUCCESSES ....................... 27
    LOVE YOUR BODY .......................................... 27

**CHAPTER 6: BREAKFAST** ..................................... 28
    PARFAIT WITH VARIETIES OF BERRIES FOR BREAKFAST .. 28
    BURRITO FOR BREAKFAST .............................. 28
    STUFFED PORTOBELLO BROILERS ................. 29
    BACON, EGG & CHEESE CASSEROLE ............. 30

VANILLA AND MARSHMALLOW SMOOTHIE ................. 30
PUMPKIN ALMOND PANCAKES ................................ 31
EGGS WITH SALSA AND AVOCADO ......................... 31
BAKED EGGPLANT PUREE ........................................ 32
PEANUT BUTTER GRANOLA ..................................... 32
BLUEBERRY YOGURT ................................................ 33
UNFORGETTABLE SLOW-COOKER TATER TOTS ........ 33
BREAKFAST BURRITO ............................................... 34
STUFFED CHICKEN WITH ASPARAGUS & BACON ..... 35
BASIL STUFFED CHICKEN BREASTS ......................... 35
LOW CARB PORK MEDALLIONS ............................... 36
EASY MOZZARELLA & PESTO CHICKEN CASSEROLE .. 36
BROCCOLI & CHEDDAR KETO BREAD RECIPE ......... 37
BACON-WRAPPED CHICKEN TENDERS WITH RANCH DIP
.................................................................................. 37
FARMHOUSE BEANS & SAUSAGE ............................ 38
MEAT-LOVER PIZZA CUPS ........................................ 38
5 MINUTE 5 INGREDIENT CHEESY BACON CHICKEN .. 39
BAKED PESTO CHICKEN ........................................... 39
PIZZA CHICKEN CASSEROLE .................................... 40
KETO CAULIFLOWER AU GRATIN ............................. 40
BOOSTED KETO COFFEE .......................................... 41
SUGAR-FREE, LOW CARB DRIED CRANBERRIES ...... 41
ORIGINAL ALMOND PORRIDGE ............................... 42
SPINACH SCRAMBLED EGG ..................................... 42
BELL PEPPER FRITTATA ............................................ 43
COCONUT PANCAKE ................................................ 44
AVOCADO TUNA SALADS ........................................ 44
VEGGIE QUICHE ....................................................... 45
BROCCOLI TURKEY CASSEROLE ............................... 45
STRAWBERRY ROLLS ................................................ 46
EGGS WITH AVOCADO, SALSA, AND TURKEY BACON (5.8G) ....................................................................... 47
HERBED SCRAMBLED EGGS (1.6G) ......................... 47
CREAM CHEESE SPINACH OMELETTE ..................... 47
BAKED CORNED BEEF OMELETS (5G NET CARBS) .. 48
BROCCOLI FRITTATA ................................................ 48
SOFT SCRAMBLED EGGS WITH LOBSTER ............... 49
ALASKAN SALMON OMELET .................................... 50
COTTAGE CHEESE SCRAMBLE ................................. 50
LOW CARB MAC 'N CHEESE ..................................... 51
CREAM CHEESE PANCAKES (2.5G NET CARBS) ...... 51
CRUSTLESS BREAKFAST TARTS WITH MUSHROOMS AND GOAT CHEESE ................................................. 52
SHRIMP SALAD WITH EGGS .................................... 53

| | |
|---|---|
| Bacon Meat Rolls | 53 |
| Grilled Steak With Red Pepper | 54 |
| Grilled Shrimp With Mint Sauce | 54 |
| California Grilled Chicken | 55 |
| Coriander Lime Grilled Salmon | 55 |
| Grilled Zucchini Salad | 56 |
| Grilled Fennel With Mozzarella And Caper And Lemon Dressing | 56 |
| Avocado Wrapped In Bacon | 57 |
| Grilled Dumplings On Fine Coleslaw With Bacon | 57 |
| Adana Kebab Recipe | 58 |
| Wings Recipe With Sauce | 59 |

## CHAPTER 7: LUNCH .................................. 61

| | |
|---|---|
| Chef Salad | 61 |
| Blackened Chicken Salad | 61 |
| Cobb Salad | 62 |
| Turkey & Cranberry Salad | 62 |
| Chicken Naan | 62 |
| Chinese Chicken Salad | 63 |
| BLT Salad | 63 |
| Turkey & Cream Cheese | 63 |
| Italian Meat & Cheese | 64 |
| Feta Spinach Salad | 64 |
| Roast Beef & Cheese | 64 |
| Salmon Avocado Lunch | 65 |
| Sautéed Greens And Poached Eggs | 65 |
| Roasted Rack Of Lamb, Fennel, Cauliflower, And Celery | 66 |
| Bowl Of Berries | 66 |
| Chocolate Pudding | 67 |
| Mexican Dip | 67 |
| Rib-Eye And Pepper | 68 |
| Fiesta Bean Dips | 68 |
| Slow Cooker Squash | 69 |
| Slow Cooker Taco Soup | 69 |
| Stuffed Bell Peppers | 70 |
| Low Carbohydrate Zucchini Fries | 71 |
| Garlic Chicken | 71 |
| Roasted Salmon With Coconut Aminos And Vegetables | 72 |
| Tuna Casserole | 73 |
| White Lasagna Stuffed Peppers | 74 |
| Creamy Basil Baked Sausage | 74 |
| Easy Taco Casserole Recipe | 75 |

| | |
|---|---|
| Parmesan Chicken Tenders | 75 |
| Bacon Wrapped Chicken Tenders With Ranch Dip | 76 |
| Stuffed Pork Chops – 5 Ingredients | 76 |
| Super Easy Spicy Baked Chicken | 77 |
| Lemon Parmesan Broccoli Soup | 78 |
| Keto Chili Dog Pot Pie Casserole | 78 |
| Low Carb Crock Pot Pizza Casserole | 79 |
| Low Carb Taco Casserole | 79 |
| Irish Chicken And Rosemary Salad | 80 |
| Roasted Chicken With Fennel And Brussels Sprouts | 81 |
| Beef And Anchovy Chowder | 82 |
| Liverwurst Stew | 83 |
| Bratwurst with Sauerkraut | 84 |
| Excellent Pork And Broccoli Surprise | 84 |

## CHAPTER 8: DINNER .................................. 86

| | |
|---|---|
| Apricot-Glazed Brisket | 86 |
| Asian Lobster Salad | 86 |
| Garlic Shrimp With Avocado Dip | 87 |
| Baked Salmon With Bok Choy & Red Bell Pepper Purée | 88 |
| Traditional Beef Stroganoff | 88 |
| Greek Salad With Chicken | 90 |
| Baked Chicken With Artichokes | 91 |
| Baked Goat Cheese And Ricotta Custards | 91 |
| Baked Meatballs | 92 |
| Baked Salmon With Bok Choy And Mixed Greens | 92 |
| Brisket With Mushrooms | 93 |
| Breaded Scrod With Basil-Mustard Sauce | 93 |
| Broiled Lobster With Garlic Oil | 94 |
| Broiled Orange-Chili Chicken Breasts | 95 |
| Buffalo Chicken Egg Salad | 95 |
| Beef And Vegetable Stew | 96 |
| Barbecue Sauce | 96 |
| Baked Tofu With Chipotle Marinade | 97 |
| Barbecue Chicken Pizza | 97 |
| Basic Steamed Lobster With Drawn Butter | 98 |
| Asian Style Tuna Salad | 98 |
| Lamb Stew | 98 |
| Tandoori Chicken | 99 |
| Fish with Tomato Basil Sauce | 100 |
| Chicken Parmesan | 100 |
| Marsala Chicken | 101 |
| Mustard Chicken | 101 |
| Stuffed Green Peppers | 102 |

| Entry | Page |
|---|---|
| Chicken With Olives | 102 |
| Turkey With Delicious Bacon | 103 |
| Teriyaki Beef | 103 |
| Dijon Pork Chops With Grapes | 104 |
| Chicken Stuffed With Sundried Tomatoes | 104 |
| Chicken Stuffed With Cheesy Bacon | 105 |
| Stuffed Turkey Rolls | 105 |
| Grilled Spicy Sesame Chicken | 106 |
| Italian Style Pork Chops | 106 |
| Pollo Con Queso | 107 |
| Baked Chicken Lebanese Style | 108 |
| Tilapia With Garlic Lemon Flavor | 109 |
| Shrimp Curry | 109 |
| Korean Beef Bulgogi | 110 |
| Salmon With Basil Tomato | 110 |
| Rich Balsamic Glaze On Filets Mignon | 111 |
| Beef London Broil | 111 |
| Crab Frittata | 112 |
| Yellow Squash Casserole | 113 |

## CHAPTER 9: MAINS ..............114

| Entry | Page |
|---|---|
| Asparagus And Leek Soup | 114 |
| Chocolate And Hazelnut Mousse | 114 |
| Crispy, Spicy Cauliflower | 115 |
| Asian Vegetable Bowl | 115 |
| Banana & Coconut Rum | 116 |
| Breakfast Sausage Sauteed With Red & Green Peppers | 116 |
| Cajun Pork Chops | 117 |
| Key Lime Mousse | 117 |
| Cauliflower Potato Salad | 118 |
| Greek Salad | 118 |
| Cheese Sauce | 119 |
| Cream Soup With Chicken And Mushrooms | 119 |
| Cream Soup From Zucchini With Salmon | 120 |
| Fried Chicken With Feta Inside, Baked With Mushroom Sauce And Cheese | 121 |
| Friends | 121 |
| Protein Variation "Cordon Blu" | 122 |
| Chicken Fillets With Mozzarella And Tomatoes | 123 |
| Basturma With Creative Cheese | 124 |
| 9Greek Type Salad | 124 |
| Boiled Lobster + Sauce | 124 |
| Boiled Point Kyiv In Dietary Interpretation | 125 |
| Delicious Sausage And Egg Casserole | 126 |
| Satisfying Pork Stew | 126 |
| Tempting Breakfast Casserole With Tomato And Spinach | 127 |
| Slow-Cooker Lemon And Olive Chicken | 127 |
| Scrumptious Breakfast Pie | 128 |
| Chicken Fajita Soup | 128 |
| Tender Autumn Oxtail Stew | 129 |
| Delightful Carnitas & Paleo Nachos | 130 |
| Tasty Tarragon Lamb Shanks With Cannellini Beans | 130 |
| Mouthwatering Chicken And Kale Soup | 131 |
| Slow Cooker Frittata | 131 |
| Appetizing Orange Chicken | 132 |
| Simple And Delicious Chicken Enchiladas | 132 |
| Easy Heart-Warming Caramel Rolls | 133 |
| Creamy Reuben Soup | 133 |
| Tasty Slow-Cooked Pesto Chicken Salad | 134 |
| Delicious Stuffed Poblano Peppers | 135 |
| Yummy Cheesy Roasted Brussels Dip | 135 |
| Delicious Slow-Cooked Italian Beef | 136 |
| Delightful Garlic Butter Chicken With Cream Cheese Sauce | 136 |
| Slow-Cooked Brats | 137 |
| Low-Carb Slow-Cooked Pizza | 138 |
| Easy Italian Zucchini Meatloaf | 138 |
| Easy Slow-Cooker Chicken Roast | 139 |
| Canneloni with Meat And Mushrooms | 139 |
| Eggplant Lasagna | 140 |
| Hot Wings | 141 |
| Beef Veggie | 142 |
| Sausage, Bell Pepper, And Onion Pizza | 142 |
| Beef Fajitas | 143 |
| Baked Quesadillas | 144 |

## CHAPTER 10: SIDES .............. 145

| Entry | Page |
|---|---|
| Red Beans Grill For 1 | 145 |
| Vegetable Skewers And Grilled Cheese | 145 |
| Mustard Sauce | 146 |
| Quiche with Spinach, Mushrooms & Feta | 146 |
| Eggs Baked In Avocado | 147 |
| Crunchy Chocolate Covered Strawberries | 148 |
| Fish Pie | 148 |
| Pancakes With Berries & Whipped Cream | 149 |
| Sausages Stuffed Mushrooms | 149 |
| Salmon With Avocado Salsa | 150 |
| Brie & Caramelized Onion Burger | 150 |
| Baked Meatballs And Green Beans | 151 |

- Balsamic And Thyme Pearl Onions ................... 152
- Broccoli Florets With Lemon Butter Sauce ..... 152
- Broccoli Rabe Parmigiano ............................... 153
- Browned Pumpkin With Maple And Sage.......... 154
- Brussels Sprouts With Bacon And Parmesan ... 154
- Brussels Sprouts With Lemon And Parmesan ... 155
- Buffalo Chicken Salad ..................................... 155
- Buffalo Hot Wing Cauliflower ...................... 157
- Caesar Salad Dressing ..................................... 157
- Peanut Cole Slaw ........................................... 158
- Pecan and Gorganzola Salad............................ 158
- Pepper Ranch Salad Dressing .......................... 159
- Philly Cheesesteak Salad ................................ 159
- Pineapple Slaw................................................ 160
- Quick Fixin Taco Salad ................................... 160
- Ranch Dressing With Blue Cheese Variation..... 160
- Sante Fe Beef And Hot Pepper Salad ................ 161
- Asme (Tahini) Dressing.................................... 162
- Butternut Squash And Escarole Gratin........... 162

## CHAPTER 11: SEAFOODS .................................. 164

- Tuna Salad ..................................................... 164
- Stuffed And Wrapped Shrimp........................... 164
- Quick Steamed Red Snapper............................. 165
- Simple Shrimp Dip........................................... 165
- Iceberg Salad with Shrimp................................ 166
- Shrimp and Mushroom Cowder ....................... 166
- Cod With Oregano .......................................... 167
- Ritz Fish.......................................................... 167
- Lori's Oil Poached Fish.................................... 168
- Catfish In Creamy Shallot Sauce ..................... 168
- Grilled Fish In Grape Tomato Sauce ................ 169
- Baked Tilapia .................................................. 170
- Crispy Baked Fish............................................ 170
- Crusted Salmon with Herbs ............................. 171
- Sautéed Salmon............................................... 171
- Spiced Tilapia ................................................. 172

## CHAPTER 12: POULTRY .................................... 173

- Flavorful Fried Chicken .................................. 173
- Delectable Whole Roast Chicken .................... 173
- Divine Buffalo Wings ..................................... 174
- Flavorsome Honey Lime Chicken Wings ........... 175
- Delightful Coconut Crusted Chicken Tenders .. 175
- Well-Tasted Popcorn Chicken.......................... 176
- Easy Chicken Strips ........................................ 177
- Savory Sriracha Chicken Drumsticks................. 177
- Chinese-Style Honey Garlic Chicken ................. 178
- Rich Parmesan Crusted Chicken Breasts........... 179
- Chicken Low Carb Meal Prep Bowls ................. 180
- This Tasty Low Carb Soup Recipe Is Loaded With Healthy Vegetables And Hen. ......................... 181
- Pecan Chocolate Cake ..................................... 182
- Low-Carb Chicken Alfredo with Baron Verulam .................................................................... 182
- Low Carb Whole Grain Pie Crust ..................... 183
- Low Carb Satay Beef Meal ............................... 184
- Low Carb Meatball Burrito............................... 185
- Yummy Chicken Pot Pie .................................. 186
- Tasty Classic Spiced Chicken Breasts................. 187
- Titanic Tomato Chicken Stew .......................... 188
- Rich Chicken Salsa. .......................................... 189
- Elegant Orange Spice Chicken ......................... 189
- Excellent Chicken And Potatoes Dish .............. 190
- Quick Spicy Chicken Curry .............................. 191
- Excellent Eggplant Thai Style Chicken ............ 192

## CHAPTER 13: MEAT ........................................... 194

- Jamaican Jerk Pork Roast ............................... 194
- Chinese-Style Pulled Pork................................ 194
- Fantastically Delicious Pork Stew With Poblano Peppers ........................................................... 195
- Chili-Lime Pork Spare Ribs .............................. 196
- Kalua Pork And Cabbage.................................. 196
- Very Famous Cider-Glazed Pork....................... 197
- Phenomenal Baby Back Pork Ribs .................... 197
- Sky-High Garlic And Lime Pork Chops............. 198
- Generous Ranch Pork Chops............................ 199
- Steak Pizzaiola................................................. 199
- Sweet And Spicy Meatballs .............................. 200
- Beef Ragu........................................................ 201
- Corned Beef And Cabbage ................................ 201
- Ancho-Beef Stew .............................................. 202
- Cider Braised Beef Pot Roast ........................... 202
- Cajun Pot Roast .............................................. 203
- Sloppy Joes ..................................................... 204
- Moroccan Beef Lettuce Wraps ......................... 204
- Steak Fajitas ................................................... 205
- Beef And Eggplant............................................ 205
- Barbecue Pulled Beef........................................ 206
- Chili With Beef ................................................ 207
- Thit Bo Xao Dua .............................................. 207

THE BEST MEATLOAF..........................................208
SUPER DELICIOUS MEATBALLS..............................208
ROLLED FLANK STEAK .......................................209
FOOLPROOF RIB ROAST......................................209
LONDON BROIL ................................................210
GERMAN ROULADEN .........................................210
JALAPENO STEAK .............................................211
MEXICAN BEEF SUPREME ...................................211

## CHAPTER 14: VEGETABLES ..................................213

SUPREME AIR-FRIED TOFU ..................................213
NOT YOUR AVERAGE ZUCCHINI PARMESAN CHIPS......213
OUTSTANDING BATTER-FRIED SCALLIONS ................214
DELECTABLE FRENCH GREEN BEANS WITH SHALLOTS AND
ALMONDS ......................................................215
SUPER-HEALTHY AIR-FRIED GREEN TOMATOES .........215
LUSCIOUS AIR-FRIED BROCCOLI CRISPS ..................216
VEGGIE TUNA SALAD ........................................217
CREAMY GREEN BEANS ......................................217
STIR-FRIED STEAK WITH ASPARAGUS......................218
THE GREAT GAZPACHO ......................................218
MEXICAN SURPRISE............................................219
CHEESY KALE AND TOMATO CHIPS ........................220
SUPER STACKED EGGPLANTS ...............................221
TURNIPS AND CAVIAR AFTERNOON SNACK ...............221
ROASTED VEGETABLES IN HERBS...........................222
SALMON CROQUETTES .......................................222
RED GRAPEFRUIT SALAD .....................................223
STUFFED CHERRY TOMATOES ..............................224
SCRAMBLED EGG BURRITOS SERVED WITH BLACK BEAN
SALSA............................................................224
LEMON CRANBERRY MUFFINS ..............................225
FLORENTINE HASH SKILLET .................................226
WHOLE-GRAIN WAFFLES IN CHERRY SAUCE .............227
SMOKED TOFU AND QUINOA SALAD ......................228
EGG SALAD BENTO BOX .....................................229

## CHAPTER 15: SOUPS AND STEWS ......................231

AMAZING JALAPENO LIME CHICKEN SOUP ...............231
TERRIFIC CREAM OF RED BELL PEPPER SOUP ...........231
BRILLIANT ITALIAN SAUSAGE AND PEPPER SOUP .......232
REMARKABLE JALAPENO BACON CHEDDAR SOUP .......233
SURPRISING AVOCADO CHICKEN SOUP....................234
OUTSTANDING TACO SOUP..................................235
VERY GOOD BROCCOLI CHEESE SOUP WITH CHICKEN .235
HUNGARIAN MUSHROOM SOUP WITH FRESH DILL ....236

CREAMY GARLIC MUSHROOM SOUP .......................237
SUPERB FRENCH ONION SOUP .............................238
SOUP WITH PORK AND FENNEL (IN A SLOW COOKER) 238
LOW CARB CHICKEN NOODLE SOUP ......................239
CREAMY SALMON SOUP WITH COCONUT MILK ........240
CREAMY CHEESE SOUP WITH BROCCOLI ..................240
GINGER PUMPKIN SOUP......................................241
CREAMY CHEESE SOUP WITH VEGETABLES ..............242
SPICY SAUSAGE AND PEPPER SOUP .......................242
SOUP WITH RED PEPPER AND CAULIFLOWER............243
SPICY LOW-CARB SPINACH SOUP ..........................244
358.CREAMY ZUCCHINI SOUP WITH SALMON CHIPS..244
PUMPKIN SOUP WITH COCONUT AND CURRY ...........245
QUICK SEAFOOD CHOWDER..................................246
ATKINS DIET SOUP............................................246
BLUE CHEESE AND BACON SOUP ..........................247
VERSATILE VEGETABLE SOUP................................248
ROASTED RED PEPPER SOUP ...............................249
LOW CARB BEEF STEW.......................................250
HEARTY BEEF STEW..........................................251
BEEF CHUCK AND VEGETABLE STEW ......................251

## CHAPTER 16: SNACKS ......................................253

APRICOT-APPLE CLOUD ......................................253
ARTICHOKE WITH THREE KINDS OF CHEESE .............253
PEANUT BUTTER GRANOLA BAR WITH STRAWBERRIES
AND YOGURT PARFAIT.......................................254
BLACKBERRY PEACH COMPOTE ............................254
BAKED BRIE....................................................255
INDIAN CHICKEN CURRY .....................................255
AVOCADO SALSA ..............................................256
CHICKEN WINGS...............................................256
CAULIFLOWER MUSHROOM RISOTTO .....................257
COCONUT ORANGE CREAMSICLE FAT BOMBS...........258
CORNDOG MUFFINS..........................................258
LAYERED FRIED QUESO BLANCO ..........................259
RASPBERRY LEMON POPSICLES ............................260
NEAPOLITAN FAT BOMBS ...................................260
ATKINS SPECIAL BURGER ...................................261
ATKINS SPECIAL GRILLED CHICKEN .......................261
BLUEBERRY BLISS.............................................262
HAM SALAD – SIMPLE VERSION...........................263
BANANA MUFFIN DELIGHT .................................263
CRISPY APPLE..................................................264
ATKINS CHICKEN WRAP SPECIAL..........................264
SALAD WRAPPINGS WITH CHICKEN.......................265

| | |
|---|---|
| Atkins Special Soup | 265 |
| Atkins Mahi-Mahi | 266 |
| Pork Delight With Poblano Pepper | 266 |
| Almonds And Strawberries | 267 |
| Apple And Cheese Snack | 267 |
| Avocado with Strawberries | 267 |
| Apples and Almond Butter | 268 |
| Asparagus and Ham | 268 |
| Atkins Rye Biscuits with Ham | 268 |
| Balls Of Cheese With Bacon | 268 |
| Celery And Hummus | 269 |
| Celery Stalk With Peanut Butter | 269 |
| Cheese With Avocado | 269 |
| Taco Salad | 270 |
| Shrimp Gumbo | 270 |
| Roast Beef And Mixed Greens With Pickled Okra And Radishes | 271 |
| Pork Tenderloin With Tomatoes And Green Olives | 272 |
| Pumpkin-Spice Brownies | 272 |
| Spicy Turnip Fries | 273 |
| Kale Chips | 273 |
| Ham N' Cheese Frittata | 274 |
| Roast Chicken And Vegetable Stew | 275 |
| Baked Spaghetti | 275 |
| Beef And Been Entrée | 276 |
| Blondies | 276 |
| Brandy Mochaccino | 277 |
| Bruschetta Style Tomato Turkey Salad | 277 |
| Butterscotch Fudge | 277 |
| Ceviche | 278 |
| Chicken Bacon Club Salad | 278 |
| Chicken, Peas, Pecans & Grapes Salad | 279 |
| Chili Relleno With Or Without Chicken | 279 |
| Chocolate Chip Muffins | 280 |
| Chocolate French Silk Pie | 280 |
| Zucchini Crisp | 281 |
| Cinnamon Churros | 281 |
| Guacamole Bacon Stuffed Pepper Poppers | 282 |
| Tomato-Mozzarella Melt | 282 |
| Roast Beef, Red Bell Pepper And Provolone Lettuce Wraps | 283 |
| Chocolate Coconut Haystacks | 283 |
| Cereal Treat | 284 |
| Spiced Coconut Bark | 284 |
| Double Chocolate Express Smoothie | 285 |
| Zesty Oven Baked Fries | 285 |
| Oven-Baked Carrot Fries | 286 |
| Zesty Baked Fries | 286 |
| Baked Fresh Chili Fries | 287 |
| Spicy Baked Sweet Potato "Fries" | 287 |
| Garlic Oven Fries | 288 |
| Peppery Turnip "Fries" | 288 |
| Oven-Baked Fries | 289 |
| Spicy 'Fries' | 289 |
| Baked Spicy French Fries (Ww Core) | 290 |
| Twice Baked French Fries | 290 |
| Baked Sweet Potato Fries | 291 |
| Sweet Potato Fries | 291 |
| Oven-Baked French Fries | 292 |
| Garlicky French Fries | 292 |

**CHAPTER 17: DESSERTS ..................................294**

| | |
|---|---|
| Panna Cotta | 294 |
| Raspberry Parfait | 294 |
| Brownie Drops | 295 |
| Chocolate Walnut Cookies | 296 |
| Caprese Salad | 296 |
| Baked Brie With Tomatoes And Nuts | 297 |
| Carrot Nut Muffins | 297 |
| French Quesadillas | 298 |
| Chocolate Coconut Smoothie | 298 |
| Mint Chocolate Smoothie | 299 |
| Coffee Cake Muffins | 299 |
| Atkins Almond Flour Pancakes | 300 |
| Cinnamon Pancakes | 301 |
| Bacon & Egg Muffins | 301 |
| 460. Strawberry & Lime Smoothie | 302 |
| 461. Instant Pot Carrots Sweet And Spicy | 302 |
| Cinnamon Sour Cream Coffee Cake | 303 |
| Cinnamon Chocolate Smoothie | 304 |
| Cream Soda (Phase 1) | 305 |
| Blackberry Yogurt Nuts (Phase 2) | 305 |
| Cherry Plum Bread Pudding (Phase 3) | 305 |
| Cream Cheese Energy Balls (Phase 4) | 306 |
| Classic Almond Flour Pound Cake | 306 |
| Flourless Chocolate Pecan Torte | 307 |
| Chocolate Torte Cake | 308 |
| Chocolate Angel Food Cake | 309 |
| Cheesecake | 309 |
| 473. Pumpkin Cheesecake | 311 |
| Strawberry Cocktail | 312 |
| Frozen Coffee Slush | 313 |

| | |
|---|---|
| VANILLA COCONUT MILKSHAKE | 313 |
| CARROT JUICE / CARROT MILKSHAKE | 314 |
| MUSHROOM SOUP – REFERRED FROM DR. ATKINS WEBSITE | 314 |
| SPINACH AND CUCUMBER SOUP – AUTHOR'S CREATION | 315 |
| CHEESY OMELET | 315 |
| B. YELLOW SQUASH AND GRUYERE FRITTATA | 316 |
| GARDEN FRESH SALAD | 316 |
| SWEET AND SOUR BROCCOLI SALAD | 317 |
| LETTUCE AND GRAPE SALAD | 318 |
| CRUSTLESS SPINACH, ONION AND FETA QUICHE | 318 |
| 3 MINUTE CHOCOLATE CAKES INGREDIENTS: | 319 |
| 3 MINUTE WPI CHOCOLATE CAKE | 320 |
| MAGICALLY MOIST ALMOND CAKE | 320 |
| SIMPLY DELICIOUS SUGAR-FREE CHEESECAKE | 321 |
| WALNUT BROWNIES | 322 |
| ALMOND COOKIES | 323 |
| EASY-PEASY CHEESECAKE | 323 |
| PEANUT BUTTER COOKIES | 324 |
| CHOCOLATE FROSTY | 324 |
| NO-BAKE COOKIES | 325 |
| RASPBERRY SMOOTHIE | 325 |
| PECAN MACAROONS | 326 |
| CHOCOLATE CAKE | 326 |
| LEMON CREAM PIE | 326 |
| PUMPKIN SQUARES | 328 |
| CHOCOLATE WALNUT CAKE WITH CHOCOLATE FUDGE FROSTING | 328 |
| FLUFFY CREAM CHEESE FROSTING | 329 |
| YELLOW ANGEL FOOD CAKE | 329 |
| SUISSE BUTTERCREAM FROSTING | 330 |
| SPONGE CAKE /LEMONY CREAM CHEESE FROSTING | 330 |
| SPICE & NUT CAKE | 331 |
| QUICK PIE CRUST | 332 |
| RASPBERRIES SMOOTHIE | 332 |
| BLUEBERRY SMOOTHIE | 332 |
| STRAWBERRY SMOOTHIE | 333 |
| RASPBERRY SMOOTHIE AND AVOCADO | 333 |
| CHOCOLATE SMOOTHIE | 333 |

**CONCLUSION .................................................. 334**

# Introduction

There is a lot of debate around whether carbohydrates are suitable for the body or not, especially in weight loss because of the introduction of different diets like the Ketogenic, Dukan, South Beach, and Atkins diets.

The idea that carbohydrates are bad for people has left the world confused since there are numerous benefits to consuming carbohydrates. They are essential to maintain the health of the body and to maintain a healthy weight. Most experts believe that people need to understand that every carbohydrate is not the same. The quality, type, and quantity of carbohydrates in your diet are what will make a difference to you. It is essential to reduce the amount of free sugar from one's diet.

Therefore, people should focus more on consuming healthy carbs and those carbs that provide fiber. Fiber is perfect for your health, and numerous studies prove the same. This chapter provides all the information you will need to know about carbohydrates. You will also learn more about the benefits of consuming carbs, healthy sources of carbs, and how you should monitor your intake if you want to maintain a healthy weight.

## What Are Carbs?

There are three macronutrients or macros that you must consume as a part of your diet, and carbohydrates are among them.

The other two macros are protein and fat. You should never expect any food to have only one of these macronutrients since most foods are a combination of fats, proteins, and carbohydrates. However, the proportion of the macros found in these foods will vary.

## Sugar

Most adults and children consume a form of sugar called free sugars. These sugars are added to biscuits, chocolate, breakfast cereals, fizzy drinks, flavored yogurt, and other foods and drinks. You can even add these sugars at home when you cook. These sugars are also found in the food that you consume in restaurants. The sugar in maple, golden, agave syrups, blossom nectars, and unsweetened fruit juices, smoothies, vegetable juices, and honey is also considered free sugar. The sugar found naturally in fruit, vegetables, and milk is not regarded as free sugar.

## Starch

Most food that comes from plants contains a large amount of starch. Food likes rice, bread, pasta, and potatoes also have a lot of starch, and these foods slowly release energy for your body throughout the day.

Fiber

There is a diverse range of compounds that you can find in the cell walls of the food that you obtain from plants. These compounds are known as fiber. The best fiber sources are whole grain bread, beans and lentils, whole-wheat pasta, and vegetables.

## Why Do We Need Carbs?

There are several reasons why it is important to consume carbohydrates:

Energy

For most people, carbohydrates are the primary source of energy. If you eat a balanced diet, you will provide your body with at least 4 kilocalories of life for every gram of carbohydrates you eat. The carbohydrates are broken down in your body into glucose, and the bloodstream absorbs this glucose. Once the sugar is in the bloodstream, it will enter the cells in your body by using the insulin produced by the body. Your body will use glucose to have energy, and this energy will be used when you perform any activity, including breathing. If your body does not use any glucose, it will be stored in your muscles and liver in the form of glycogen. If you consume too many carbohydrates, the excess glucose is stored as fat in your body. This fat will be used to produce energy in the long run. Carbohydrates that are rich in starch will release more sugar into your body.

Disease Risk

Vegetables, legumes, whole grains, whole wheat, and fruits are all excellent sources of fiber. This compound is an essential part of a balanced and healthy diet. Fiber will reduce the risk of constipation, lower cholesterol levels in the body, and improve bowel health. Numerous studies and research show that foods rich in fiber are associated with a lower risk of bowel cancer, cardiovascular diseases, and type 2 diabetes. Most people do not consume enough fiber. The average person only consumes around 19 grams of wool when they consume 30 grams of fiber a day.

Calorie Intake

Most carbohydrates contain fewer calories when compared to fats. Starchy foods are rich in fiber, and they also help to maintain your weight. When you replace sugary, fatty foods and drinks with food rich in fiber, you can reduce your caloric intake, thereby improving your chances of losing weight. You can keep your hunger satiated by consuming foods that are rich in fiber. You will still have to watch your portion sizes because you should always avoid overeating. It is also essential to protect your fat intake when you cook your meals. If you consume too much fat in your meals you will increase your caloric intake.

# CHAPTER 1:

# Shopping Guide For Atkins Diet

How to Shop When You Are on Atkins Diet?

You should find yourself frequenting the perimeter of grocery stores if you are going through the Atkins Diet plan.

Clearing your pantry of every possible unhealthy ingredients and food is highly recommended. Skip the aisles of bread, breakfast cereals, sodas, juices, and ice cream.

Shopping organic under the Atkins Diet is unnecessary, so you do not need to blow up your budget. You can just stick to buying the least processed food options that you can afford.

Make a weekly meal plan before hitting the grocery stores and buy in bulk as much as possible.

Once your cart is full of healthy and acceptable Atkins Diet foods, there won't be room for any unnecessary item.

You get to stick to your diet and save money at the same time.

Base your shopping list around possible meals that include fatty protein sources with vegetables or nuts and other healthy fats.

Here is an overview of allowed foods under the Atkins Diet that you may include in your shopping list.

- Omega-3 enriched and pastured eggs are highly recommended.
- Chicken, pork, beef, lamb, and bacon are acceptable protein meat sources.
- Fatty fish and seafood like sardines, salmon, and trout are okay, too.
- Also include spinach, asparagus, kale, broccoli, and other low-carb vegetables.
- Walnuts, almonds, sunflower seeds, and macadamia nuts.
- Other healthy fats such as Avocado or Avocado oil, coconut oil, and extra virgin olive oil.
- Your dairy options include full-fat yogurt, cheese, butter, and cream.

As for beverages, water should always be your go-to drink. But the Atkins Diet also considers green tea and coffee as healthy alternatives and sources of antioxidants, as well.

Cross out beers and other drinks with high carbohydrate contents from your shopping list.

However, other alcoholic beverages with no added sugars such as dry wines are okay in small quantities.

## Check The Label

Just because a food is marked as having zero carbs does not mean it is free of carbohydrates. Manufacturers can round off the content to zero if they contain less than 0.5 grams of any carbohydrate. You will only find out if the product has some fractional carbs by going through the ingredients list.

It is best to make it a habit always to check the package label of each food item when shopping.

## What Should We Eat?

Now let us breakdown your food list based on the four phases of the Atkins Diet. What you should eat primarily depends on the number of net carbs that you are allowed each day.

Whatever you decide to eat, remember never to skip a meal. Eating is an essential part of the Atkins Diet for you to achieve your weight loss goal. Keeping your stomach full by eating throughout the day reduces the risk of hunger pangs and sudden unhealthy food choices. You may eat three main meals a day or up to five small meals.

You will find that you need to adjust to your appetite as it decreases while on the Atkins Diet. Always eat to your satisfaction without getting stuffed. Eat a small low-carb snack whenever you do not feel hungry during mealtimes. The key is not to go for more than four waking hours without food or skipping a full meal entirely.

Food for Phase 1

You should eat a high-protein and high-fat diet with low-carb leafy greens or other vegetables as you need to keep your daily carbs intake at 20 grams for two weeks. Eating vegetables is significantly less than the daily 300 grams of carbohydrates that the Food and Drug Administration recommends.

During Phase 1, you have to prioritize your protein intake in every meal. Not only does protein play a vital role in losing weight, but it also protects your lean muscle mass to ensure that your weight loss would mainly be due to losing only fat. Your target is to have 4- to 6-ounce servings of protein at least three times each day.

Eggs, Poultry, Red Meat, Fish and Shellfish

You can have your eggs whichever way you want them—fried, poached, soft or hard-boiled, scrambled, omelet, or deviled are all acceptable. You may also enjoy them mixed with vegetables or topped with herbs and feta cheese.

Poultry and meat products may not have any net carbs but aim to eat different healthy diets. You may have chicken, turkey, duck or quail, and beef, lamb, or pork alternately. Some processed meats are allowed, such as bacon and ham, but do not forget to count carbs as these are cured with sugar.

Fish and shellfish also do not have net carbs. Salmon, tuna, sardines, trout, flounder, sole, cod, herring, and halibut are recommended.

These fish types are excellent sources of iron, potassium, calcium, and vitamins B2 and D.

Meanwhile, shrimp, lobster, crabmeat, squid, and clams are rich in omega-3, iron, zinc, magnesium, and copper. Mussels and oysters are also allowed, but these have higher carbohydrates content and must be limited to about 4 ounces in a day.

Fats and Oils

Aside from being a flavorful aide in weight loss, fats also help your body absorb specific vitamins better. Two to 3 tablespoons of pure and natural fat is allowed each day. Mayonnaise, butter, sunflower, safflower, and preferably cold-pressed of expeller-pressed vegetable oils are recommended. Olive oil should be used for sautéing only, while sesame and walnut oil can be used as a dressing but not for cooking.

Artificial Sweeteners

Up to three packets of sugar substitutes such as stevia, saccharin, and sucralose are allowed per day. Take note that one pack is equal to 1 gram of net carbs.

Cheese

You may consume up to 4 ounces of cheese daily. An ounce of cheese, about the size of a 1-inch cube, contains about 1 gram of carbs. Take your pick from among cheddar, parmesan, mozzarella, feta, goat, Gouda, Swiss, cream cheese, or bleu cheese.

Vegetables

At least 12 to 15 grams of your daily net carbs should come from vegetables. Choose from among vegetables with high-fiber, nutrient-dense, foundation vegetables: alfalfa sprouts, artichoke, arugula, asparagus, beet greens, bell pepper, bok choy, broccoli, broccoli rabe, broccolini, Brussels sprouts, button mushroom, cabbage, cauliflower, celery, chicory greens, collard greens, cucumber, dill, eggplant, endive, escarole, fennel, garlic, green beans, Haas avocado, the heart of palm, jicama, kale, kohlrabi, leeks, lettuce, mung beans sprouts, okra, olives, onion, Portobello mushroom, pumpkin, radicchio, radish, rhubarb, sauerkraut, scallion, shallot, snow peas, spaghetti squash, spinach, Swiss chard, tomato, turnip, watercress, yellow squash, and zucchini.

You may substitute 3 grams of your net carbs from foundation vegetables with 3 grams of net carbs from nuts or seeds if you plan to extend your induction phase for more than two weeks.

Herbs and Spices

Add more flavor to your food through these herbs and spices: basil, black pepper, cayenne pepper, chives, cilantro, dill, garlic, ginger, oregano, parsley, rosemary, sage, and tarragon. Just make sure that you are getting the sugar-free versions.

Salad Dressings and Garnishes

Only up to 3 grams of net carbs per serving from salad dressing is acceptable, so make sure yours does not contain sugar. Always read the labels first or create your balsamic vinegar, bleu cheese, Caesar, Italian, lemon or lime juice, ranch, or red wine vinegar dressing.

You may also garnish your salad with bacon, cheese, sour cream, hard-boiled egg, or mushrooms.

Beverages

It is common to lose water weight during the induction phase to stay hydrated at all times. Drink at least 64 ounces of water daily to flush out the by-products of burning fat and avoid electrolyte imbalance and constipation. Having enough fluid in your system also helps with weight loss. You may swap 16 ounces of water with regular or decaffeinated coffee or tea and another 16 ounces with low-sodium chicken, vegetable, or beef broth. Other water alternatives include club or diet soda, soy or almond milk, and zero-calories flavored seltzer.

Food for Phase 2

After the Induction phase, you are encouraged to slowly add healthier carbohydrates into your diet with your increased daily net carbs of 25 to 45 grams. That equates to an additional 5 grams of net carbs per week.

Phase 2 is often referred to as a point of freedom and variety in your Atkins Diet journey. You can say hello to about a month of being happily well-fed. Whole food carbohydrates such as low-carb fruits, berries, vegetables, and nuts are recommended as you try to find your carb balance. You are also allowed to eat legumes, potatoes, oats, rice, and other healthier grains.

Of course, you still need to eat primarily natural and unprocessed foods. But you will have more convenient food options. Unprocessed foods are an even bigger help for those trying to stick to this diet and stay on track toward their weight loss goals amid their busy schedules.

Below is a list of foods that you can add to your diet during Phase 2:

•Fruits and fresh berries, including cantaloupe, honeydew, blackberries, blueberries, boysenberries, cranberries, raspberries, gooseberries, and strawberries.

•Nuts and seeds such as almonds, brazil nuts, cashews, macadamias, peanuts, pecans, pistachios, sunflower seeds, and walnuts. Butter versions of these nuts and seeds are also okay.

•Cooked or canned legumes, including black beans, chickpeas, great northern beans, kidney beans, lentils, lima beans, navy beans, and pinto beans.

- Dairy products such as cottage cheese, mozzarella cheese, ricotta cheese, heavy cream, and Greek, plain, whole milk, or unsweetened yogurt.
- Lemon juice, lime juice, tomato juice, and other juices.

# CHAPTER 2:

# Convenience Foods

Many of the above-mentioned acceptable foods on the list are sold as pre-packaged items at supermarkets, grocery stores, and convenience stores. Just make sure to take note of the serving sizes of each pack. Some of these convenience foods even come as a grab and go foods. There are super convenient Atkins bars and shakes in various flavors that are all allowed during Phase 2.

Food for Phase 3

You are now very close to your weight goal and can consume 50 to 70 net carbs each day. Continue to up your carbohydrate intake until your weight loss slows down. Also, add more variety to your diet to include more fruits, whole grains, and starchy vegetables.

Food for Phase 4

You just need to keep eating a low-carbohydrate diet of about 75 net carbs daily to maintain your ideal weight. By this time, you may not even need to count your net carbs because you would probably know by heart just how much you can eat without regaining weight. Congratulations and happy eating!

# CHAPTER 3:

# Keys To Success On Atkins

Some people find it reasonably easy to cut back on carbs and have great success without any problems on the Atkins diet. Other people, however, have more difficulty switching to the Atkins diet. It can be a surprise to go from eating much of your caloric intake in carbs to moving to a very low-carb diet, but with the following keys to success, you will be able to transition more smoothly.

First, make sure to make the best use of your net carbs. Remember, net carbs are the total number of carbohydrates in your food minus the dietary fiber. The remainder is the net carb for that food. Since the thread has almost no impact on your blood sugar, it is unnecessary to cut down fiber. It is best to get your full allotment of net carbs, especially in phase 1. Make sure you eat all your net carbs!

Second, make sure to eat plenty of vegetables. In phase 1, most of your net carbs (12 to 15 grams) will be found in the vegetables you eat.

Make sure to keep salt in your diet. As your body transitions from carb-burning for energy to fat burning, you may suffer from headaches, lightheadedness, cramps, or a feeling of weakness or lethargy if you do not get enough salt. By making sure that there is adequate sodium intake, you should be able to avert these symptoms as your body adapts to the new eating way.

Also, as important as salt, is to drink plenty of water. Most people go through life dehydrated and don't even know it. It is important to note that when you are thirsty, it may feel like being hungry. That is one reason some people overeat. Instead of eating when you get a sign of hunger pains, start with a glass of water. Also, there is an easy key to see if you are dehydrated: check your urine color. You want to make sure that your urine is light yellow or clear. If your urine is dark, it means that you aren't getting enough liquid. You should get at least 64 ounces a day, but larger people and people who are very active will need more.

Protein has a way of filling you up longer. It takes longer to digest than simple carbs, so you will feel fuller longer when you get enough protein, which helps you stick to the plan (especially in the induction phase). Make sure to eat 4 to 6 ounces of protein with every meal.

Make sure to get enough fat to feel full. It can be challenging to have most of your diet be primarily fats and proteins because eating fat has gotten a bad rap in our society. However, eating fat will help you control your carb intake, and the fats that are recommended in the Atkins diet are right for you!Eating processed foods with a lot of fat is not necessarily good, but eating fats from vegetable oils, olive oils, and lean meats is essential. Just don't go overboard. You should make sure that you feel full after eating, but don't go overboard eating fats.

Check all your foods for hidden carbs, especially if you are eating processed foods. Many things have sugars added for flavor, especially condiments such as ketchup, salad dressings, etc. Ensure you know all these hidden carbs in your foods, use low-carb foods (and still read the label), and stay within your net carb count. You may be surprised by what you find when you become an expert label reader.

Watch your calorie counts. Although you don't have to count calories on the Atkins diet, you mustn't overeat either. If you follow Atkins but eat 3,000 calories a day, your body will have fats to burn for fuel from your food instead of your stored fat. And this will hinder your weight loss. Most women should eat between 1500 and 1800 calories and most men between 1800 and 2200 calories. Your portions should be sensible, not humongous. You know when you get into a restaurant, and they fill massive plates? Those portions are too big. Eating moderate portions will help you maintain a reasonable amount of food.

Make sure to stay moving. Regular exercise, even taking a walk, will help you lose weight faster. If you do no movement, it will be harder for the value to come off, no matter what diet plan you follow.

Another tip that many people have found especially helpful is to plan your foods. When you know what you are going to eat and when it is easier to succeed on a diet, after all, you won't be surprised by that 3 pm hunger strike that always made you want to go to the vending machine before. Now, when you have a sensible snack already ready for you to eat, you won't be tempted by junk. If you have planned for your food, you will be prepared to face the day without fear of getting hungry.

One of the essential tips to follow on the Atkins diet is to track the foods you eat. That is especially important for tracking your net carbs. Study after study has found that people who follow what they eat have more success with a weight loss plan (any weight loss plan) than those who do not. So, keeping track of your food will do several things for you. First, it will help you track your net carbs and make sure you aren't eating more carbohydrates than you think you are. It will help you see patterns that you may not have noticed. If you aren't losing any weight, can you attribute it to a particular food? If you don't feel well, is it because you aren't getting enough protein? These things can be the difference between success and failure in any diet. Lastly, it will tell you if you are overeating. After all, no matter what plan you are on, you will not lose weight if you fill food. It is as simple as that. So tracking can be the make-or-break habit for the diet.

If you follow these tips, the Atkins diet will be much easier to follow, and you will have tremendous success as a result. And now that you have all the necessary information, let's dive into exactly what each phase of the diet requires. That is the meat and potatoes of what Atkins is.

# CHAPTER 4:

# Atkins In The Modern World

When you're on the go, at a restaurant, or even at work, you may be faced with tempting options that are not necessarily adaptable to the Atkins program. Donuts, bagels, and Danishes pop up on breakfast carts and, chances are the menu at the local restaurant is not focused on conforming to your diet plan. However, none of these need to be a problem; if the menu doesn't adapt to your diet, you can always adapt to the situation. As long as you know the proper strategies, there's still a way to handle things.

## Be Prepared

If you have a hard time resisting the pastries in the conference room at work, make sure you don't show up for the conference hungry. If you've fortified yourself with a hearty mushroom omelet for breakfast, you can indeed find the resolve to resist the workplace temptations. If your meal needs to be on the go, check out the cafeteria menu. Is there anything on there you can eat? If not, try brown-bagging it to make sure you always have a healthy option on hand.

## Fast Food Establishments

Fast food establishments often get a bad rap from the health industry in general, but surprisingly, most of the main course choices, like burgers and chicken fingers, are Atkins friendly; it's the extras you need to be wary of. Try to plan your order ahead of time, try not to add the sides, like French fries and onion rings, when you see them in the restaurant.

## Restaurants

If you eat regularly at a particular restaurant, the staff will probably be more than happy to accommodate your dietary requirements. Inform the waiter that you're on a sugar-free program and can tolerate no sugar whatsoever. This way, you won't have to worry about hidden sugars cropping up in menu choices.

Avoid breading, sauces, and flour used as a thickener. Be aware that carbohydrates can lurk in surprising places. There can be grain or flour in hamburgers or bread crumbs in fried chicken.

Don't be shy about inquiring firmly about what is in a particular dish. Waiters will usually be more than compliant; after all, you are the one responsible for deciding their tips.

When you begin to explore restaurants that can make exceptional dishes with acceptable ingredients, you'll start to realize how many options you have. Roast beef, duck, lobster, and poached salmon are all examples of upscale entrees that can be eaten without going off your diet.

If the breadbasket is tempting, consider asking for a tray of veggies instead. If someone else at the table wants the bread, try and keep the basket at the far end of the table, rather than under your nose.

### Parties

If you're going to an ice cream party, there may be a chance that you find nothing acceptable to eat. In this case, let your host know, and ask what they are planning to serve. If nothing fits into the plan, make sure you have loaded up on a salad and high protein entree before leaving or bringing some food along.

### Atkins On The Go

Life on the road can be challenging. Living out of suitcases, dealing with time changes, and checking in and out of hotels can all throw off your usual patterns, but your diet need not be one of them. If you're planning on doing some traveling, there are plenty of ways to include the Atkins diet in your travel plans.

### En Route

Whether flying, driving, or taking a train, it's essential to make sure you've brought some suitable food along. If that's not an option, check ahead to make sure there will be low carb options available on the way. It may be a good idea to visit the airport's salad bar to stock up on some greens and chicken. Bring along club soda, bottled water, coffee, or herb tea if you're driving or on a train, or ask for it on the plane. Atkins shakes, and bars are great options, and the bars are easy to transport.

### Dine-In, Dine Out

If you're ordering from room service, be clear about what you don't want. Specify that you don't wish to toast with your eggs or rolls with your dinner. If any offending items arrive on the room service cart, politely ask the waiter to take them with him on his way out. Place the tray outside your door as room as you're done to prevent grazing. Try to control your urge to peek into the bar refrigerator, which is likely to be a minefield of starchy snacks. If you think this may be difficult, consider refusing the key to the fridge.

### Dining Meccas

When you're in areas with lots of culinary hot spots, it can be hard to go without sampling some local fare. To enjoy without overdoing it, have a low carb shake or eggs for breakfast and a protein-rich salad for lunch. That should leave room to enjoy the local foods in moderation. Try and choose a specialty prepared without sauces and heavy breading.

## Stay In Motion

If you're on a leisurely vacation, there's a good chance you're getting in lots of exercises. However, if you're going to spend a lot of time in a conference room or car, it's a good idea to find some other ways of getting in some fitness activities. If the hotel you're in does not have a fitness center, bring good walking shoes, and get out exploring your surroundings.

Snacks for the Road

If you are planning to be on the road for a while, here are some low carb options to consider packing instead of the chips and cookies:

1. Sliced veggies and cream cheese

2. Cheese slices, string cheese, or cheese cubes

3. Trail mix

4. Deviled or hard-boiled eggs

5. Almonds

6. Olives

7. Popcorn and nut mix

8. Beef jerky or turkey jerky (cured, without sugar)

9. Berries

10. Celery sticks with peanut butter

11. Sugar-free candies and snack cakes

Also, remember to stay hydrated on the road. Make sure everyone in the car has their water bottle. Plan your route so you can find spots to stop and eat, or just walk and stretch your legs along the way. Try and eat a low carb snack or healthy meal once every two to three hours to keep hunger in check. Pack snacks like the ones list above and are sure to have plenty of ice and a cooler to keep refrigerated items cool.

## CHAPTER 5:

# How To Stay Consistent On The Atkins Diet

The long roads of diet programs are packed with bodies of people who got sidetracked and fell by the wayside. If you were to ask these people what happened, you would hear stories of how they lost motivation along the way, despite their best efforts. How do you keep yourself from ending that way? Here are nine tips to keep you consistent till the end.

Find Your Why

Why do you need to lose weight? What was the turning point?

Answering the above questions is a great way to find you why; the reasons you want to lose weight. Once you have figured that out, write them down, so they serve as a daily reminder to stick to your plans.

### Be Realistic With Your Goals

The excitement of starting a weight loss program can tempt us to draft impossible and unattainable goals. I know this because I've been there.

Despite what the weight loss commercials say, losing 30lbs in one month is downright impossible. Besides, the frustration that comes with achieving such an unattainable goal can put a damper on your enthusiasm.

So how do you avoid this?

Simply set realistic and attainable goals. Believe me. Nothing compares to that feeling of accomplishment that comes with knowing you are crushing your goals. And as a bonus, you are more likely to continue with your plan for the long-term.

### Focus On Your Goal's Process

Setting goals can be a double-edged sword. On the one hand, it makes you look forward to the result of your hard work. On the other hand, since the outcome is so far away, you can easily get derailed and lose motivation. To ensure you don't come out on the losing end, you need to enjoy the process.

How?

Let's assume one of your goals is to incorporate exercise into your weight loss program. Merely saying I will start exercising is vague and comes with no immediate urgency. Besides, you will be less likely to put it to fruition anytime soon.

Instead of the above vague term, you could say I will do squats for 20 minutes, four times a week. Now, this is something you can easily keep track of.

## Keep A Journal

By now, you should know the brain is not a good memory keeper. So relying on it is equivalent to doing you more harm than good, especially when it comes to weight loss. Absolutely nothing is more motivating than seeing your progress in black and white.

Therefore, get a journal to track down your daily food intake, whether the food is prepared by you or not. Your journal should also record weekly measurements of your weight. Doing this is a great way to keep you accountable.

Don't also forget to take pictures! Those before and after weight loss pictures on social media will never are uncool.

## Find Your Tribe

It's much more fun and more comfortable losing weight when doing it with people of like minds. The encouragement, accountability, and motivation you will receive could provide the necessary support for your journey. So ensure you have a tribe to lean on.

Your tribe could comprise of your partner, a dear friend, or a fellow gym-goer. Of you could do exercises together, share tips and recipes, and be each other's cheerleaders. Also, joining an online Atkins community can offer the same benefits.

## Show Up For Yourself

If you are desirous of losing weight, you have to be committed to the process. Once you have written down your attainable goals, it's time to show up for yourself. A great way to do this is to join a gym. Getting a gym membership means you are likely to commit yourself to your plan so you won't lose out on your investment.

Also, telling others about your weight loss plan is another option. That could be as simple as announcing it on social media or just telling your loved ones. Do remember, the more people you tell, the greater your commitment.

In any case, you have been showing up for other people; isn't it time you do the same for yourself?

## Be Kind To Yourself

No matter how committed you are there will be days you'll be tempted to chuck the deuces at your diet program and gorge on Ben & Jerry's. When that happens, please understand that it is not the end of the world.

Beating you up and having self-defeating thoughts could make you burn out and give up. Realize that humans are not perfect. We make mistakes all the time. But we are always given another opportunity to wipe the slate clean and begin again.

Just dust yourself up and try again.

## Celebrate Your Successes

Weight loss is hard work. And hard work needs to be recognized and rewarded if you want to keep at it. Please don't put off the celebrations until the very end; celebrate all your little achievements as they happen.

Kept to your goal of doing squats four times a week? Then treat yourself to a massage or go to the movies. Knowing that there is a reward waiting for you will motivate you to work harder. Nothing beats the feeling of accomplishment and pride that comes with knowing you are on the right track.

A note of warning here. Don't use food as a reward. It could defeat the very purpose you started losing weight in the first place. Also, rewarding yourself is not an excuse to splurge on unnecessary things. On the flip side, stay away from 'rewards' that give you no thrill whatsoever.

## Love Your Body

Having a positive body image is one factor that tends to be glossed over in weight loss programs. But it is just as important as exercising or eating the right foods. When you love your body, you are more likely to engage in wholesome activities to keep it healthy.

If you find it difficult to love your body, you could do the following activities:

1. Speak positive words of affirmation to your body – do this in front of a mirror

2. Wear well-tailored clothes

3. Exercise

4. Quit comparing yourself to other people, especially those in magazines and TVs

5. Treat yourself to something special like getting a manicure

6. Cut off from toxic people

Remember, if you hate your body, you won't lose weight. It's as simple as that.

# CHAPTER 6:

# Breakfast

## Parfait with Varieties Of Berries For Breakfast

Preparation time: 10 minutes

Cooking Time: 50 minutes

Serving: 2

Ingredients:

- 12 tbsp. whipped cream
- Six fresh strawberries
- 30 gr. Raspberries
- 300 gr. Greek yogurt
- 3 tsp. vanilla extract
- 4 bar of almonds and cranberries red Atkins daybreak

Directions:

1. In a blender, blend half the strawberries with half the raspberries and half the Splenda.
2. Chop the remaining raspberries into large pieces and place them in the puree.
3. In a large whipping bowl, use an electric mixer at medium speed to combine the cream, remaining scoop of Splenda, and vanilla; beat until smooth peaks.
4. Add the yogurt and beat until you get firm peaks.
5. In four cups, alternate the layers of the blackberry mixture, the cream filling, and the chopped Day Break, and place at least two layers of each.
6. Top each with some remaining strawberries and serve.

Nutrition:

Carbohydrates: 8.1 grams

Proteins: 15.8 grams Fat: 21.3 grams

## Burrito For Breakfast

Preparation time: 5 Minutes

Baking Time: 15 Minutes

Servings: 2

Ingredients:

1. One red pepper
2. 1 tbsp. chili powder
3. Two whole tortilla
4. Four eggs
5. 1 tbsp. vegetable oil

6. One red chili pepper

7. Two long onion

Directions:

1. Beat the eggs, salt, and cayenne pepper in a bowl.

2. On medium heat, cook the tortillas 1 minute on each side until they are browned on the edges.

3. Cover with aluminum foil to keep warm.

4. Add oil, red pepper, long onion, and jalapeños.

5. Cook until vegetables are tender, about 3 minutes.

6. Add eggs and continue cooking, whipping until eggs are cooked, about 2 minutes.

7. Place the tortillas on a plate.

8. Divide the eggs between the tortillas, season with hot sauce, and roll carefully.

Nutrition:

Carbohydrates: 24.4 grams

Proteins: 19.1grams

Fat: 21.1 grams

## Stuffed Portobello Broilers

Preparation Time: 10 minutes

Cooking time: 20 minutes

Serving: 2

Ingredients:

- Four eggs
- ¼ cup mozzarella cheese, shredded
- 8 oz. chicken breast, deboned and cooked
- ¼ teaspoon Italian seasoning
- 3 tbsp. scallions, chopped
- ¼ teaspoon black pepper
- 2 tbsp. olive oil, extra virgin
- ¼ teaspoon salt
- 6 cups Portobello mushrooms

Directions:

1. Preheat your broiler. Line a baking sheet with foil.

2. Slice the chicken lengthwise in half before thinly cutting them crosswise.

3. Sauté the scallions and chicken in oil over medium heat for about 4 minutes.

4. Add the eggs and continue cooking until firm.

5. Arrange the mushroom caps with their ribbed side up on the baking sheet. Season with pepper, salt, and herbs, and then broil them for 7 minutes. Make sure to turn the caps once during the cook.

6. Remove the mushrooms from the oven and fill them with the egg mixture. Place cheese on top

before placing them back in the broiler.

7. Cook for a minute or until cheese is melted.

Nutrition:

15.1 grams of protein,

1.2 grams of fiber,

10.2 grams of fat,

165 calories

2.7 grams of net carbohydrates.

## Bacon, Egg & Cheese Casserole

Preparation time: 15 Minutes

Cooking time: 15 Minutes

Serving: 2

Ingredients:

- 12 eggs
- Six slices of bacon
- 4 ounces of sour cream
- 4 ounces of heavy cream
- 10 ounces cheddar cheese, shredded
- 1/3 cup of chopped green onions
- Salt
- Pepper
- Cooking spray

Directions:

1. Preheat your oven to 350° F.
2. Fry the bacon in a skillet. Set aside on paper towels and cool. Crumble into bacon bits after cooling.
3. In a bowl, place the eggs, sour cream, heavy cream, salt, and pepper. Blend well with a hand mixer.
4. Prepare a baking dish or pan and spray with cooking spray.
5. Place a single layer of cheese in the pan. Cover the cheese with the egg mixture.
6. Now top everything with the crumbled bacon.
7. Bake in the oven for few minutes. Eliminate from the oven when the edges are browned and serve garnished with chopped green onions.

Nutrition:

Calories 437 Fat 38 g Protein 43 g

Carbohydrates 2 g

## Vanilla and Marshmallow Smoothie

Preparation time: 10 Minutes

Cooking time: 25 Minutes

Servings: 2

Ingredients:

- ½ cup of coconut milk
- 1 cup of water

- 3 cups of ice
- 2 tbsp. of chia
- 1 tsp. vanilla extract
- 2 tbsp. collage hydrosol
- honey to taste

Directions:
1. Place the ingredients in your blender or food processor.
2. Blend until creamy smooth. Enjoy

Nutrition:

Calories 257

Fat 18.7 g

Protein 8.1 g

Carbohydrates 17.9 g

## Pumpkin Almond Pancakes

Preparation Time: 5 minutes

Cooking time: 10 minutes

Serving: 2

Ingredients:

- 4 oz. vanilla whey protein powder
- ½ cup pumpkin puree, canned
- Four eggs, beaten
- 1 tsp. Double-acting baking powder, sodium aluminum sulfate
- 1 cup creamed cottage cheese
- ¼ cup almond flour, blanched
- ½ teaspoon pumpkin pie spice
- ¼ cup whole grain soy flour, dry

Directions:
1. Combine the protein powder, pumpkin pie spice, almond flour, baking powder, and soy flour in a bowl.
2. Add the remaining ingredients and mix until well blended.
3. Grease a skillet using butter.
4. Pour ¼ cup of the batter into the skillet and cook over medium heat. Once bubbles form in the middle, flip the pancakes over and cook until firm.
5. Repeat the procedure with the remaining batter.

Nutrition:

Each serving contains 21 grams of protein, 1.8 grams of fiber, and 8.4 grams of fat, 183 calories, and 4.3 grams of net carbohydrates.

## Eggs With Salsa And Avocado

Preparation Time: 5 minutes

Cooking time: 10 minutes

Servings: 1

Ingredients:

- Two eggs

- ½ Avocado, peeled, deseeded, and sliced.
- 1 oz. salsa
- 4 oz. turkey sausage
- 1/8 cantaloupe melon, sliced

Directions:
1. Fry eggs in a pan.
2. Arrange Avocado on the bottom of a plate. Place eggs on top, followed by salsa.
3. Cook sausage over high heat until browned on all sides. Serve with egg stack and cantaloupe slices.

Nutrition: Each serving contains

35.9 grams of protein,

5.9 grams of fiber,

28.9 grams of fat,

474 calories

12.8 grams of net carbohydrates.

## Baked Eggplant Puree

Preparation time: 15 Minutes

Cooking time: 40 Minutes

Serving: 2

Ingredients:
- 16 tomatoes
- One cucumber
- 2 Tsp. ground pepper
- 1 Tsp. Salisaubergine olive oil
- One clove (s) garlic.
- Ground coriander

Directions:
1. Preheat the oven to high temperature. Make deep cuts in the aubergines and place them on a baking tray. Bake until smooth, about 30 to 40 minutes.
2. Let them cool until they can be manipulated, about 15 minutes for large aubergines and picas (or briefly pass through the blender or food processor), and place in a medium bowl.
3. Mix with oil, garlic, and cilantro. Salt and pepper to taste. Serve the mixture to accompany raw vegetable snacks such as cucumber sticks or cherry tomatoes.

Nutrition:

Carbohydrates: 1.8 grams

Proteins: 0.5 grams Fat: 10.6 grams

## Peanut Butter Granola

Preparation time: 10 minutes

Cooking time: 47 minutes Total time: 57 minutes

Servings: 2

Ingredients:
- Nonstick spray

- 4 cups oats
- ⅓ cup of cocoa powder
- ¾ cup peanut butter
- ⅓ cup maple syrup
- ⅓ cup avocado oil
- 1½ teaspoons vanilla extract
- ½ cup cocoa nibs
- 6 ounces dark chocolate, chopped

Directions:
1. Preheat your oven to 300 degrees F.
2. Spray a baking sheet with cooking spray.
3. In a medium saucepan, add oil, maple syrup, and peanut butter.
4. Cook for 2 minutes on medium heat, stirring.
5. Add the oats and cocoa powder, mix well.
6. Spread the coated oats on the baking sheet.
7. Bake for 45 minutes, occasionally stirring.
8. Garnish with dark chocolate, cocoa nibs, and peanut butter.
9. Serve.

Nutrition:

Calories 134

Total Fat 4.7 g

Saturated Fat 0.6 g Cholesterol 124mg

Sodium 1 mg Total Carbs 54.1 g

Fiber 7 g Sugar 3.3 g Protein 6.2 g

## Blueberry Yogurt

Preparation time: 2 Minutes

Baking time: 0 Minutes

Servings: 1

Ingredients:
- 39 gr. Blueberries
- 130 gr. Greek yogurt

Directions:
1. Add the blueberries to Greek yogurt and enjoy it.

Nutrition:

Carbohydrates: 7.6 grams

Proteins: 8.7 grams Fat: 13.2 grams

## Unforgettable Slow-Cooker Tater Tots

Preparation time: 10 Minutes

Cooking time: 8 hours

Servings: 1

Ingredients:
- 15 oz. Tater Tots
- 3 oz. Canadian bacon, diced
- One onion, chopped

- ½ cup cheddar cheese, shredded
- 1/8 cup Parmesan cheese, grated
- Six eggs
- ½ cup milk
- 2 Tbsp. All-purpose flour
- ½ tsp. salt
- 1/4 tsp. pepper

Directions:
1. Grease the stoneware insert with butter or ghee and add, one at a time in layers, 1/3 of the Tots, onion, bacon, and cheeses. Repeat with the two remaining thirds.
2. In a large bowl, mix all the remaining ingredients. Pour the mixture over the layered ingredients.
3. Cover and cook on Low for 6-8 hours.
4. You can prepare this overnight and enjoy a ready-made breakfast in the morning!

Nutrition:

Protein: 40.9g

Fat: 37.6g

Carbohydrate: 12g

Fiber: 38.3g

Total Calories: 654

## Breakfast Burrito

Preparation time: 10 Minutes

Baking time: 10 Minutes

Servings: 1

Ingredients:
- Four low carb tortillas
- 1/2 cup cheddar cheese, shredded
- 3 Spring Onions or scallions, large, diced
- One whole red tomato, medium, chopped
- 4 oz. canned green chili peppers
- 1/8 tsp. cayenne or red pepper
- 1 tbsp. canola vegetable oil
- Eight whole eggs, large
- 1/4 tsp. black pepper
- Nine sprigs cilantro, fresh
- 1 serving tomatillo salsa
- 1/2 tsp. salt

Directions:
1. Preheat your oven to 160C/325 F.
2. Wrap the tortillas in a large foil & heat in the preheated oven for 5 to 10 minutes. Over medium-high heat settings in a medium nonstick skillet; heat the oil. Add in the green onions, tomato, chiles, pepper & salt; sauté for 3 to 5 minutes.

3. Push this mixture to the side of the pan. Add eggs & cayenne to the skillet. Cook until soft, creamy curds form, for a minute or two, stirring now and then using a rubber spatula.
4. Add vegetable mixture into the eggs; stir well.
5. Evenly divide the mixture among warm tortillas, sprinkle with 2 tbsp. Of cheese, 1 tbsp. Of salsa & fresh cilantro. Roll up the tortillas. Serve & enjoy!

Nutrition:

333 Calories

168 Calories

23.9g Protein

## Stuffed Chicken With Asparagus & Bacon

Preparation time: 5 minutes

Cooking Time: 40 minutes

Serving: 2

Ingredients:

- 2 - Chicken tenders about 1 lb.
- 1/8 - tsp. salt , 1/4 - tsp. pepper
- 3 - Asparagus spears about .5 lb.
- 2 - Pieces bacon about .5 lb.

Directions:

1. Preheat oven to 400.
2. Spot 2 chook tenders to complete the system of the whole lot.
3. Season with pretty salt and pepper.
4. Incorporate three spears of asparagus.
5. Overlay the bacon over the fowl and asparagus to shield every piece of it together.
6. Warmth for 40mins until the hen is cooked through, the asparagus is clean, and the bacon is new.

Nutrition:

Calories 377g,

Fat 25g

Carbs 3g,

Protein 32g

## Basil Stuffed Chicken Breasts

Preparation time: 20 minutes

Cooking Time: 45 minutes

Serving: 2

Ingredients:

- 1 - bone-in, skin-on chicken breasts, 2 - tbsp. cream cheese
- 1 - tbsp. shredded cheese, 1/4 - tsp. garlic paste
- 3-4 - fresh basil leaves finely chopped, black pepper

Directions:

1. Preheat the oven to 375F.
2. Make the stuffing by joining the cream cheddar, cheddar, garlic paste, basil, and dull pepper.
3. Carefully strip back the skin on one side of the chicken chest and detect the half stuffing inside.
4. Smooth it down and supersede the skin
5. Repeat for the other piece of chicken.
6. Cook on a getting ready plate for 45 minutes or until the inward temperature of 165F has been come to.

Nutrition:

Calories 152g, Fat 15g

Carbs 8gSugar 12g Protein 22g

## Low Carb Pork Medallions

Preparation time: 15 minutes

Cooking Time: 30 minutes

Serving: 2

Ingredients:

- 1/2 - lb. pork tenderloin
- 1 1/2 - medium shallots (chopped nice), 1/4 - cup oil

Directions:

1. Diminish the hamburger into half-inch thick cuts.
2. Hack the shallots and notice them on a plate.
3. Warm the oil in a skillet press every piece of red meat into the shallots on the two angles.
4. Detect the hamburger cuts with shallots into the warm oil and get ready supper till achieved.
5. You will find that a piece of the shallots will expand for the span of cooking. At the same time, they'll even now present delightful taste to the meat.
6. Essentially cook supper the red meat until it's cooked through.
7. Present with veggies.

Nutrition:

Calories 53g  Fat 5g, Carbs 1g

Sugar 2g  Protein 6g

## Easy Mozzarella & Pesto Chicken Casserole

Preparation time: 30 minutes

Cooking Time: 30 minutes

Serving: 2

Ingredients:

- 1/8 - cup pesto, 8 - oz. cream cheese softened
- 1/8 - 1/2 - cup heavy cream
- 4 - oz. mozzarella cubed
- 1 - lb. cooked cubed chicken breasts
- 4 - oz. mozzarella shredded

Directions:

1. Preheat stove to 400. Sprinkle a tremendous supper dish with a cooking shower.
2. Unite the underlying three fixings and mix them until smooth in a bread bowl.
3. Incorporate the chicken and cubed mozzarella. Trade to the goulash dish.
4. Sprinkle the decimated mozzarella to complete the process of everything.
5. Plan for 25-30 minutes. Present with zoodles, spinach, or squashed cauliflower

Nutrition:

Calories 452g at 26g,

Carbs 11g Sugars 5g, Protein 39g

## Broccoli & Cheddar Keto Bread Recipe

Preparation time: 20 minutes

Cooking Time: 35 minutes

Serving: 2

Ingredients

- 1 - Egg beaten
- 1/4 - cup shredded cheddar cheese
- 1/4 - cup fresh raw broccoli florets chopped
- 1 - tbsp. coconut flour
- 1/2 - tsp. baking powder
- 1/4 - tsp. salt

Directions:

1. Preheat broiler to 350. Shower a portion skillet with a cooking splash.
2. Blend every one of the fixings in a medium bowl. Fill the portion skillet.
3. Heat for 30-35 minutes or until puffed and brilliant. Cut and serve.
4. To Reheat Microwave or warmth in a lubed griddle.

Nutrition:

Calories 443g Fat 29.8, Carbs 5.8g,

Sugars 2.1g, Protein 37.2g

## Bacon-Wrapped Chicken Tenders With Ranch Dip

Preparation time: 20 minutes

Cooking Time: 35 minutes

Serving: 2

Ingredients:

- 2- chicken tenderloins about .25 lb., 2 - slices of bacon

Ranch Dip Ingredients:

- 1/8 - cup sour cream, 1/3 - cup mayo, 1/2 - tsp. salt
- 1/8 - tsp. each garlic powder onion powder, parsley, and dill

Directions:

1. Preheat the broiler to 400.

2. Wrap every chicken delicate firmly in a bit of bacon. I extended the bacon as I folded it over the chicken.
3. Spot on a heating sheet. Prepare for 35-45 minutes until the bacon is fresh, and the chicken is thoroughly cooked.
4. In the meantime, mix the elements for the plunge. Present with the cooked chicken.

Nutrition:

Calories 204g, Fat 15g, Carbs 0.1g, Sugar 3.2g, Protein 13g

## Farmhouse Beans & Sausage

Preparation time: 15 minutes

Cooking Time: 30 minutes

Servings: 2

Ingredients:

- 2 - cups gluten-free chicken broth
- 2 16 - oz. frozen green beans
- 1 16 - oz. chicken sausage, sliced
- ½ - onion, diced
- 2 - teaspoons Herb mare
- salt & pepper to taste

Directions:
1. Spot all fixings in the Instant Pot. Spot top on and close, ensuring the steam vent is shut.
2. Utilize manual setting and set at 6 minutes.
3. When cook time is done, utilize the fast discharge strategy to let off steam.

Nutrition:

Calories 297.6g,

Fat 8.2g,

Carbs 38.2g,

Sugars 4.8g,

Protein 19.4g

## Meat-Lover Pizza Cups

Preparation time: 15 minutes

Cooking Time: 35 minutes

Serving: 2

Ingredients:

- 2 - deli ham slices
- 1/8 - lb. bulk Italian sausage
- 2 - Tbsp. sugar-free pizza sauce
- 1/2 - cups grated mozzarella cheese
- 4 - pepperoni slices
- 1/8 - cup cooked and crumbled bacon

Directions:
1. Preheat stove to 375 F. Dark-colored Italian frankfurters in

a skillet, depleting abundance oil.

2. Line 12-container biscuit tin with ham cuts. Gap frankfurter, pizza sauce, mozzarella cheddar, pepperoni cuts, and bacon disintegrate between each container, in a specific order.

3. Prepare at 375 for 10 minutes. Cook for 1 minute until cheddar air pockets and tans and the meat garnishes' edges look firm.

4. Take pizza containers out from the biscuit tin and set on a paper towel to keep the bottoms from getting wet. Appreciate promptly or refrigerate and reheat in toaster broiler or Microwave.

Nutrition:

Calories 520g, Fat 29g, Carbs 38g, Sugars 4g, Protein 26g

## 5 Minute 5 Ingredient Cheesy Bacon Chicken

Preparation time: 10 minutes

Cooking Time: 40 minutes

Serving: 2

Ingredients:

- 1 2/3 to 6 - chicken breasts, cut in half widthwise
- 2/3 - tbsp. seasoning rub
- 1/8 - pound bacon, cut strips in half
- 1 1/3 - oz. shredded cheddar
- sugar-free barbecue sauce, optional, to serve

Directions:

1. Preheat stove to 400. Splash a massive rimmed preparing sheet with a cooking shower.

2. Rub the two sides of chicken bosoms with flavoring rub. Top each with a bit of bacon. Prepare for 30 min on the best rack until the chicken is 160 degrees, and the bacon looks firm.

3. Take the plate out from the broiler and sprinkle the cheddar over the bacon. Set back in the broiler for around 10 min until the cheddar is bubbly and brilliant. Present with grill sauce.

Nutrition: Calories 345g, Fat 23g, Carbs 1g, Sugar 4.1g, Protein 29g

## Baked Pesto Chicken

Preparation time: 20 minutes

Cooking Time: 40 minutes

Serving: 2

Ingredients

- 2 - chicken breasts about 1.5 lb., sliced in half widthwise to make eight pieces
- 1 1/2 - tbsp. basil pesto
- 4 - oz. mozzarella thinly sliced or shredded
- 1/4 - tsp. salt, 1/4 - tsp. black pepper

Directions:

1. Preheat stove to 350.
2. Splash making a ready dish with cooking shower. Spot chicken inside the base in a solitary layer and sprinkle with the salt and pepper. Spread the pesto on the bird. Put the mozzarella to finish everything.
3. Prepare for 35-forty five minutes till the chook is a hundred and sixty stages, and the cheddar is excellent and bubbly. You can hear it for a few minutes toward the conclusion to darker the cheddar inside the event you want.

Nutrition:

Calories 287.5g, Fat 16g, Carbs 4.3g, Sugars 1.8g, Protein 30.3g

## Pizza Chicken Casserole

Preparation time: 10 minutes

Cooking Time: 50 minutes

Serving: 2

Ingredients:

- 1.5 to 2 - lb. cooked chicken breast sliced or cubed
- 8 - oz. cream cheese
- 1 - tsp. dried minced garlic
- 1 - cup marinara sauce no sugar added
- 8 - oz. shredded mozzarella

Directions:

1. Preheat oven to 350.
2. Put the chicken in the backside of a 9x13 baking dish.
3. Combine cream cheese and garlic. Drop small spoonfuls onto the bird. Pour the sauce on the pinnacle. Sprinkle with the shredded mozzarella.
4. Bake for 30 min or till the cheese is melted and bubbly.

Nutrition:

Calories 258.1g, Fat 14.1g, Carbs 3.1g, Sugars 0.7g, Protein 28.1g

## Keto Cauliflower Au Gratin

Preparation time: 25 minutes

Cooking Time: 55 minutes

Serving: 2

Ingredients:

- 1/2 - large head of cauliflower, trimmed and cut into florets
- 1 - small red onions, thinly sliced
- 1 - tablespoons olive oil
- 1 - tablespoons balsamic vinegar
- 1/2 - tablespoon granular erythritol
- 1/3 - cup heavy cream
- 1/4 - cup finely grated parmesan
- 1/4 - teaspoon sea salt, more to taste
- 1/8 - teaspoon black pepper, more to taste
- 1/2 - cup shredded gruyere or gouda cheese

Directions:

1. Preheat the broiler to 350°F.
2. Put the olive oil in a significant skillet over medium warmth. When the dish is hot, upload the onions to the field and cook dinner till delicate and sensitive, around 15mins.
3. Include the balsamic vinegar and erythritol if utilizing, to the field with the onions, and blend to consolidate. Cook for a further 5 minutes.
4. Upload cauliflower florets to the pan and blend it with the onions.
5. In a touch bowl, is part of the large cream, parmesan cheddar, salt, and pepper? Pour the aggregate over great of the cauliflower.
6. Sprinkle the gruyere over high-quality and prepare for 40 minutes or until the cauliflower is touchy, and the splendid is first-rate dark-colored and bubbly.

Nutrition: Calories 230g, Fat 17g, Carbs 11.9g, Sugars 0.4g, Protein 9.2g

## Boosted Keto Coffee

Preparation time: 15 minutes

Cooking Time: 30 minutes

Serving: 1

Ingredients:

- 8 - ounces dark roast coffee
- 1 - tablespoons butter flavored coconut oil
- 1 - scoop Keto Zone French Vanilla
- 1 - scoop Collagen Peptides
- 2 - teaspoons monk fruit sweetened caramel syrup
- Splash coconut milk

Directions:

1. Pour all the ingredients into a blender or milk frothier and Blend till smooth and creamy. ENJOY!!

Nutrition:

Calories 296g, Fat 23g, Carbs 16g, Sugars 2.1g, Protein 15g

## Sugar-Free, Low Carb Dried Cranberries

Preparation time: 35 minutes

Cooking Time: 3hrs. 10 minutes

Serving: 1

INGREDIENTS

- 2 to 12 - ounce bags fresh cranberries
- 1 - Cup granular erythritol
- 3 - Tablespoons avocado oil
- ½ - teaspoon pure orange extract

Directions:

1. Preheat the stove to 200°F. Line two rimmed preparing sheets with material paper.
2. Wash and dry the cranberries and expel any sautéed or delicate berries. Cut the cranberries into equal parts and add them to a blending bowl.
3. Include the sugar, avocado oil, and orange concentrate if utilizing. Hurl to coat the majority of the berries equitably.
4. Line the berries in single layers over the heating sheets.
5. Heat for 3 to 4 hours, turning the racks part of the way through.

Nutrition:

Calories 208.8g, Fat 22.5g, Carbs 0.8g, Sugars 0.1g, Protein 1.6g

## Original Almond Porridge

Preparation time: 5 minutes

Cooking Time: 2 minutes

Serving: 2

Ingredients:

- 1/4 cup unsweetened almond milk
- 1/3 cup ground almond
- 1/4 tsp. cinnamon
- 1-Tbsp. butter

Topping:

- 2 Tbsp. sliced roasted almond

Directions:

1. Pour the almond milk into a microwave-safe bowl. Microwave it for 2 minutes.
2. Add the almond flour to the bowl and microwave again for a minute.
3. When it is done, remove from the microwave, and then quickly stir in butter and cinnamon. Mix well.
4. Serve and enjoy warm.

Nutrition:

Each serving contains 144 Calories, 4.8 g Net Carbs, 13.1 g Fats, 4.2 g Protein

## Spinach Scrambled Egg

Preparation time: 5 minutes

Cooking Time: 10 minutes

Serving: 2

Ingredients:

- 1/2 tsp. coconut oil
- two organic eggs
- 1-cup spinach
- 1/2 Tbsp. Chopped onion ring
- 1/4 tsp. pepper

Directions:

1. Crack the eggs and drop into a bowl. Using a fork, beat until incorporated, then sets aside.

2. Preheat a saucepan over medium heat, and then pour coconut oil into the saucepan.

3. Once it is hot, stir in the chopped onion and sautés until wilted and aromatic.

4. Add spinach to the saucepan and cooks until wilted.

5. Pour beaten egg over the spinach, and then quickly stir the eggs until becoming scrambles.

6. Season with pepper, then cooks until the egg is set but still soft.

7. Transfer to a serving dish, then serves immediately.

Nutrition:

Each serving contains 76 Calories, 1g Net Carbs, 5.5 g Fats, 5.8 g Protein

## Bell Pepper Frittata

Preparation time: 1hr. 45 minutes

Cooking Time: 30 minutes

Serving: 2

Ingredients:

- Three organic eggs
- 1 tsp. minced garlic
- 1 1/2 Tbsp. chopped onion
- 1/3 cup sliced red bell pepper
- 1/3 cup yellow bell pepper
- 1 tsp. Olive oil
- 1/4 cup sliced zucchini
- 1/8 cup plain yogurt
- 1/3 tsp. pepper

Directions:

1. Crack the eggs, and then place in a bowl. Add yogurt to the eggs, and then beat until incorporated.

2. Preheat a pan over medium heat, then pours olive oil into it.

3. Once it is hot, stir in the chopped onion and minced garlic, then sautés until wilted and aromatic.

4. Add bell pepper and zucchini into the pan, then sautés until wilted.

5. Pour the egg mixture over the bell pepper, and zucchini then spread evenly. Remove from heat, then covers with aluminum foil.

6. Preheat an oven to 325°F, then bakes the frittata for an hour.

7. After an hour, takes the pan out from the oven, and then uncover it.

8. Return to the oven back then bakes for 30 minutes until the frittata's top is lightly golden.

9. Remove from the oven, and then transfer to a serving dish.

10. Cut the frittata into wedges, and then serve. Enjoy!

Nutrition:

Each serving contains 100 Calories, 6.4 g Net Carbs, 5.9 g Fats, 5.9 g Protein

## Coconut Pancake

Preparation time: 5 minutes

Cooking Time: 5 minutes

Serving: 2

Ingredients:

- 1/4 cup coconut flour
- Two organic eggs
- 1/8 cup of coconut milk
- 1/2 tsp. coconut oil

Directions:

1. Place the real ingredients in a mixing bowl.
2. Using a whisker, mix until incorporated.
3. Preheat a pan over medium heat, and then brush the pan with coconut oil.
4. Drop about 2 Tbsp. Of the mixture into the pan and make a pancake.
5. Cook the pancake for about 2 minutes, then flips it. Cook again for another 2 minutes or until both sides of the pancakes are lightly golden.
6. Repeat with the remaining mixture, then arranges the pancakes on a serving dish.
7. Serve and enjoy warm.

Nutrition:

Each serving contains 83 Calories, 2 g Net Carbs, 7.2 g Fats, 3.4 g Protein

## Avocado Tuna Salads

Preparation time: 15 minutes

Cooking Time: 20 minutes

Serving: 2

Ingredients:

- 1 ripe avocados
- 1/2 cup cooked chopped tuna
- 1/8 cup diced tomato
- 1/2 Tbsp. Chopped onion
- 1/4 tsp. pepper
- 1/2 tsp. olive oil
- 1 1/2 tsp. lemon juice

Directions:

1. Preheat a skillet over medium heat, and then pour olive oil into it.
2. Once it is hot, stir in chopped onion, then sautés until translucent and aromatic.
3. Add tuna and tomato to the skillet, then sautés until wilted.
4. Season with pepper and lemon juice, and then stir well.
5. Remove the tuna from heat, and then let it cool for a few minutes.
6. Cut the avocados into halves, and then discard the seeds.
7. Scoop out the avocado flesh, and then combine it with the cooked tuna.
8. Fill the halved avocado with the tuna and avocado mixture, then arranges on a serving dish.

9. Serve and enjoy right away.

Nutrition:

Each serving contains 214 Calories, 8.4 g Net Carbs, 15.8 g Fats, 12.1 g Protein

## Veggie Quiche

Preparation time: 30 minutes

Cooking Time: 20 minutes

Serving: 2

Ingredients:

- 1/3 Tbsp. olive oil
- 1 Tbsp. chopped onion
- 1 tsp. minced garlic
- 1/2 cup chopped kale
- 1/8 cup diced bell pepper
- 1/3 cup diced tomato
- 1 organic eggs
- 2 organic egg whites
- 1/2 Tbsp. Milk
- 1/4 tsp. Oregano
- 1/4 tsp. black pepper

Directions:

1. Preheat an oven to 425°F, then coat eight muffin cups with cooking spray. Set aside.
2. Preheat a skillet over medium heat, then pours olive oil into it.
3. Once it is hot, stir in the chopped onion minced garlic, then sautés until aromatic and translucent.
4. Add kale, bell pepper, and tomato, then stirs until wilted. Remove from heat.
5. Crack the eggs, and then place them in a bowl.
6. Pour milk into the eggs, then seasons with oregano and black pepper.
7. Add the sautéed vegetables to the egg mixture, and then mix well.
8. Divide the mixture into the eight prepared muffin cups, then bake for 20 minutes or until the eggs are set.
9. Remove the quiche from the oven, and then let them cool for a few minutes.
10. Take the quiche out from the cups, then arrange on a serving dish.
11. Serve and enjoy immediately.

Nutrition:

Each serving contains 95 Calories, 5.4 g Net Carbs, 5.1 g Fats, 7.6 g Protein

## Broccoli Turkey Casserole

Preparation time: 40 minutes

Cooking Time: 30 minutes

Serving: 2

Ingredients:

- 1-cup broccoli florets
- 1/2 cup grated cheddar cheese
- 1/2 cup shredded cooked turkey
- four organic eggs
- 3/4 tsp. black pepper
- 1/8 cup chopped onion
- 1 1/2 tsp. butter

Directions:

1. Preheat an oven to 325°F, then coats a casserole dish with cooking spray. Set aside.
2. Preheat a skillet over medium heat, then place butter in it.
3. Once the butter is melted, stir in chopped onion and broccoli, then sauté until the onion is aromatic, and the broccoli is crispy.
4. Add cooked turkey to the skillet, and then mix well.
5. Transfer the mixture to the prepared casserole dish, then spreads evenly. Set aside.
6. Crack the eggs, and then place in a bowl.
7. Season the eggs with pepper, then beats until incorporated.
8. Pour the egg mixture over the broccoli and turkey, and then sprinkle grated cheese on top.
9. Bake the casserole for 30 minutes until the eggs are set.
10. Remove the casserole from the oven, then serve warm.

Nutrition:

Each serving contains 337 Calories, 3.7 g Net Carbs, 22.8 g Fats, 29.2 g Protein

## Strawberry Rolls

Preparation time: 5 minutes

Cooking Time: 10 minutes

Serving: 2

Ingredients:

- 1 organic egg
- 1/2 tsp. olive oil
- 1 1/2 Tbsp. almond flour
- 1/4 cup strawberry

Directions:

1. Crack the eggs and drop in a bowl.
2. Add almond flour to the egg, then using a whisker, mix the egg, and almond flour until incorporated, then sets aside.
3. Preheat a pan over medium heat, and then make four omelets on it.
4. Transfer the omelets to a flat surface, and then set aside.
5. Place the strawberries in a blender, and then blend until smooth.
6. Brush each omelet with strawberry, and then roll them.
7. Arrange on a serving dish, and then serve immediately.

Nutrition:

Each serving contains 70 Calories, 1.9 g Net Carbs, 5.1 g Fats, 4.5 g Protein

## Eggs With Avocado, Salsa, And Turkey Bacon (5.8g)

Preparation time: 15 minutes

Cooking Time: 5 minutes

Serving: 2

Ingredients:

2. 2 pcs Large eggs
3. ½ pc Sliced Hass avocado
4. 1 Ounce Salsa
5. 2 Ounce Turkey bacon

Directions:

1. Fry turkey bacon slices until crispy.
2. Cook the eggs. That can be fried, scrambled, or poached. Set aside.
3. Layer the eggs, avocado, and bacon, and then top it with salsa.

Nutrition:

Calories 75

Protein 7 grams

Fat 5 grams

## Herbed Scrambled Eggs (1.6g)

Preparation time: 10 minutes

Cooking Time: 10 minutes

Serving: 2

Ingredients:

- 6 pcs Large eggs 2 Tablespoon Heavy cream
- 1 tbsp. unsalted butter
- ¼ TeaspoonSalt
- 1/8 Teaspoon
- Black pepper
- Fresh parsley
- 1 Teaspoon Chives or tarragon

Directions:

1. Whisk eggs with cream, herbs, salt, and pepper in a bowl.
2. Melt the butter into a non-stick pan, and then pour in the eggs. Let the eggs cook for 1 minute without stirring.
3. Stir eggs to form soft creamy small curds. Remove eggs before they turn brown.
4. Serve immediately.

Nutrition:

Calories 105g

Protein 7 grams

Fat 11.5 grams

## Cream Cheese Spinach Omelette

Preparation time: 10 minutes

Cooking Time: 5 minutes

Serving: 1

Ingredients:

- Cream cheese 2 oz.
- Chopped fresh spinach leaves ¼ cup

- Large eggs 2 pcs
- Toasted sesame seed oil ¼ teaspoon

Directions:

1. Mix cream cheese and spinach, then set aside.
2. Beat two eggs in a separate bowl and set aside as well.
3. Use toasted sesame seed oil and lightly grease the frying pan.
4. Preheat the pan over medium heat, and then pour in the eggs.
5. Cook eggs for 1 minute, then flip it on the other side.
6. Spread cream cheese mixture onto the cooked side of the egg.
7. Fold egg in half. Wait at least 1 minute for the cream cheese mixture to melt.
8. Remove from heat and serve immediately.

Nutrition:

Calories 150 Protein 9 grams Fat 6.5 grams

## Baked Corned Beef Omelets (5g Net Carbs)

Preparation time: 30 minutes

Cooking Time: 20 minutes

Serving: 2

Ingredients:

- Large eggs 2 pcs
- Thinly sliced corned beef 3 ounce
- Heavy cream 1 cup
- Grated mozzarella cheese 1 cup
- Chopped green onion 1 tbsp.
- Lawry's Seasoned salt ½ teaspoon

Directions:

1. Preheat oven to 325 degrees.
2. Mix cream, beaten eggs and seasoned salt together.
3. Tear the sliced corned beef into smaller pieces.
4. Add corned beef, cheese, and onion into the egg mixture.
5. Pour the mixture into a greased baking dish.
6. Bake without cover for 45 minutes or until the top is golden brown.

Nutrition:

Calories: 102.1 Total Fat: 6.8 g

Protein: 7.9 g Saturated Fat: 2.3 g

## Broccoli Frittata

Preparation time: 20 minutes

Cooking Time: 20 minutes

Serving: 2

Ingredients:

- Non-fat cottage cheese ½ cup
- Dried dill ½ teaspoon

- Fat-free egg substitute 2 cups
- Frozen chopped broccoli 10-ounce
- Olive oil 1 tsp.
- Margarine 2 teaspoon
- Diced onion one pc

Directions:

1. Use a non-stick frying pan to sauté onions in oil for 5 minutes over medium heat.
2. Add broccoli and dried dill, then sauté for another 5 minutes.
3. Mix eggs and cottage cheese in a large bowl, then add the broccoli mixture into it.
4. Wipe clean the frying pan, and then let it stand for 2 minutes.
5. Swirl one teaspoon of margarine onto the pan to grease it.
6. Pour in just half of the egg mixture. Lift and rotate the pan, so the eggs are distributed evenly.
7. Set heat to low and cover the pan. Wait until the top portion is cooked.
8. Put cooked eggs onto a serving plate and cut evenly into wedges.
9. Repeat steps 4-9 with the remaining one teaspoon margarine and egg mixture.

Nutrition:

Calories 185

Protein 13.4 grams

Fat 11.6 grams

## Soft Scrambled Eggs With Lobster

Preparation time: 20 minutes

Cooking Time: 15 minutes

Serving: 2

Ingredients:

- Unsalted butter 6 Tablespoons
- Seeded red bell pepper ½ pc
- Heavy or whipping cream 5 Tablespoons
- Freshly cooked lobster meat
- (torn into 1/2-inch pieces) 12 ounces
- Large eggs - lightly beaten nine pcs
- Fresh chives – snipped 2 Tablespoons
- Salt
- Black Pepper

Directions:

1. Melt two tablespoons of the butter in a small skillet over medium heat.
2. Sauté the bell pepper into the skillet for 2 minutes.
3. Add lobster meat and continue sautéing until lobster is warm enough. Put in chives and cook for 30 seconds more, then remove skillet from heat. Set aside.
4. Melt another two tablespoons of butter in a giant skillet, but this time over low heat.
5. Put in the eggs and just half the cream.

6. Scramble the eggs by stirring with a rubber spatula to make soft creamy curds.
7. Continue by adding the remaining half of the cream and the last 2 Tablespoons of butter to the eggs.
8. Stir the eggs until the texture is very thick and creamy.
9. Add salt and pepper to taste.
10. Get the lobster mixture and quickly fold just until evenly distributed.
11. Serve immediately.

Nutrition:

Calories 279

Protein 28 grams

## Alaskan Salmon Omelet

Preparation time: 10 minutes

Cooking Time: 10 minutes

Serving: 2

INGREDIENTS:

- Flaked salmon 8 ounce
- Large eggs 2 pcs
- Sour cream 2 Tablespoons
- Unsalted Butter 2 Tablespoons
- Fresh tarragon 1/2 teaspoon
- Salt
- White Pepper

DIRECTIONS:

1. Beat the eggs together with sour cream and minced tarragon. Add salt and pepper.
2. Melt the butter using a non-stick, oven-safe skillet over medium heat. Make sure the melted butter completely covers the bottom surface of the skillet.
3. Pour the egg mixture into the skillet and cook until the base is set.
4. Arrange salmon on top of the omelet. Remove from heat.
5. Preheat oven to 375 degrees.
6. Place the skillet on the top shelf of the oven for about 10 minutes.
7. Carefully fold the omelet in half.
8. Slide the omelet onto a serving plate. Serve immediately.

Nutrition:

Calories 224 Protein 32.74 grams

Fat 6.56 grams

## Cottage Cheese Scramble

Preparation time: 10 minutes

Cooking Time: 50 minutes

Serving: 2

INGREDIENTS:

- Whole eggs ¼ cup
- Cottage cheese ½ cup

- Instant nonfat dry milk 1/3 cup
- Water ¼ cup
- Unsalted Butter 2 Tablespoons
- Chopped chives 1 Tablespoon
- Salt ¼ teaspoon
- Black pepper

DIRECTIONS:

1. Whisk together eggs, cottage cheese, nonfat dry milk, water, salt, pepper, and chives in a large bowl.
2. Melt the butter in a large skillet over medium heat.
3. Pour the egg mixture into the skillet, stirring continuously to make soft and creamy curds.
4. Serve immediately.

Nutrition:

Calories 298

Fat 24 grams

## Low Carb Mac 'N Cheese

Preparation time: 10 minutes

Cooking Time: 50 minutes

Serving: 2

INGREDIENTS:

- Cauliflower 16 oz.
- Cream cheese 4 oz.
- Cheddar cheese 4 oz.
- Colby jack cheese 4 oz.
- Heavy cream 2 tbsp.
- Minced Garlic 1 tsp.
- Chopped bacon six slices
- Chopped green onion ¼ cup
- Chicken bouillon 1 tsp.
- Black pepper ½ teaspoon

Directions:

1. Place cauliflower in a glass dish and cook in microwave until tender.
2. Chop cooked cauliflower in small pieces using a food processor.
3. Combine cream cheese, cheddar cheese, Colby jack, cream, and minced garlic in a medium pot over medium heat. Stir continuously until smooth.
4. Stir in chopped cauliflower, bacon, green onion, chicken bouillon, and black pepper to the cheese sauce.
5. Serve warm.

## Cream Cheese Pancakes (2.5g Net Carbs)

Preparation time: 10 minutes

Cooking Time: 3 minutes

Serving: 2

INGREDIENTS:

- Cream cheese 2 oz.
- Whole eggs 2 pcs

- Stevia sweetener one packet
- Cinnamon1/2 teaspoon

DIRECTIONS:

1. Put all ingredients in a blender to make a batter. Blend until smooth, and then set aside for 2 minutes.
2. Pour 1/4 of the batter into a hot pan to make 6-inch sized pancakes. Use cooking spray or butter to grease the pan.
3. Cook one side for 2 minutes, flip and cook the other side for 1 minute.
4. Repeat steps 1-4 for the rest of the batter.
5. Serve with sugar-free syrup and fresh berries.

Nutrition:

Calories 185g

Protein 7 grams

Fat 5 grams

## Crustless Breakfast Tarts With Mushrooms And Goat Cheese

Preparation time: 30 minutes

Cooking Time: 25 minutes

Serving: 2

INGREDIENTS:

- Goat cheese4 oz.
- Half-and-half¼ cup
- Finely grated Parmesan2 Tablespoons
- Sliced Crimini mushrooms12 oz.
- Olive oil2 tsp.
- Spike seasoning1 tsp.
- Fresh-ground black pepper
- Whole eggs8 pcs
- Sliced green onions two pcs
- Grated Mozzarella cheese6 Tablespoons

Directions:

1. Cut, crumble, and soften the goat cheese into a mixing bowl.
2. Preheat oven to 375F/190C. Spray the tart pan with olive oil.
3. Mix milk, half-and-half into the goat cheese, and then add in the Parmesan cheese.
4. Beat the eggs in a separate bowl.
5. Gradually add the beaten eggs into the goat cheese mixture while stirring continuously.
6. Cook sliced mushrooms over medium-high heat until all the liquid has evaporated and mushrooms are starting to brown. Divide mushrooms evenly in the tart pan.
7. Stir in the custard mixture on top of the mushrooms.
8. Sprinkle minced green onions on top of each tart, followed by mozzarella cheese.

9. Bake for about 25 minutes. Cook just until the top portions of tarts start to brown. Serve hot.

Nutrition:

Calories 185g

Protein 7 grams

Fat 5 grams

## Shrimp Salad With Eggs

Preparation time: 10 minutes

Cooking Time: 0 minutes

Serving: 2

Ingredients:

- 200 grams of seafood;
- A bunch of green salad;
- Vegetable oil (100 g);
- 2 eggs;
- Vinegar and lemon juice (2 tablespoons each);
- Some mustard;
- Spice.

Directions:

1. Boil shrimps and eggs, peel, and cut into cubes. Tear the salad. Put everything in a bowl.
2. Prepare the sauce - mix oil, mustard, vinegar, lemon juice, and spices in a jar. Close the lid tightly.
3. Shake the mixture.
4. Add dressing to the salad and mix.

Nutrition:

Calories 185g Protein 7 grams Fat 5 grams

## Bacon Meat Rolls

Preparation time: 25 minutes

Cooking Time: 20 minutes

Serving: 2

Ingredients:

- A pound of beef
- Two cloves of garlic
- 250 grams of smoked bacon
- Oil
- Spice

Directions:

1. Slice the bacon in broad stripes. Beef, beat with spices.
2. Pass the garlic through a garlic squeezer.
3. Place the bacon on a strip of beef and spin the roll so that it is inside. Pound the resulting roll onto a toothpick.
4. Fry the rolls on both sides for several minutes. The crust should be golden.
5. Transfer toasted rolls onto a baking sheet, bake until tender (about 20 minutes).

Nutrition:

Calories 185g Protein 7 grams Fat 5 grams

## Grilled Steak With Red Pepper

Preparation time: 15 minutes

Cooking Time: 0 minutes

Serving: 2

Ingredients

- Three-piece steak
- Three roasted red peppers

For Sauce

- 1 tbsp. Worcestershire sauce
- 2 tbsp. honey
- 4 tbsp. balsamic vinegar
- 3 tbsp. of ketchup or hot sauce
- 1 tsp. of Dijon mustard
- 3 tbsp. olive oil
- 1 tsp. of granulated sugar
- Salt
- Black pepper

Directions:

1. Mix the ingredients for the sauce in a deep bowl. Place roasted peppers on each steak and wrap it in roll form.
2. Cut the rolls in half and thread the bottle. Grill the steaks. When cooking both sides, apply with a brush from the sauce. Take your steaks to the serving plate.

Nutrition:

Calories 185g Protein 7 grams Fat 5 grams

## Grilled Shrimp With Mint Sauce

Preparation time: 20 minutes

Cooking Time: 15 minutes

Serving: 2

Ingredients:

- 250 g shrimp

For Sauce

Half of fresh mint

- 1-2 shallots
- 1 1/2 cloves of garlic
- 1 tablespoons apple cider vinegar
- One tea glass of olive oil
- 1/2 tsp. of sugar
- 1 tsp. of salt
- 1/2 tsp. of red paprika

Directions:

1. For the sauce, put all ingredients except olive oil into the blender and run the blender. Slowly add olive oil and have a thick consistency.
2. Extract the shrimps and put them in a deep dish. Hover over the sauce and find all sides. Wrap the stretch film and leave in the refrigerator for at least 2-3 hours. Pass the prawns to the bottle. Cook on the overheated grill. Serve hot.

## California Grilled Chicken

Preparation time: 20 minutes

Cooking Time: 40 minutes

Servings: 2

Ingredients:

- 1/3 c. balsamic vinegar
- 1/2 tsp. Garlic Powder
- 1 tbsp. honey
- 1 tbsp. extra virgin olive oil
- 1 tsp. Italian spice
- Kosher salt
- Freshly ground black pepper
- 2 boneless chicken breast without the skin
- 2 slices of mozzarella
- 2 slices of avocado
- 2 tomato slices
- 1 tbsp. freshly cut basil for garnish
- Balsamic glaze for drizzling

Directions

1. In a small bowl, whisk balsamic vinegar, garlic powder, honey, oil, and Italian spices and season with salt and pepper. Pour the chicken and marinate for 20 minutes.
2. When you are ready to grill, heat the grill to medium-high. Grate the oil grills and chicken until charred and cooked through, 8 minutes each side.
3. Top chicken with the mozzarella, avocado, and tomato and lid grill melt, 2 minutes.
4. Garnish with basil and then drizzle with some balsamic glaze.

## Coriander Lime Grilled Salmon

Preparation time: 5 minutes

Cooking Time: 20 minutes

Servings: 2

Ingredients:

- 1/8 c. balsamic vinegar
- 1/4 tsp. Garlic Powder
- 1/2 tbsp. honey
- 1/2 tbsp. extra virgin olive oil
- 1/2 tsp. Italian spice
- Kosher salt
- Freshly ground black pepper
- 1 boneless chicken breast without the skin
- 1 slices of mozzarella
- 1 slices of avocado
- 1 tomato slices
- 1/2 tbsp. freshly cut basil for garnish
- Balsamic glaze for drizzling

Directions:

1. Season salmon with salt and pepper. Heat the grill and place the salmon meat side down on the grill. Cook for 8 minutes, then turn and cook on the other side until the salmon is cooked through another 6 minutes. Let rest for 5 minutes.
2. In the meantime, prepare the sauce: inside a medium saucepan over medium heat, add butter, lime juice, honey, and the garlic. Mix it until butter is melted and all ingredients are combined. Turn off heat and add cilantro.
3. Pour salmon over the sauce and serve.

## Grilled Zucchini Salad

Preparation time: 25 minutes

Cooking Time: 10 minutes

Serving: 2

Ingredients:

- 1 zucchini
- 1 1/2 tablespoons mild olive oil
- 1/2 tbsp. balsamic vinegar
- 25 g of hazelnuts
- 7 1/2 g fresh basil
- 5 g of fresh mint
- 75 g burrata

Directions:

1. Cut the zucchini into 1 cm long slices. Season with salt and pepper and sprinkle with olive oil. Heat the grill pan and grill the zucchini slices in 4 minutes. Turn halfway. Put the zucchini slices in a bowl, mix with the balsamic vinegar and let stand until use.
2. Heat a pan without oil or butter and roast the hazelnuts until golden brown for 3 minutes over medium heat. Cool on a plate and chop roughly.
3. Cut basil leaves and mint roughly. The stems of basil finely chopped. They have a lot of taste. Mix the zucchini with the herbs and the rest of the oil. Tear the burrata to pieces.
4. Divide first the zucchini and then the burrata over the plates. Sprinkle with the roasted hazelnuts and herbs - season with (freshly ground) pepper and possibly salt.
5. Serving suggestion:
6. The salad tastes great with chicken from the oven.

Nutrition:

320 kcal

## Grilled Fennel With Mozzarella And Caper And Lemon Dressing

Preparation time: 22 minutes

Cooking Time: 8 minutes

Serving: 2

Ingredients:

- 125 g cherry tomatoes on the branch
- 1 1/2 tbsp. mild olive oil
- 1 fennel tubers
- 15 g pine nuts
- 1/4 lemons
- 1/4 tbsp. liquid honey
- 1 1/2 tbsps. extra virgin olive oil
- 25 g capers
- 1 balls mozzarella

Directions:

1. Preheat your oven temperature to 200 ° C. Place the cherry tomatoes on a baking sheet covered with baking paper on a branch, drizzle with mild, mild olive oil, and sprinkle with pepper. Approximately 8 minutes.
2. Heat grill pan. Cut the green and tops of the fennel tubers. Finely chop the green. Leave the stump on the fennel and cut the fennel lengthwise into thin slices. Sprinkle with the

remaining olive oil and grill for 3 minutes in the grill pan.

3. Heat a pan without oil or butter and roast the pine nuts golden brown over medium heat. Let it cool on a plate.
4. Scrub the lemon, rub the yellow skin and squeeze out the fruit. Mix the juice and rub with the honey and extra virgin olive oil. Add the capers and fennel green.
5. Quarter the mozzarella. Spread the grilled fennel on the plates, place the ¼-ball mozzarella, and a sprig of roasted tomatoes on each plate, and spread the dressing and pine nuts on top.
6. Variation Tip:
7. Dive it! Use the green fennel sprouts to make a yogurt dip. Finely chopped with a little mint and honey and Tada: Your homemade dip is ready.

## Avocado Wrapped In Bacon

Preparation time: 22 minutes

Cooking Time: 15-30 minutes

Serving: 2

Ingredients:

- 1 avocados (ripe)
- 7-10 strips of bacon

Directions:

1. For the avocado wrapped in bacon-wrapped bacon, first, preheat the oven to 180 ° C. Cover a baking tray with baking paper.
2. Halve the avocado and remove the kernel. Carefully remove the pulp (preferably with a tablespoon). Then cut lengthwise into approximately 1 cm thick slits.
3. Wrap each column with a strip of bacon and place it on the baking sheet. Put the avocado wrapped in bacon in the oven for about 15 minutes until the bacon is crispy. Best observe because every range is a little different.

Tip

The bacon-wrapped avocado is ideal as a starter, snack, or side dish. It can also be prepared as a grill on the grill.

## Grilled Dumplings On Fine Coleslaw With Bacon

Preparation time: 22 minutes

Cooking Time: 30-60 minutes

Serving: 2

Ingredients:

Dough:

- 62 1/2 grams of butter
- 75 grams of flour (handy)
- 125 grams of quark
- One egg

Salt Filling:

- 100 grams cracklings
- One onion
- One bunch of parsley

- Coriander
- One clove of garlic
- Salt
- Pepper
- Marjoram

Lovage coleslaw:

- 450 grams white cabbage
- 50 grams of bacon grease
- One sliced onion
- 1 1/2 tbsp. butter
- 1/2 tsp. caraway (whole)
- 62 1/2 ml white wine
- Wine vinegar
- Oil
- Salt
- Pepper
- 1 tbsp. sugar (or honey)

Directions:

For the dough:

1. Knead all the ingredients quickly and chill.

For the fruitful:

2. Chop the pieces, pluck and chop parsley, remove garlic from the skin, and press through the press. Chop the onion and sauté; pour the remaining ingredients and then season.
3. Form the dough into a roll and then cut into small pieces. Just press the pieces of dough. Put some filling on the dough and form dumplings. Dumpling in boiling water, bring to a boil and, with the lid closed, pull for about 7 minutes.

For the coleslaw:

1. Roast onion with bacon, add caraway with sugar or honey, add the cut cabbage with white wine, and softly. Marinate with white wine vinegar, oil, salt, and pepper.

## Adana Kebab Recipe

Preparation time: 45 minutes

Cooking Time: 25 minutes

Serving: 2

Ingredients:

- 116 2/3 grams of ground beef
- 100 grams of lamb minced meat
- 1/3 clove of garlic
- 2/3 pieces of onions
- 1/3 teaspoon of chili peppers
- 1/3 teaspoon black pepper
- 1/3 tablespoon hot pepper paste
- 1/8 bunch of parsley

The Tip of Adana Kebab Recipe

Lubricating the grill wire will help the meat to taste more when cooking. You can obtain tail oil from your butcher and taste your kebab for this lubrication.

Adana Kebab Recipe Cooking Suggestion

Always put a baking tray under the wire shelf and the kebabs will be greased. Running in a finless program will prevent the meat from drying out.

Directions:

1. Chop the onions into cubes. Filter the water into a deep container.

2. Crush the garlic and mix with onions. Stir the lamb minced meat and veal minced meat and blend with the onion and garlic mixture.

3. Chili, pepper, and hot pepper paste mixture to the mixture.

4. Add the oil. Finely chop the parsley and then add to the mixture.

5. Let the mortar rest in the cupboard for 2-3 hours.

6. Lubricate the oven grill with tail oil from the butcher or butter with butter.

7. Heat the oven to 200 degrees in a fanless program.

8. Spread the meat to the flat skewers.

9. Index on the wire shelf. Cook for 20-25 minutes. Enjoy your meal!

10. Adana Kebap Recipe Service Suggestion

11. If you wish, you can put onions, tomatoes, peppers, or thinly sliced eggplant slices on the grill and enrich your food. If you put lavash bread on the meats close to cooking, it will absorb the fat and strengthen the flavor.

## Wings Recipe With Sauce

Preparation Time: 20 minutes

Cooking Time: 50 minutes

Serving: 2 people

Ingredients:

- 1-kilogram chicken wing
- 4 tbsp.sunflower oil
- 4 tbsp. of milk
- 2 tbsp.yogurt
- 1 tsp. tomato paste
- 1 tsp. hot sauce
- Two cloves of garlic
- 1/2 teaspoon of grape vinegar
- 1/2 teaspoon of honey
- One bay leaf
- 1 tsp. of oregano
- 1 tsp. fresh ground black pepper
- 1 tsp. of salt
- One sprig of fresh rosemary

Directions:

1. Wash the chicken wings in plenty of water and remove excess water with paper towels.

2. Grate the garlic. Mix sunflower oil, milk, yogurt, tomato paste, hot sauce, and honey in a large bowl.

3. Add grated garlic, bay leaf, thyme, freshly ground colored black pepper,

extracted rosemary branches, and salt. Mix all the ingredients.

4. Put the chicken wings in the sauce mixture you prepared and place them in a single row on the oven tray.

5. Bake in a preheated 180-degree oven for 45-50 minutes. Serve hot wings, which draw the sauce and flavored with spices.

Nutrition:

203 calories, 30.5 grams of protein, and 8.1 grams of fat

# CHAPTER 7:

# Lunch

## Chef Salad

Preparation Time: 20 minutes

Cooking Time: 10 minutes

Serving: 2 people

Ingredients:

- 2 slices deli ham, divided
- 2 slices deli turkey, divided
- 2 slices deli roast beef, divided 1 cup cheese, divided
- 3 slices cucumbers (1.8 g)
- Iceberg lettuce (1.6 g per cup)

Directions:

1. Arrange meat, cheese & toppings on a salad.
2. Serve with your favorite low carb dressing.
3. Check the label of the deli meat - sometimes, sugar is added.

Nutrition:

Carb Count: Recipe Total 3.4 g, Per Serving 1.7 g

## Blackened Chicken Salad

Preparation Time: 20 minutes

Cooking Time: 30 minutes

Serving: 1

Ingredients:

- Cooked, cubed chicken
- 2 tbsp. each soy sauce & vinegar six slices cucumber (1.8 g) 1/4 cup chopped tomato (2.8 g) bacon, cooked, cooled & crumbled
- 4 tbsp. balsamic vinegar mixed with 6 tbsp. olive oil, divided
- Romaine lettuce (1.9 g per cup)

Directions:

1. Combine soy sauce & vinegar. Pour into skillet. Add chicken.
2. Heat on high until chicken chars a bit.
3. Serve with salad. Drizzle vinegar & oil over the salad.

Nutrition:

Carb Count: Recipe Total 5.5 g, Per Serving 2.7 g

## Cobb Salad

Preparation Time: 5 minutes

Cooking Time: 20 minutes

Serving: 2 people

Ingredients:

- Cooked & crumbled bacon
- 6 boiled eggs, chopped, divided 1/2 cup cheese, divided
- Romaine lettuce (1.9 g per cup)

Directions:

1. Arrange bacon, cheese & eggs on a bed of lettuce.
2. Enjoy with your favorite low carb dressing.

Nutrition: Carb Count: Recipe Total 1.9 g, Per Serving 0.8 g

## Turkey & Cranberry Salad

Preparation Time: 5 minutes

Cooking Time: 5 minutes

Serving: 2 people

Ingredients:

- Sliced Turkey deli meat (or chicken)
- Boston or Bibb lettuce (1.4 per cup)
- 4 tbsp. red wine vinegar mixed with
- 4 tbsp. olive oil, divided (3.6 g)
- 1 tbsp. cranberry relish (2 g)
- 1/4 cup chopped walnuts, divided (5 g)

Directions:

1. Arrange turkey on a bed of lettuce. Combine vinegar, oil & relish.
2. Drizzle vinegar & oil over the salad. Sprinkle with walnuts.

Nutrition:

Carb Count: Recipe Total 8. 4 g, Per Serving 4.2 g

## Chicken Naan

Preparation Time: 20 minutes

Cooking Time: 50 minutes

Serving: 2 people

Ingredients:

- 1/8 cup plain yogurt (1.4 g)
- 1/2 tsp. chili powder (0.7 g) salt to taste
- 1 tbsp. lemon juice (1.3 g)
- Four portions of chicken, cooked & cubed
- 1/4 cup chopped tomato (2.8 g)
- Romaine lettuce (1.9 g per cup)

Directions:

1. Combine yogurt, chili powder, salt, lemon juice & cilantro. Warm chicken.
2. Serve with yogurt dressing, tomatoes & lettuce.

Nutrition: Carb Count: Recipe Total 8.1 g, Per Serving 2 g

## Chinese Chicken Salad

Preparation Time: 10 minutes

Cooking Time: 30 minutes

Serving: 2

Ingredients:

- 1/3 tsp. crushed red pepper (0.7 g)
- One garlic clove, crushed (0.9 g)
- 1 1/2 tbsp. soy sauce
- 1/8 cup sesame oil
- 1/2-pound bean sprouts (1.5 g) 2 tbsp. white vinegar
- 1 packets artificial sweetener
- 1/4 tsp. dry mustard (0.1 g)
- 1/8 cup napa cabbage, thinly sliced (1.2 g)
- 1/2 cup romaine lettuce (1.9 g)
- 1-pound chicken, cooked, cut into bite-sized pieces

Directions:

1. Mix red pepper, garlic, soy sauce, sesame oil, vinegar, sweetener, and mustard.
2. Mix lettuce & cabbage. Add chicken & dressing to lettuce beds.

Nutrition: Carb Count: Recipe Total 5.6 g, Per Serving 1.4 g

## Blt Salad

Preparation Time: 10 minutes

Cooking Time: 10 minutes

Serving: 2

Ingredients:

- Six strips bacon, cooked
- 1 cup iceberg lettuce (1.6 g)
- 1/2 cup tomato (5.8 g)
- 1 tbsp. mayo, divided

Directions:

Place three strips of bacon onto lettuce with tomato & mayo.

Nutrition:

Carb Count: Recipe Total 7.4 g, Per Serving 3.7 g

## Turkey & Cream Cheese

Preparation Time: 20 minutes

Cooking Time: 50 minutes

Serving: 2 people

Ingredients:

- 4 tbsp. cream cheese, divided
- 1 thick slices of tomato (4 g)

Directions:

1. Turkey lunch meat, divided Spread cream cheese on a tomato slice, pile on meat & enjoy.
2. For variety, replace tomato with an apple slice (1/4 apple: 5 g).

Nutrition:

Carb Count: Recipe Total 4 g, Per Serving 2 g

## Italian Meat & Cheese

Preparation Time: 10 minutes

Cooking Time: 20 minutes

Serving: 2

Ingredients:

- Salami slices
- Ham slices
- Provolone cheese slices
- Two slices tomato (3 g)
- 4 tbsp. balsamic vinegar mixed with 1 tbsp. olive oil, divided (3.6 g)
- Romaine lettuce (1.9 per cup)

Directions:

Arrange meat, cheese, and tomato on lettuce. Drizzle with vinegar/oil.

Nutrition:

Carb Count: Recipe Total 8.5 g, Per Serving 4.2 g

## Feta Spinach Salad

Preparation Time: 20 minutes

Cooking Time: 20 minutes

Serving: 2

Ingredients:

- One medium red pepper, cut into strips (8 g)
- 1 tsp. salt 3 tbsp. white vinegar black pepper
- 1 cup fresh spinach (2.4 g)
- 8 ounces feta cheese, crumbled

Directions:

1. Heat olive oil over medium-high heat. Add red peppers & cook until tender. Remove.
2. Add vinegar, pepper, 1 tbsp. oil, and 1/2 tsp. salt. Add spinach & vinegar mix to a bowl.
3. Sprinkle feta cheese overall. Optional, add grill chicken.

Nutrition:

Carb Count: Recipe Total 10.4 g, Per Serving 2.6 g

## Roast Beef & Cheese

Preparation Time: 20 minutes

Cooking Time: 30 minutes

Serving: 2 people

Ingredients:

- Roast beef
- Slices cheddar cheese 1/4 cup onions (3.4 g)
- 1/2 cup green pepper (3.6 g)

Directions:

1. Sauté onions & green peppers. Arrange meat, cheese, onions & peppers on half a sub.
2. Broil in the toaster oven until cheese has melted. Serve with Horseradish Sauce (Beat 1/4 cup light cream until soft peaks form & fold in 1-2 tbsp.

horseradish). Optional: Serve on a slice of wheat bread for an additional 11 g of carbs.

Nutrition:

Carb Count: Recipe Total 7 g, Per Serving 3.5 g

## Salmon Avocado Lunch

Preparation Time: 20 minutes

Cooking Time: 50 minutes

Serving: 2 people

Ingredients

- Cold Salmon, 4 ounce
- A Hass Avocado
- Salt according to taste

Directions:

1. Slice salmon into four pieces and avocado into 4-inch pieces.
2. Cover Avocado Pieces with Salmon and add salt.
3. Serve and enjoy

Nutrition:

Calories 160

Total Fat 15 g

Total Carbohydrate 9 g

Protein 2 g

## Sautéed Greens And Poached Eggs

Preparation Time: 20 minutes

Cooking Time: 50 minutes

Serving: 2 people

Ingredients:

- 2 tbsp. unsalted butter
- Two eggs, poached
- Salt according to taste
- 2-3 cups kale
- 2 tbsp. sliced almond

Direction:

1. Cook the greens ingredients in the pan containing water.
2. Discard water and add butter.
3. Toss it well in the butter, and then add nuts and salt according to taste.
4. Add eggs with nuts and enjoy this delicious recipe.

Nutrition:

Calories 143

Saturated fat 3.1 g

Carbohydrate 0.7 g

Protein 13 g

## Roasted Rack Of Lamb, Fennel, Cauliflower, And Celery

Preparation Time: 20 minutes

Cooking Time: 50 minutes

Serving: 2 people

Ingredients:

- A Rack of organic lamb, one and a half pound
- 1 tbsp. of fresh thyme, sage, turmeric, rosemary, and oregano, finely chopped
- 1 tbsp. of ghee
- 2 cups of fennel, sliced
- Salt according to taste
- 2 cups of cauliflower, finely chopped
- 2 cups of celery, sliced

Directions:

1. Preheat oven to 350F.
2. Add ghee over the lamb mark the top lamb.
3. Add vegetables to the pan and add lamb over the top.
4. But make sure that the marked fat side is facing up.
5. Bake for 45 minutes until completely done.
6. Now place it in the oven over low heat and cook for more than 3 minutes until making crisp.
7. Now serve this delicious recipe.

Nutrition:

Calories 294

Saturated fat 9 g

Protein 25 g

## Bowl Of Berries

Preparation Time: 20 minutes

Cooking Time: 50 minutes

Serving: 2 people

Ingredients:

- 1/4 cup of raspberries
- 1/4 cup of blueberries
- 1/4 cup of strawberries
- 1/4 lime juice
- ¼ cup of fresh basil, finely chopped

Directions:

1. Remove stems from berries and chop them in a bowl.
2. Mix lemon juice with berries.
3. Topping with chopped basil, and it's ready to serve.
4. Serve this delicious recipe.

Nutrition:

Calories 57

Total Fat 0.3 g

Dietary fiber 2.4 g

Protein 0.7 g

## Chocolate Pudding

Preparation Time: 20 minutes

Cooking Time: 50 minutes

Serving: 2 people

Ingredients:

- 2 tbsp. stevia
- 2 cups coconut oil, divided
- 1 tbsp. vanilla powder
- 1/2 tbsp. of gelatin, grass-fed
- 1/2 tbsp. of MCT oil
- 1/3 cup of chocolate powder
- 1/8 cup of macadamia nuts
- 2 tbsp. of butter, without salt

Direction:

1. Heat a cup of coconut oil along with stevia and gelatin in the pan.
2. Heat oil over medium temperature until they are completely dissolved.
3. Add remaining cups of coconut oil to the blender with vanilla, butter, oil, and chocolate powder.
4. Give it few high-speed pulses until completely dissolved.
5. Now add coconut mixture to the blender and blend until form smooth puree.
6. Now pour back the puree into a tin container and refrigerate it for an hour.
7. Serve this delicious recipe with a topping of nuts.

Nutrition:

Calories 546

Saturated fat 19 g

Total Carbohydrate 61 g

Protein 4.9 g

## Mexican Dip

Preparation Time: 20 minutes

Cooking Time: 50 minutes

Serving: 2 people

Ingredients:

- Processed cheese (1/2 loaf, about 1/2 pound, cubed)
- Beef tamales (6, husked and mashed)
- Tomatoes and green chilies (1/2 can, about 14.5 ounces, diced)

Direction:

1. Combine the entire ingredient to slow cooker and switch heat to high.
2. Heat it until cheese is melted. Now switch to low heat and let it keep over the stove to keep it warm for serving.
3. Serve with tortilla chips.

Nutrition:

Calories 45

Total Fat 3.1g

Saturated Fat 1.5g

Sugars 0.5g

Protein 1.8g

## Rib-Eye And Pepper

Preparation Time: 20 minutes

Cooking Time: 30 minutes – 1hour

Serving: 2 people

Ingredients

- 1 tbsp. of cooking oil (1 tbsp.)
- Beef rib-eye steak(4 each of 10 ounces)
- 1 Red bell pepper, finely chopped
- One green bell pepper, finely chopped
- 1 Onion, sliced
- Four cloves of Garlic, finely minced
- Fajita seasoning (3 tbsp.)
- One lime juice

Direction:

1. Take a large pan and add oil to it. Switch to high heat. Lightly burn the steak on both sides.
2. Add red bell pepper, green bell pepper, garlic, and onion to the same pan and sauté it for about 5 minutes to get the desired doneness.
3. Combine steak and seasoning and put them back in the pan.
4. Squeeze the lime juice gradually over the whole pan to cover steaks and bell peppers.
5. Let it simmer for about 30 minutes – 1 hour.
6. Turning steaks from time to time, so get the desired doneness.

Nutrition:

Calories 291 Total Fat 22 g

Saturated fat 10 g Protein 24 g

## Fiesta Bean Dips

Preparation Time: 20 minutes

Cooking Time: 50 minutes

Serving: 2 people

Ingredients:

- Sour cream (1 cup)
- Condensed nacho cheese soup (1 can, about 10.75 ounces)
- Refried beans (1 can about 10 ounces)
- Chunky-style salsa (1 jar about 8 ounces)

Directions:

1. Take a small pan and add cheese soup, sour cream, salsa, and refried beans.
2. Set the pan to medium-high heat.
3. Cook and mix until the mixture is thoroughly warm. It will take about 10 minutes.

Nutrition:

Calories 30 Calories from Fat 10

Total Fat 1g Protein 1g

## Slow Cooker Squash

Preparation Time: 20 minutes

Cooking Time: 1hour and 10 minutes

Serving: 2 people

Ingredients:

- Summer Squash (4 pounds yellow, sliced)
- Onion (1 small, chopped)
- Butter (1/4 cups, cubed)
- Processed cheese (1/4 pound, cubed)

Directions:

1. Add onion and squash to a pot and fill with water just to cover these.
2. Let it boil. Let it simmer for about 10 minutes until tender.
3. Drain and place in the sink. Make a layer of butter cubes, cheese cubes over squash mixture in a slow cooker.
4. Switch the cooker to low heat and cook until tender.
5. Cook until butter makes a creamy sauce with cheese. That will take about 1 hour. Do not mix.

Nutrition:

Calories 17

Total Carbohydrate 3.1 g

Sugar 2.5 g

Protein 1.2 g

## Slow Cooker Taco Soup

Preparation Time: 20 minutes

Cooking Time: 8 minutes

Serving: 2

Ingredients:

- Ground beef (1 pound)
- Tomato sauce (1 can about 8 ounces)
- Water (2 cups)
- Peeled and Diced tomatoes (2 cans, about 14.5 ounces)
- Green chili pepper (1 can about 4 ounces)
- Taco seasoning (1package, about 1.25 ounce)
- Onion (1, finely chopped)
- Chili beans with liquid (1 can about 16 ounces)
- Kidney beans with liquid (1 can about 15 ounces)
- Whole kernel corn with liquid (1 can about 15 ounces)

Directions:

1. Take a small pan and add ground beef. Cook over medium-high heat until browned. Drain and keep it aside.
2. Add the ground beef chili beans, taco seasoning mix, green chili pepper, diced tomatoes, water, corn, tomato sauce, kidney beans, and onion to the slow cooker and mix.

3. Reduce heat to low and cook for about 8 minutes.

Nutrition:

Total Calories 265

Total Fat 5 g

Saturated Fat 2 g

Protein 19 g

## Stuffed Bell Peppers

Preparation Time: 15 minutes

Cooking Time: 45 minutes

Servings: 2 servings

Stuffed bell peppers sound like regular food, but you can make this dish exciting by adding great stuff. The best part about is this dish is that it is a satisfying meal and can be prepared quickly. Bell peppers work great with a beef filling. This way, you would be able to get a sufficient protein intake and get the vegetables' nutrients.

Ingredients:

- 1/3 lb. lean beef grounded
- 1/8 C chopped onion
- 1/8 t Paprika powder
- 1/8 t black pepper
- Salt as per taste
- One green chili
- One beaten egg
- Six bell peppers
- One can diced tomatoes (19 ounces)
- One jar salsa (15 ounces)
- 1/3 T cilantro
- shredded cheddar cheese

Directions:

1. Take a bowl and combine the egg, beef, onion, paprika, black pepper, green chili, and salt in a bowl.
2. Now add in the rice and mix well.
3. Now it is time to cut the peppers in halves. Remove the membrane and the seeds.
4. Take an ovenproof baking dish. Place the tomatoes on the bottom of the word.
5. Now place the halved peppers on top of the tomatoes.
6. Now put the beef mixture in each pepper and top the mix with salsa.
7. Cook the peppers in a pre-heated (375 degrees F) oven for 40 -45 minutes till the meat is cooked.
8. Now once the peppers are cooked, top them with cheese and broil them till the cheese melts.

Nutrition:

Calories: 147 per serving

Total fats: 5.8 g

Cholesterol: 47mg

Protein: 16.1g

Total Carbohydrates: 7.7 g

## Low Carbohydrate Zucchini Fries

Preparation Time: 30 minutes

Cooking Time: 25 minutes

Servings: 2 servings

There are times when you need a break from the regular lunch and want something extra light. You just would not want to opt for potato fries when you want to stick to a low carbohydrate diet. Well, this does not mean that you have to ban fries. You can come up with the idea of trying out Zucchini fries. They are a great replacement and would satisfy your craving for fries as well.

Ingredients:

- 2/3 Zucchini
- 1/3 T salt
- 1/8 t black pepper
- 1/8 t paprika
- one egg
- 1/8 C ground almonds
- 1/8 grated cheese
- 1/8 t dried herb seasoning

Directions:

1. Make sure that you pre-heat the oven to 475 degrees F.
2. The zucchini needs to be cut into 3-inch lengths, and then every piece has to be cut into nine fries. Take a colander and place the zucchini fries in it. That will help the excess water drain out. It would take about one hour to remove the excess liquid from the zucchini.
3. Take a bowl and add in the eggs, parmesan cheese, herb seasoning, black pepper, and paprika.
4. Now make sure that you rinse off the salt from the zucchini and dry them with a paper towel's help.
5. Dip the zucchini in the egg mixture and coat with grounded almonds.
6. Place the coated zucchini fries on a baking tray and bake them for 25 minutes till they are crisp and brown.

Nutrition:

Calories: 78

Total fats: 5.5 g

Cholesterol: 55mg

Protein: 4.3g

Total Carbohydrates: 4.1g

## Garlic Chicken

Preparation Time: 20 minutes

Cooking Time: 35 minutes

Servings: 2 servings

Ingredients:

- ¼ C olive oil
- Two crushed garlic cloves
- ¼ C flaxseed meal
- ¼ C Parmesan cheese
- ¼ t black pepper
- ¼ t Paprika
- Four boneless and skinless chicken breast

Directions:

1. The first step is to preheat the oven to a temperature of 425 degrees F.
2. Take a pan and add the olive oil to it. Sauté the garlic in the oil for about 2 minutes and then transfer that oil to a bowl.
3. Take another bowl and combine Parmesan cheese with the seasoned bread crumbs.
4. Sprinkle the black pepper and Paprika onto the chicken breasts and then dip in the garlic mixture and olive oil.
5. Now coat the breasts with bread crumb and cheese mixture. Make sure that the chicken is coated well on both sides.
6. Now place the chicken in a baking dish and bake for about thirty to thirty-five minutes.

Nutrition:

Calories:146 per serving

Total fats: 14.8 g

Cholesterol: 0

Protein: 1.3g

Total Carbohydrates: 2.1 g

## Roasted Salmon With Coconut Aminos And Vegetables

Preparation Time: 15 minutes

Cooking Time: 12 minutes

Servings: 2 servings

Ingredients:

- ¼ C coconut amino
- 1 T toasted sesame oil
- 1 T olive oil
- Three chopped green onions
- Two cloves garlic
- Four center-cut salmon fillets
- ½ C green beans
- 2 C mushrooms
- Three sliced red bell peppers,
- One green chili
- Salt as per taste
- ¼ t black pepper
- ¼ t Paprika

Directions:

1. Preheat your oven to 450 degrees F.
2. You will need three rimmed baking pans. Make sure that you place all three baking pans in the oven. One pan will accommodate the Salmon, and the other two are for the vegetables.
3. Take a blender and add in the onions, garlic, green chili, black pepper, salt, red chili flakes, oil, and

the coconut amino. You need to blend the ingredients for about 25 seconds.

4. Now remove the mixture from the blender and add to a bowl. Brush the salmon on both sides with the sauce.

5. Now take another bowl and add the mushrooms, bell peppers, and green beans. Add the remaining sauce on top of the vegetables and mix well.

6. Now take out the pans that you had placed in the oven. You should put the Salmon in the larger pan, and the vegetables can be placed in the smaller pans.

7. Now place all three pans in the oven and cook for about 12 minutes.

Nutrition:

Calories: 106 per serving

Total fats: 7.3 g

Cholesterol: 0

Protein: 2.6g

Total Carbohydrates: 9.0 g

## Tuna Casserole

Preparation Time: 10 minutes

Cooking Time: 30 minutes

Servings: 2 servings

Ingredients:

- 2/3 cans of tuna drained (6 ounces)
- 1/3 bag French cut green beans (16 ounces)
- 2 2/3 small fresh chopped mushrooms
- 1/3 chopped stalk of celery
- 2T onion chopped
- 2/3 T butter
- 1/8 C chicken broth
- 1/4 Cheavy cream
- Salt as per taste
- 1/8 t black pepper
- 1/8 t Paprika powder
- 1/8 green chili minced
- 1/8 C shredded cheddar cheese

Directions:

1. Take a pot and cook the beans as per the packet instructions.

2. Take another skillet and add butter to the skillet. Now sauté the onions, celery, and mushrooms in the butter until they become soft and turn brown.

3. Now add broth to the skillet having the vegetables and bring to a boil.

4. When just half the liquid is left in the skillet having the vegetables, add it. Bring this mixture to a boil.

5. Once you have added the cream to the vegetables, and then let them cook on low heat. You need to thicken this sauce.

6. When the sauce has thickened up, adds salt, pepper, paprika, and minced green chili.

7. Now add the sauce to the beans. Make sure that all the excess liquid is drained out from the beans before you add the sauce.

8. Now add the tuna to the sauce.

9. Place the tuna and sauce in a casserole and top with cheddar cheese.
10. Bake the mixture for about 30 minutes.

Nutrition:

Calories: 242 per serving

Total fats: 17.4 g

Cholesterol: 59mg

Protein: 19.3g

Total Carbohydrates: 1.5 g

## White Lasagna Stuffed Peppers

Preparation Time: 10 minutes

Cooking Time: 30 minutes

Servings: 2 servings

Ingredients

- 2/3 - large sweet peppers halved and seeded
- 1/3 - tsp. garlic salt divided
- 4 - oz. ground turkey
- 1/4 - cup ricotta cheese
- 1/3 - cup mozzarella
- 2 2/3 - cherry tomatoes

Directions:

1. Preheat stove to 400.
2. Put the split peppers in a preparing dish. Sprinkle with 1/4 tsp. garlic salt. Partition the ground turkey between the peppers and press into the bottoms. Sprinkle with another 1/4 tsp. garlic salt. Heat for 30 minutes.
3. Gap the ricotta cheddar between the peppers. Sprinkle with the rest of the 1/2 tsp. garlic salt. Sprinkle the mozzarella to finish everything. Put the cherry tomatoes in the middle of the peppers, if utilizing.
4. Prepare for an extra 30 minutes until the peppers are mollified, the meat is cooked, and the cheddar is brilliant.

Nutrition:

Calories 281, fat 11 grams

## Creamy Basil Baked Sausage

Preparation Time: 30 minutes

Cooking Time: 3 minutes

Servings: 2 servings

Ingredients:

- 3 - lb. Italian sausage chicken, turkey, or pork
- 8 - oz. cream cheese
- ¼ - cup basil pesto
- ¼ - cup heavy cream
- 8 - oz. mozzarella

Directions:

1. Preheat broiler to 400. Shower a huge meal dish with the cooking splash. Put the frankfurter in the heating dish. Prepare for 30 minutes.

2. In the meantime, blend the cream cheddar, pesto, and overwhelming cream.

3. Spread the sauce over the frankfurter. Top with mozzarella. Prepare for an extra 10 minutes or until the hotdog is 160 degrees when checked with a meat thermometer.

4. Discretionary: Broil for 3 minutes to toast the cheddar to finish everything. Watch it always. It can consume effectively.

Nutrition:

Carbs 87g Protein 31g Fat 663 Calories.

## Easy Taco Casserole Recipe

Preparation Time: 30 minutes

Cooking Time: 20 minutes

Servings: 2 servings

Ingredients:

- 2 - lb. ground turkey or beef
- 2 - tbsp. taco seasoning
- 1 - cup salsa
- 16 - oz. cottage cheese
- 8 - oz. shredded cheddar cheese

Directions:

1. Preheat stove to 400.
2. Blend the ground meat and taco flavoring in a vast meal dish. Mine is 11 x 13. Prepare for 20 minutes.
3. In the interim, combine the curds, salsa, and one measure of the cheddar. Put aside.
4. Take off the meal dish from the stove and cautiously channel the cooling fluid from the meat. Separate the meat into little pieces. A potato masher works incredible for this. Spread the curds and salsa blend over the heart. Sprinkle the rest of the cheddar to finish everything.
5. Return the meal to the stove and heat for an extra 15-20 minutes until the meat is cooked thoroughly and the cheddar is hot and bubbly.

Nutrition:

Calories: 281.9

Sugars: 1.5 g

Dietary Fiber: 4.4 g

## Parmesan Chicken Tenders

Preparation Time: 4hrs

Cooking Time: 3hrs 30 minutes

Servings: 2 servings

INGREDIENTS:

- 1 2.5 - lb. bag chicken tenderloins
- ¾ - cup butter
- 1⅛ - cup parmesan cheese
- ¾ - tsp. garlic powder
- Salt, to taste

Directions:

1. Soften the margarine in a skillet and include the parmesan cheddar and garlic powder (and salt, if utilizing). Plunge the chicken in the blend and spot on a treat sheet. Prepare at 325 degrees F for 20-30 minutes (until the chicken is never again pink inside and the juices run clear). Don't over bake!

2. We have likewise utilized these for Sunday lunch. My mother set them up for chapel; at that point, heated them on our stove's "warm" setting for about 3½ hours while we were no more. Worked incredibly!

Nutrition:

Calories: 306.0

Total Fat: 8.6 g

Total Carbohydrate: 9.8 g

## Bacon Wrapped Chicken Tenders With Ranch Dip

Preparation time: 50 minutes

Cooking Time: 45 minutes

Serving: 2

Ingredients:

- 12- Chicken tenderloins about 1.5 lb.
- 12 - slices of bacon
- Ranch Dip Ingredients:
- 1/3 - cup sour cream
- 1/3 - cup mayo
- 1 - tsp. each garlic powder onion powder, parsley, and dill
- ½ - tsp. salt

Directions:

1. Preheat the broiler to 400.

2. Wrap every chicken delicate firmly in a bit of bacon. I extended the bacon as I folded it over the chicken.

3. Spot on a heating sheet. Prepare for 35-45 minutes until the bacon is fresh, and the chicken is thoroughly cooked.

4. In the meantime, mix the elements for the plunge. Present with the cooked chicken.

Nutrition:

7 g Fat, 9 g Protein

118 calories

## Stuffed Pork Chops – 5 Ingredients

Preparation time: 25 minutes

Cooking Time: 20 minutes

Serving: 2

Ingredients:

- 12 - thin-cut boneless pork chops, about 2 - 2.5 pounds
- 4 - garlic cloves

- 1 ½ - tsp. salt
- 2 - Cups baby spinach, about 2.5 oz.
- 12 - Slices provolone cheese (about 8 oz.)

Directions:

1. Preheat the range to 350.
2. Press the garlic cloves via a garlic press into a touch bowl. Add the salt and mix to consolidate. Spread the garlic rub on one aspect of the beef hacks. Turn 6
3. Slashes garlic aspect down onto an expansive rimmed heating sheet. Gap the spinach between the ones six cleaves. Crease the cheddar cut down the center, and placed them over the spinach. Put second pork lower over each with the garlic facet up.
4. Heat for 20 mins. Spread each pork cleave with another cut of cheddar. Back for a further 10-15 mins or till the meat is a hundred and sixty stages while checked with a meat thermometer.

## Super Easy Spicy Baked Chicken

Preparation time: 10 minutes

Cooking Time: 50 minutes

Serving: 2

Ingredients:

- 4 - ounces cream cheese cut into large chunks
- ½ - cup salsa
- ½ - teaspoon sea salt
- ¼ - teaspoon black pepper freshly ground
- 1 - pound boneless, skinless chicken breasts
- 1 - teaspoon parsley finely chopped, for garnish (optional)

Directions:

1. Preheat stove to 350° Fahrenheit.
2. Spot cream cheddar and salsa in a little, overwhelming weight pan. Spot over low warmth and cook, blending habitually, until cream cheddar melts and joins with the salsa. Blend in ocean salt and pepper. Expel from warmth. Mastermind chicken bosoms in a heating dish. Pour arranged cream cheddar sauce over best, covering the bosoms.
3. Prepare in the preheated stove for 40-45 minutes, or until the focus of chicken bosoms achieve 180° Fahrenheit. Take it off from a furnace and sprinkle with parsley, whenever wanted, before serving.

Nutrition:

Calories 225

Protein 30 grams

Fat 11 grams

## Lemon Parmesan Broccoli Soup

Preparation time: 10 minutes

Cooking Time: 0 minutes

Serving: 2

Ingredients

- to 3 - lbs. of fresh broccoli florets
- 4 - cups of water
- 2 - cups unsweetened almond milk
- ¾ - cup parmesan cheese
- 2 - tbsp. lemon juice

Directions:

1. Put the broccoli and water in a substantial pan. Spread and cook on medium-high until the broccoli is delicate.
2. Save one measure of the cooling fluid and dispose of the rest.
3. Include half of the broccoli, the saved cooking fluid, and almond milk into a blender. Mix until smooth.
4. Come back to the pot with whatever is left of the broccoli. Include the parmesan and lemon squeeze and warmth until hot.
5. I didn't include salt or pepper; however, you might need to have a bit. Simply season to taste.

Nutrition:

371 Calories, 28.38g Fats, 11.67g Net Carbs, and 14.63g Protein

## Keto Chili Dog Pot Pie Casserole

Preparation time: 30 minutes

Cooking Time: 35 minutes

Serving: 2

INGREDIENTS

- 1 - batch Slow Cooker Kickin' Chili
- 2 – tbsp. butter
- 8 - grass-fed beef hot dogs, sliced
- 1 ½ - cups shredded sharp cheddar cheese
- 1 ½ - cups shredded mozzarella cheese
- 1 - batch Low Carb Cheddar Biscuit Dough (minus the sausage)

Directions:

1. Set up the stew early. You can radically decrease the cook time of this formula by changing over the bean stew to a stovetop formula.
2. Warmth the spread in a vast ovenproof skillet over medium heat. When the distance is liquefied and the dish is hot, add the cut wieners to the container and cook until they have a decent singe on them.
3. Pour the whole clump of bean stew over the cooked wieners.
4. Blend the cheddar and mozzarella cheeses and sprinkle them over best of the bean stew.
5. Set up the scone mixture as indicated by the headings (less the hotdog)

6. Preheat broiler to 350°
7. Drop vast scoops of the bread mixture over the meal.
8. Heat for 30 minutes or until the bread topping is brilliant darker.

## Low Carb Crock Pot Pizza Casserole

Preparation time: 30 minutes

Cooking Time: 35 minutes

Serving: 2

Ingredients

- 1 - pound ground pork
- 1 - pound ground beef
- 2 - tablespoon pizza seasoning
- 1 - cup diced peppers onions, olives, mushrooms or other pizza toppings
- 1 - can diced tomatoes drained
- 1 - jar pizza sauce
- 2 - cups shredded mozzarella cheese
- 30 - pepperoni slices

Directions:

1. Dark colored ground meats with seasonings with pizza flavoring over medium warmth.
2. Include veggies or pizza garnishes other than pepperoni for 2-3 minutes till dampness is cooked out. Blend in depleted diced tomatoes.
3. Pour meat into the goulash simmering pot. Spread out over the slow cooker.
4. Pour sauce over meat and spread out equitably.
5. Sprinkle equitably with cheddar.
6. Top with pepperonis. You have two additional items - appreciate inspecting.
7. Put the top on and cook for two hours on high or 3-4 hours on low.

## Low Carb Taco Casserole

Preparation time: 30 minutes

Cooking Time: 35 minutes

Serving: 2

INGREDIENTS

- 1 - pound ground beef
- ¼ - cup chopped onion
- 1 - jalapeno minced
- 1 - packet taco seasoning or homemade
- ¼ - cup water
- 2 - ounces cream cheese
- ¼ - cup salsa
- 4 - eggs
- 1 - tablespoon hot sauce
- ¼ - cup heavy whipping cream
- ½ - cup grated cheddar

- ½ - cup grated pepper-jack cheese

Directions:

1. Preheat broiler to 350 degrees. Shower an 8x8 preparing dish with the non-stick splash.
2. Dark colored the ground hamburger in a huge skillet over medium warmth.
3. Add the onions and jalapeno to the meat and cook until onion is translucent. Channel any oil.
4. Mix in the taco flavoring and water and cook for 5 minutes.
5. Include the cream cheddar and salsa and mix to join.
6. Break the eggs in a medium combining bowl and race with the hot sauce and overwhelming cream.
7. Pour the meat blend into the readied preparing dish and best with the egg blend.
8. Sprinkle with cheddar and heat for 30 minutes or until eggs are set.
9. Cool 5 minutes before cutting and serving.

## Irish Chicken And Rosemary Salad

The right combination of proteins, cheese, and vegetables has quite a zesty but not overbearing flavor and will give you enough energy for the day!

Preparation time: 10 minutes

Cooking Time: 20 minutes

Serving: 2

Ingredients:

- Eight button mushrooms, sliced
- 6 oz. blue cheese or Irish cheese, crumbled
- Six hard-boiled eggs, coarsely chopped
- Three medium celery stalks, chopped
- 2/3 cups mayonnaise
- 2 lbs. chicken breasts
- 2 cups red cabbage, thinly sliced
- Ten cherry tomatoes, quartered
- 1/8 tsp. freshly ground black pepper
- 1/8 tsp. dried tarragon
- 1/3 medium cucumber, sliced
- 1 cup cauliflower florets
- 1 ½ tsp. fresh rosemary, chopped
- ¾ lb. Boston lettuce, torn into bite-sized pieces
- ½ cup yellow squash or zucchini, chopped
- ¼ tsp. salt
- ¼ cup of water
- ¼ cup heavy cream

Directions:

1. Preheat a grill, then season chicken with freshly ground black pepper and salt. Grill until meat is no longer pink and until juices are clear or for about 10 minutes.

2. In a large bowl, toss celery, lettuce, cabbage, chopped cucumber, sliced mushrooms, tomatoes, diced eggs, and chopped zucchini to make the salad.

3. In a medium bowl, combine heavy cream, mayonnaise, rosemary, tarragon, salt, pepper, and water. Whisk until everything blends well, and then add cheese to make the dressing.

4. Pour dressing over the salad and make sure to toss well. Top mixture with sliced grilled chicken slices.

Nutrition:

342Cal.

31gCarbs.

19gFat.

## Roasted Chicken With Fennel And Brussels Sprouts

What's good about chicken is that it is full of protein that promotes muscle growth instead of fats. It is also a natural anti-depressant—that's why parents/guardians usually make chicken soup when a child is not feeling well. It's because chicken increases the body's happy hormones or the Serotonin levels in the brain to keep a person feeling calm and reasonable.

Preparation time: 10 minutes

Cooking Time: 1 hr. 15 minutes

Serving: 2

Ingredients:

- One 5 to 6 lb. roasting chicken
- Olive oil
- Kosher salt
- Freshly ground black pepper
- Brussels sprouts, to taste
- A large bunch of fresh thyme
- Four carrots, cut into chunks
- 2 Tbsp. butter
- One lemon, cut in half
- One large yellow onion, sliced thickly
- One head garlic, cut in half
- One fennel bulb tops removed then cut into wedges

Directions:

1. Preheat the oven to 425 degrees.

2. Rinse the chicken thoroughly and remove any excess fat. Pat dry and season with salt and pepper liberally.

3. Stuff the chicken with lemon, garlic, and half a bunch of thyme, and then brush it with butter, salt, and pepper outside.

4. Tie the legs with a kitchen string, and then make sure to tuck its wings under its body and put the

Turn once halfway through the cooking time. Cut into slices, and then set aside.

onions, carrots, and fennel in the pan.

5. Toss extra thyme, salt, pepper, and olive oil together with the rest of the ingredients and spread the mixture evenly to the pan's bottom before placing the chicken on top.

6. Proceed to roast the chicken for an hour and a half or until the juices have run clear, then move the chicken and the vegetables to another platter and cover for around 20 minutes with aluminum foil.

7. Slice the chicken before serving and serve with vegetables on the side. Enjoy!

Nutrition:

387 calories; protein 31g

## Beef And Anchovy Chowder

Preparation time: 10 minutes

Cooking Time: 50 minutes

Serving: 2

Ingredients:

- 5 pounds of beef chuck stew meat, boneless and cut into 1 ½ inch cubes
- Four large garlic cloves, roasted and minced
- 3 Tbsp. Virgin Olive Oil, divided
- 3 Tbsp. Anchor Chili Powder. If this is not available, go for Mexican Style Chili Powder
- 2 tsp. kosher salt
- One medium yellow onion, chopped
- One can of diced tomatoes mixed with green chilies
- ¾ cup dry red wine
- ½ tsp. freshly ground black pepper

Directions:

1. Heat oven to 325 degrees.

2. Mix beef with salt and pepper, then toss.

3. Heat half a teaspoon of oil in a Dutch oven, and then cook onions until lightly browned. Add 1/3 of the beef, and then cook until brown on all sides or for around 5 minutes.

4. Transfer to another bowl, and then repeat the process with the rest of the beef and oil.

5. Add the last 1 ½ tsp. of oil to the oven and cook the rest of the onions until lightly browned. Add wine, tomatoes, chili powder, and garlic, and then simmer. Bring back the beef and the juices that have been accumulated to the oven.

6. The cover mixture then bakes for around 2 ½ hours. Don't forget to stir once halfway through the cooking period or until beef is tender.

7. Serve topped with green onions or shredded cheese, if you prefer.

Nutrition:

387 calories; protein 36g

## Liverwurst Stew

Instead of using soy sauce that's full of sodium, you can opt for coconut amino instead. Those have low acid content and are certified to be raw and gluten-free, and are also low in the glycemic index because of its sap.

Preparation time: 25 minutes

Cooking Time: 20 minutes

Serving: 2

Ingredients:

- Salt and pepper, to taste
- 5 oz. grass-fed liverwurst
- Five garlic cloves, minced
- Three bay leaves
- 2 Tbsp. rice vinegar
- 2 Tbsp. lard
- 2 lbs. grass-fed beef, cubed
- 2 cups green beans, sliced
- 2 cups beef broth
- One tomato, diced
- Tbsp. red chili flakes, dried
- 1 Tbsp. paprika
- One red pepper, sliced
- One orange pepper, sliced
- One onion, diced
- One can tomato sauce
- One can tomato paste
- ½ cups carrot discs
- ½ cup coconut amino

Directions:

1. Pre-heat oven to 325 degrees, then place liverwurst, tomato paste, and tomato sauce in a blender or food processor, puree them and season the beef with salt and pepper.

2. Add a tablespoon of lard to a Dutch oven, sauté onions, carrots, garlic, and chili pepper flakes until translucent. Turn the heat to low after adding chopped tomatoes, and then simmer for a minute or two before turning the heat off.

3. Then, heat a skillet adds the other tablespoon of lard before adding the seasoned beef. Cook until browned, and then transfer to the Dutch oven.

4. Mix coconut amino with vinegar in a glass, and then pour over the beef bits to deglaze them. Move everything to the Dutch oven, then add the pureed tomato paste, tomato sauce, and liverwurst together with paprika, beef broth, and bay leaves to the range and mix thoroughly.

5. Bake the mixture for around an hour, then add the green beans and bake for 20 minutes more. Then, add the bell peppers and bake again for 10 minutes.
6. Serve with steamed cauliflower rice, if desired. Enjoy!

Nutrition:

Calories 305

Total Fat 25 g

Saturated fat 10 g

Protein 12 g

## Bratwurst with Sauerkraut

Bratwurst is a kind of sausage that's most popular in Germany, while Sauerkraut is a topping made out of cabbage gaining popularity these days. These two are a perfect fit!

Preparation time: 10 minutes

Cooking Time: 2minutes

Serving: 2

Ingredients:

- 1 pork Bratwurst
- ½ cup drained Sauerkraut

Directions:

1. Pre-heat your grill or broiler. What you want to use is up to you.
2. Broil or grill the Bratwurst. Make sure to turn a couple of times until all sides have turned brown. You may also choose just to microwave the Bratwurst for only 1 to 2 minutes.
3. Heat the Sauerkraut in the microwave while grilling the Bratwurst.
4. Then, pour Sauerkraut on top of the Bratwurst and serve.

Nutrition:

43gCarbs.

18gFat.

15gProtein.

## Excellent Pork And Broccoli Surprise

Broccoli was first planted in the Mediterranean Isles in the 6th century. It's quite beneficial because it contains high Vitamin C content. A cup of broccoli is already equivalent to the Vitamin C content of one orange!

Ingredients:

- 5 Thai chilies, chopped
- 3 tsp. sesame oil
- 3 Tbsp. almond butter
- Two pinches of sea salt
- 2 cups broccoli florets
- Two bell peppers, sliced
- 1 tsp. grated ginger
- 1 tsp. fish sauce

- 1 ½ Tbsp. coconut oil
- One ¼ lb. sliced grass-fed pork tenderloin
- ½ cup of coconut milk

Directions:

1. To prepare the sauce, mix the Thai chilies, almond butter, sesame oil, fish sauce, and coconut milk in a small bowl until well-blended, then mix bell peppers and broccoli in a small work together with ¼ cup of water. Cook for around 6 to 8 minutes in medium heat.

2. Cook ginger, green onions, and coconut oil in a skillet over medium heat for 3 minutes, then add the sliced pork and cook until both sides are brown or for 3 to 5 minutes. Make sure not to overcook, and then add the ingredients from the skillet to the wok before adding the almond sauce. Cover for around 10 minutes and simmer on low.

Nutrition:

Calories: 424 •Carbs: 23g •Fat: 25g •Protein: 26g. 424.

# CHAPTER 8:

# Dinner

## Apricot-Glazed Brisket

Preparation time: 3 Hour & 40 Minutes

Cooking Time: 3 Hour & 40 Minutes

Serving: 2

Ingredients:

- 1 pounds whole lean beef brisket
- 1/2 tsp. paprika
- 3/4 tbsp. apricot preserves, sugar-free
- 1/4 tsp. black pepper
- 1/2 tsp. salt

Directions:

1. Preheat your oven to 475 F/235 C. Season the brisket with paprika, pepper & salt.
2. Place the brisket in a Dutch oven, preferably fat side down. Scatter the carrots & onions around the brisket. Cook for 12 to 15 minutes.
3. Turn the brisket, preferably fat side up & then add approximately 1/2 cup of water; tightly cover. Decrease the oven temperature to 185 C/375 F. Cook until the brisket is fork-tender, for 3 to 4 hours.
4. Heat your broiler & remove the cooked brisket from the Dutch oven, placing it on the broiler pan. Evenly spread the jam over brisket & broil until jam is lightly browned in spots, for 5 minutes, preferably 6 inches away from the heat source. While the brisket broils, remove the carrots and onions from the cooking juices.
5. Cover the brisket with a large foil & let rest for 12 to 15 minutes before serving. Using a spoon, remove the surface fat & help with the degreased cooking juices.

Nutrition:

753 Calories  0.5g Total Carbohydrates

0.1g Sugars 58.7g Protein

## Asian Lobster Salad

Preparation time: 35 minutes

Cooking Time: 30 minutes

Serving: 2

Ingredients:

- 2 cups Chinese cabbage such as Pak-Choi or Bok-Choy, shredded

- 3/4 pound northern lobster
- Four spring onions or scallions, medium
- 1 tbsp. whole sesame seeds, dried
- 2 tbsp. tamari soybean sauce
- 1 tsp. ginger
- 1/2 sweet red pepper, small
- 1 tbsp. canola vegetable oil
- 2 tbsp. rice vinegar, sodium & sugar-Free
- 1 tsp. sesame oil

Directions:

1. Combine lobster with bell pepper, cabbage, sesame seeds & scallions in a large size serving bowl.
2. Now, whisk the rice vinegar and grated ginger, Tamari soy sauce, sesame & canola oils in a separate small-sized bowl.
3. Pour the dressing over salad & gently toss to coat. Season with salt & freshly ground black pepper.

Nutrition:

366 Calories

1.7g Saturated Fat

11.1g Total Carbohydrates

2g Sugars

46.5g Protein

## Garlic Shrimp With Avocado Dip

Preparation time: 30 minutes

Cooking Time: 25 minutes

Serving: 2

Ingredients:

- 6 shrimps, medium
- 1/4 tsp. garlic
- 1/2 California avocados, cut in half, pit removed
- One jalapeno pepper, stem & seeds removed
- 1/8 tsp. cayenne or red pepper
- 1/4 tbsp. olive oil, extra virgin
- Freshly ground black pepper to taste
- 1/8 tsp. salt

Directions:

1. For the dip: Scrape the flesh from the avocado and put it together with jalapeno into a food processor. Pulse on high settings until smooth & then season with freshly ground black pepper & salt to taste.
2. Place the shrimp in a large bowl & then rub it with oil, cayenne, minced garlic & sprinkle with salt. Soak eight wooden skewers in water for a minimum period of an hour & then evenly thread the shrimp onto each one of them, leave a small space between the shrimps.
3. Grill the shrimp until just cooked through & turns golden, for 2 & 1/2 minutes per side, preferably covered. Serve the cooked

shrimps with the avocado dip on the side.

Nutrition:

91 Calories

1g Saturated Fat

3.6g Total Carbohydrates

4.2g Protein

## Baked Salmon With Bok Choy & Red Bell Pepper Purée

Preparation time: 30 minutes

Cooking Time: 25 minutes

Serving: 2

Ingredients:

- 20 oz. Salmon, boneless
- 3 oz. roasted bell pepper strips, deli-sliced
- 1/4 tsp. each black pepper & salt
- 64 oz. Chinese Cabbage, raw
- 1 tbsp. butter stick, unsalted
- 2 oz. salsa
- 1/2 tsp. lemon peel
- 2 tbsps. light olive oil

Directions:

1. Preheat your oven to 475 F/235 C.
2. Place the butter & olive oil in an oven-safe large skillet, preferably in a single layer. Place in oven until butter melts for a couple of minutes.
3. Season the fish with pepper & salt. Place the fish in the prepared skillet, preferably flesh side down. Bake until just cooked through, for 8 to 10 minutes; carefully turn the fish once halfway. Remove from skillet & tent with foil.
4. Add in the lemon peel & chopped bock Choy to the skillet. Stir several times to coat.
5. Place in the oven for a minute until stems are warmed through & leaves are wilted.
6. Purée the salsa & peppers in a blender for half a minute. Evenly divide the greens among four plates; top each dish with a fish piece. Place a dollop of purée on top of each fish piece.

Nutrition: 451 Calories  6.4g Saturated Fat

12.3g Total Carbohydrates

6.8g Sugars  38.6g Protein

## Traditional Beef Stroganoff

Preparation time: 20 minutes

Cooking Time: 10 minutes

Serving: 2

Ingredients:

- 14 oz. boneless, raw, lean only beef steak

- 4 oz. Crimini Italian brown mushrooms, remove & discard the stems from the caps
- 1/2 tsp. Dijon mustard
- 1 oz. sour cream
- 1 tsp. bouillon beef base (made from concentrated beef stock & roasted beef)
- 1 1/2 tsp. butter stick, unsalted
- 1/2 onion, medium, peeled & cut in half
- 4 tbsp. red cooking wine
- 6 oz. broccoli
- 3/4 tsp. each salt & black pepper
- 1 2/3 tbsp. olive oil

Directions:

1. Preheat your oven on low. Cut the crimini mushroom caps into ¼" slices; set aside. Chop half onion into ¼" dice; set aside. In a small-sized bowl, combine ½ cup of water with the beef stock concentrate.

2. Place the flank steak on paper towels; pat dry & cut into ½" thick slices & season with ¼ tsp. of each pepper & salt. Over medium-high heat settings in a large oven-proof sauté pan; heat a tbsp. Of canola oil. When hot, add in the flank steak strips & sauté until the beef is browned, for 2 to 3 minutes. Now, keep the sauté pan warm inside the oven.

3. Over medium heat settings in a separate large-sized sauté pan; melt the butter & cook the onions until softened, frequently stirring for 2 to 3 minutes. Add in the mushrooms & cook until the mushroom's liquid has evaporated, for 5 to 7 minutes, stirring now and then.

4. Add in the wine & cook for 3 to 5 more minutes. Add in the beef stock; stir & cook until the mushrooms are evenly coated & the sauce has reduced, for 8 to 10 minutes. Stir in the Dijon & then the sour cream. Add in the beef & its accumulated juices. Decrease the heat settings to low & cook until the meat is heated through for more minutes. Season with ¼ tsp. of each pepper & salt; keep warm.

5. Over medium-high heat settings in a medium sauté pan; heat 2 tsp. Of olive oil. When hot, sauté the broccoli florets for 3 to 5 minutes, stirring now and then. Season with ¼ tsp. of pepper & salt again; toss until well combined.

6. Evenly divide the cooked broccoli between two large plates & serve the beef stroganoff alongside the broccoli. Enjoy!

Nutrition:

786 Calories  54.2g Total Fat

13g Total Carbohydrates

4.1g Sugars  55.9g Protein

## Greek Salad With Chicken

Preparation time: 20 minutes

Cooking Time: 15 minutes

Serving: 2

Ingredients:

- 12 oz. chicken breast, raw
- 1 tsp. oregano, dried
- Six olives Kalamata olives, cut in half
- 1 1/2 tbsp. red wine vinegar
- 1/2 head of Romaine Lettuce, cut & discard the end, chop into 1" pieces
- 1 Italian tomato, chopped & diced into ½" pieces
- 1/2 cucumber, peeled & cut in half lengthwise
- One garlic clove, finely chopped
- 1/4 cup feta cheese, crumbled
- 1 oz. Shallots, cut into ¼" thin slices
- 1/2 tsp. each salt & black pepper
- 2 1/3 tbsp. olive oil

Directions:

1. Mix chopped pieces of garlic with oregano, red wine vinegar, ½ tbsp. Water, ¼ tsp. of each pepper & salt in a small bowl.Gradually add in 2 tbsp. Of olive oil, mix well.
2. Dice half of the cucumber into ¼" pieces & place it in a large-sized bowl.Now, add the shallot pieces to the bowl with the cucumber.
3. Add the tomato pieces to the bowl, followed by the romaine lettuce & the Kalamata olives; mix well.
4. Place the chicken breast on paper towels; pat them dry & season with ¼ tsp. of each pepper & salt.Over medium-high heat settings in a medium sauté pan; heat 2 tsp. Of olive oil.When hot, sauté the chicken pieces for 3 to 4 minutes per side.Now, transfer the sautéed chicken pieces to a large plate & let rest for a couple of minutes.Once easy to handle, slice the chicken into ½" pieces; set aside.
5. Toss all of the salad ingredients together.
6. Evenly divide the salad mixture between two large plates & top each dish with the sliced chicken & the crumbled feta cheese. Serve & enjoy.

Nutrition:

449 Calories

6g Saturated Fat

12.3g Total Carbohydrates

5.4g Sugars

44g Protein

## Baked Chicken With Artichokes

Preparation Time: 10 minutes

Cooking Time: 40 minutes

Servings: 2

INGREDIENTS:

- 4 oz. boneless chicken thigh
- 1/8 tsp. salt
- 1 2/3 oz. mushroom pieces and stems
- 1/8 cup chopped onions
- 1/3 tsp. grounds oregano
- 1 tsp. garlic
- 3/4 oz. vinegar
- 1/4 tsp. rosemary
- 2/3 tbsp. extra virgin olive oil
- 1 3/4 oz. artichokes
- 1/8 tsp. black pepper
- 1/8 tsp. crushed red pepper flakes
- 1/8 serving an all-purpose low-carb baking mix

DIRECTIONS:

1. Preheat oven to 350F and grease your baking dish with oil.
2. Combine 1/4 cup of the baking mix with salt and pepper.
3. In a skillet, sear the chicken for 5 minutes and add to your greased baking dish.
4. In the same skillet, fry the onion with mushroom and stir for 4 minutes.
5. Add in the vinegar, artichokes, red pepper flakes, and rosemary.
6. Cook until it simmers and then adds to the baking dish.
7. Bake in the preheated oven for about 40 minutes.

Nutrition:

Calorie: 376

## Baked Goat Cheese And Ricotta Custards

Preparation Time: 10 minutes

Cooking Time: 30 minutes

Servings: 2

INGREDIENTS:

- 1/4 cup chopped English walnuts
- 1 cup ricotta cheese (whole milk)
- 3 tbsp. parmesan cheese (Grated)
- 12 leaves spinach
- 1/8 tsp. salt
- Two large eggs (whole)
- 6 oz. goat cheese (semisoft)
- 1/8 tsp. black pepper
- 1 1/3 Second Sprays Original Canola Cooking Spray
- 2 tbsp. basil

DIRECTIONS:

1. Heat your oven to 350F. Grease your ramekin cups using oil or butter.
2. In a mixing bowl, add in the goat cheese, walnuts, parmesan, basil, salt, egg, and pepper.

3. Mix well until smooth.
4. Add spinach on ramekin cups.
5. Pour in the cheese mix and bake in the oven for 30 minutes

Nutrition:

Calorie: 360

## Baked Meatballs

Preparation Time: 10 minutes

Cooking Time: 20 minutes

Servings: 2

INGREDIENTS:

- 1/8 lb. ground veal
- 1/8 large scallions or spring onion, sliced
- 1/8 lb. ground beef
- Two large eggs (whole)
- 1/2 tsp. garlic
- 1/8 lb. ground chicken
- 1/8 tsp. salt
- 1/8 cup parmesan cheese (grated)
- 1/3 tbsp. extra virgin olive oil
- 1/8 tsp. black pepper

DIRECTIONS:

1. Heat oven to 375°F and grease a baking sheet.
2. In a pan, heat the olive oil.
3. Add in the onion, garlic, and cook until they become brown.
4. In a bowl, mix eggs, salt, cheese, meat, and pepper.
5. Add in the fried onion and garlic and mix well.
6. Create flat patties and add to the greased baking sheet.
7. Bake for about 20 minutes.

Nutrition:

Calorie: 409

## Baked Salmon With Bok Choy And Mixed Greens

Preparation Time: 10 minutes

Cooking Time: 40 minutes

Servings: 2

INGREDIENTS:

- 1 cup shredded or chopped mixed salad greens
- 3/4 cup chopped snow peas
- 1/2 oz. salsa
- 8 oz. Chinese cabbage, halved
- 3 oz. cooked red peppers
- 1 tbsp. vinegar
- 1/16 tsp. black pepper
- 1/4 tbsp. unsalted butter stick
- 2 oz. pickled okra
- 1/16 tsp. salt
- 1/2 tbsp. extra virgin olive oil
- 6 oz. Atlantic salmon (farmed)

DIRECTIONS:

1. Preheat the oven to 475F and grease your baking tray.
2. In a skillet, heat the oil and add the butter.
3. Fry the fish for a minute. Add salt and pepper.
4. Transfer to the baking tray.
5. Bake for 10 minutes and then flip it. Bake for another 5 minutes.
6. In the same skillet, add the cabbage, okra, and red peppers, and peas.
7. Toss for 10 minutes and serve with the baked fish, greens, and salsa.
8. Add the vinegar on top.

Nutrition:

Calorie: 623

## Brisket With Mushrooms

Preparation Time: 10 minutes

Cooking Time: 2.5 hours

Servings: 2

INGREDIENTS:

- 4 lbs. beef brisket
- 15 pieces of dried porcini mushrooms
- 1 tsp. crumbled bay leaf
- Two medium onions, diced
- 1 1/2 tsp. garlic
- 14 oz. beef broth
- 1/2 tsp. salt
- 1 tbsp. extra virgin olive oil
- 1/4 tsp. black pepper

DIRECTIONS:

1. Boil the mushrooms in salted water for 5 minutes.
2. Drain well and set aside.
3. In a skillet, fry the brisket for 8 minutes.
4. Add the onion, garlic, and toss for 5 minutes.
5. Add in the mushrooms, bay leaf, beef broth, salt, and pepper.
6. Cook for about 2 hours on low heat.
7. Serve hot.

Nutrition:

Calorie: 619

## Breaded Scrod With Basil-Mustard Sauce

Preparation Time: 20 minutes

Cooking Time: 10 minutes

Servings: 2

INGREDIENTS:

- 2 lbs. Atlantic cod
- 1/4 cup fresh lemon juice

- 7 tbsp. extra virgin olive oil
- 16 tbsp. basil
- 1 tsp. leaf oregano
- Four servings Atkins Cuisine Bread
- 3 tsp. garlic
- 2 tsp. Dijon mustard

DIRECTIONS:

1. Preheat your oven to 400F and spray your baking sheet with cooking oil.
2. Marinade the cod using salt, lime juice, and pepper.
3. Let it stand in the fridge for 20 minutes or longer.
4. Combine the garlic, bread, basil, mustard, and oregano in a blender and create a crumbly mixture.
5. Arrange the cod in your baking sheet.
6. Add the bread mix on top.
7. Add a drop of oil on top and bake for 10 minutes.
8. Serve hot.

Nutrition:

Calorie: 619

## Broiled Lobster With Garlic Oil

Preparation Time: 10 minutes

Cooking Time: 10 minutes

Servings: 2

INGREDIENTS:

- 3 lbs. northern lobster
- 1/4 cup extra virgin olive oil
- 1 tbsp. unsalted butter stick
- 1 tsp. garlic
- 1/8 tsp. coarse kosher salt

DIRECTIONS:

1. Heat the broiler over medium heat.
2. Combine the melted butter, salt, garlic, and olive oil.
3. Use a brush to add the garlic mix to the lobster.
4. Boil for 5 minutes and then brush again with the garlic mix.
5. Broil for three more minutes and serve.

Nutrition:

Calorie: 303

## Broiled Orange-Chili Chicken Breasts

Preparation Time: 2 hours

Cooking Time: 12 minutes

Servings: 2

INGREDIENTS:

- 32 oz. chicken breast
- 1 tbsp. extra virgin olive oil
- 1 tsp. honey
- 1 tbsp. chili powder
- 1 tsp. orange peel
- 2 tsp. garlic
- 1/4 cup freshly squeezed orange juice
- 1/4 tsp. red or cayenne pepper

DIRECTIONS:

1. In a bowl, combine the garlic, orange juice, chili powder, oil, orange rind, honey, and cayenne pepper.
2. Place the chicken breasts and let it sit for 2 hours or longer in the fridge.
3. In a broiler, broil the chicken for 12 minutes over medium heat.
4. Serve hot.

Nutrition:

Calorie: 431

## Buffalo Chicken Egg Salad

Preparation Time: 10 minutes

Cooking Time: 20 minutes

Servings: 2

INGREDIENTS:

- 2 oz. boneless, cooked chicken thigh
- 1/2 tbsp. Red Hot Buffalo Wing Sauce
- 2 large hardboiled eggs
- 1/8 cup crumbled blue or Roquefort cheese
- 1 tbsp. real mayonnaise
- 2 2/3 stalk celery, diced

DIRECTIONS:

1. Chop the eggs into thin pieces and set aside for now.
2. Combine the chicken, mayo, and celery in a mixing bowl.
3. Add in the wing sauce and eggs.
4. Stir gently and add the cheese.
5. Coat well and serve immediately or cold.

Nutrition:

Calorie: 143

## Beef And Vegetable Stew

Preparation Time: 20 minutes

Cooking Time: 1.5 hours

Servings: 2

INGREDIENTS:

- 1/2 lbs. beef chuck
- 1/3 tsp. paprika
- 2/3 tbsp. unsalted butter stick
- 1/3 tsp. leaf dried thyme leaves
- 2/3 tsp. salt
- 1/3 tsp. black pepper
- 2/3 cloves garlic
- 1/3 tsp. rosemary (dried)
- 1/3 lb. green snap beans
- 2/3 tbsp. extra virgin olive oil
- 1/3 cup of water
- 1/3 tsp. leaf oregano
- One medium carrot
- 1/3 cup white pearl onions
- 2/3 tbsp. Thick-It-Up

DIRECTIONS:

1. Combine the thyme, rosemary, oregano, salt, paprika, and pepper.
2. Add beef to it and let it sit for 10 minutes.
3. In a large pot, heat the olive oil.
4. Fry the beef with its juice for nearly 15 minutes or until it becomes brown.
5. Add the rest of the ingredients one by one.
6. Stir well with a spoon and add your lid.
7. Cook on high heat for nearly 1 hour.
8. Make sure to stir every 10 minutes.
9. Serve hot.

Nutrition:

Calorie: 316

## Barbecue Sauce

Preparation Time: 10 minutes

Cooking Time: 20 minutes

Servings: 2 cups

INGREDIENTS:

- 1/4 cup chopped onions
- 2/3 tbsp. Worcestershire sauce
- 2 tbsp. tomato paste
- 1 tsp. cumin
- 1 tsp. chili powder
- 3/4 tsp. garlic powder
- 1/4 tsp. allspice ground
- 3/4 tsp. yellow mustard seed
- 1/8 tsp. red or cayenne pepper
- 1 tbsp. vinegar (cider)
- 1 1/2 cups unsweetened ketchup
- 2 tsp. Sucralose sweetener (sugar substitute)
- 1 tbsp. extra virgin olive oil
- 1/4 tsp. dry coffee (instant powder)

DIRECTIONS:

1. In a saucepan, heat the oil and add the onion.
2. Fry until it becomes transparent and stirs in all the spices.
3. Add in the sauces, sugar substitute, vinegar, ketchup, and coffee.
4. Stir for about 10 minutes and store in the fridge until used.

Nutrition:

Calorie: 32

## Baked Tofu With Chipotle Marinade

Preparation Time: 10 minutes

Cooking Time: 15 minutes

Servings: 1

INGREDIENTS:

- 6 oz. Firm silken tofu
- 1 serving chipotle marinade

DIRECTIONS:

1. Cut the tofu into bite-size pieces.
2. Combine with the chipotle marinade and let it sit for 30 minutes.
3. Arrange on a greased baking tray and bake in the oven for 15 minutes over 375F.

Nutrition:

Calorie: 227

## Barbecue Chicken Pizza

Preparation Time: 10 minutes

Cooking Time: 20 minutes

Servings: 2

INGREDIENTS:

- 2 2/3 oz. boneless, cooked chicken breast
- 1/3 cup shredded mozzarella cheese (whole milk)
- 1/3 cups tap water
- 1/8 tsp. salt
- One small red onion, sliced
- 2/3 tsp. Sucralose sweetener (sugar substitute)
- 1 tbsp. extra virgin olive oil
- 1/8 medium green sweet pepper
- 1 1/3 servings barbecue sauce
- 1/2 tsp. baking powder
- 2 servings all-purpose low-carb baking mix

DIRECTIONS:

1. Heat your oven to 425F and grease your pizza pan using oil.
2. Combine the baking powder, baking mix, sugar substitute, and salt in a bowl.
3. Add some water and oil and mix well.
4. Create sticky dough and let it sit for 30 minutes in a warm place.

5. Roll out in a thin circle and add to the pizza pan.
6. Bake for 10 minutes and then add the sauce.
7. Add the sweet pepper, onion, cheese, and chicken.
8. Bake for another 10 minutes.

Nutrition:

Calorie: 293

## Basic Steamed Lobster With Drawn Butter

Preparation Time: 10 minutes

Cooking Time: 20 minutes

Servings: 2

INGREDIENTS:

- 3/4 cup unsalted butter stick
- Four lobsters northern lobster
- 1/2 lemon

DIRECTIONS:

1. Cook the lobsters in boiling salted water for about 20 minutes.
2. Drain and discard the shells.
3. Serve with lemon wedges and butter on the side.

Nutrition:

Calories 125

## Asian Style Tuna Salad

Preparation time: 10 minutes

Cooking Time: 50 minutes

Serving: 2

Ingredients:

- 175-gram tuna filet
- 1 Tablespoon soy sauce
- Six radishes
- One tomato
- 30-gram water chestnuts
- Three bok choy

Directions:

1. Grill the tuna. Steam the bok choy. Stir fry together with the rest of the ingredients and soy sauce. Enjoy!

Nutrition:

Calorie: 442

## Lamb Stew

Preparation time: 10 minutes

Cooking Time: 50 minutes

Serving: 2

Ingredients:

- 400 grams lamb stewing steak
- One medium onion
- 300-gram cauliflower
- 180 milliliters beef broth

- Two turnips
- Two teaspoon pepper
- One teaspoon salt
- Three garlic cloves
- Two teaspoons dried bay leaves

Directions:

1. Place oil and lamb in a large pan and brown lamb.
2. Add in the chopped onion, cauliflower, and turnips. Pour in the beef broth and add salt, pepper, garlic, and bay leaves and stir well. Cover.
3. Turn heat down to low and allow simmering for an hour. Before serving, remove bay leaves.

Nutrition:

Calories 294

Total Fat 21 g

Protein 25 g

## Tandoori Chicken

Preparation time: 10 minutes

Cooking Time: 50 minutes

Serving: 2

Ingredients:

- 200 grams of mixed salad leaves
- 1/2 teaspoon spice turmeric ground
- 1/2 teaspoon chili powder
- 1/2 teaspoon ground cumin
- 1/2 teaspoon curry powder
- Four garlic cloves
- One teaspoon ground ginger
- 300 grams Greek yogurt
- 1 Tablespoon vegetable oil
- 16 chicken thighs
- Two red onions
- Four teaspoons ground paprika
- 4 Tablespoons lemon juice

Directions:

1. Mix the lemon juice, red onions, and paprika in a large, shallow dish. Slash each of the chicken thighs three times, turn them in the liquid, and set aside for ten minutes.
2. Mix the marinade ingredients and pour over the chicken. Give it all the right mix and then cover and place in the refrigerator for a minimum of an hour. You can do this up to a day in advance.
3. Heat your grill. Place the chicken on a rack over a baking tray and brush on a little oil. Place on grill for eight minutes on each side or until lightly charred and cooked through. Serve with a mixed salad on the side.

Nutrition:

Calories 239 Total Fat 14 g Protein 27 g

## Fish with Tomato Basil Sauce

Preparation time: 10 minutes

Cooking Time: 50 minutes

Serving: 2

Ingredients:

- 500-gram white fish fillet
- 3 Tablespoons fresh basil
- 400 gram canned tomatoes with basil
- Two garlic cloves
- 1/2 teaspoon ground paprika
- One eggplant
- One medium onion
- 1 Tablespoon olive oil

Directions:

1. Heat the olive oil in a large frying pan and stir fry together with the eggplant and onion. In about four minutes, they will begin to turn golden but won't be soft. Cover with lid and allow vegetables to steam for about six minutes. Stir in paprika, tomatoes, garlic, and salt and cook for ten minutes, until eggplant and onion are tender. Make sure to stir often.
2. Scatter the basil leaves and put the fish into the sauce. Cover and cook for six minutes until fish flakes when tested with knife and flesh are firm but moist. Tear the rest of the basil and serve with salad.

Nutrition:

Calories 29

Total Fat 0.2

Protein 1.3 g

## Chicken Parmesan

Preparation time: 10 minutes

Cooking Time: 35 minutes

Serving: 2

Ingredients:

- 1 c. crushed pork rinds
- ½ c. spaghetti sauce
- Four chicken breasts
- ½ c. mushrooms
- Two beaten eggs

Directions:

1. In one bowl, set the eggs. Set pork rinds in another bowl. Immerse the chicken in the first bowl, and then toss in the second to coat well.
2. Set a frying pan over medium heat. Heat olive oil and place in the chicken to fry.
3. Sauté the mushrooms.
4. Set in your serving plates and enjoy alongside cheese and spaghetti sauce

## Marsala Chicken

Preparation time: 10 minutes

Cooking Time: 30 minutes

Serving: 2

Ingredients:

- ¼ tsp. salt
- ¼ c. Marsala wine
- 2 lbs. boneless chicken
- 1 c. fresh mushrooms
- ¼ tsp. pepper

Directions:

1. Set a pan over a medium source of heat. Add in olive oil and heat.
2. Add in the chicken and let cook until it becomes golden brown. Add a seasoning of pepper and salt.
3. Decrease the heat intensity and allow it to cook through. Set aside
4. Set in the mushrooms and heat until browned.
5. To the mushrooms, add in the wine. You then return the chicken.
6. Heat through and serve.

Nutrition:

Calories 239 Total Fat 14 g

Saturated fat 3.8 g

Protein 27 g

## Mustard Chicken

Preparation time: 10 minutes

Cooking Time: 30 minutes

Serving: 2

Ingredients:

- 4 skinless, boneless chicken breasts
- 1/3 c. Dijon mustard
- 1 tsp. orange peel, freshly grated
- 2 tbsps. fresh dill, chopped
- Honey

Directions:

1. Set your oven to preheat at 400° F.
2. In a bowl, mix honey and mustard.
3. Add in the orange peel and dill as you stir.
4. Set aluminum foil on a baking pan.
5. Sprinkle sauce over the chicken.
6. Set on the baking sheet and bake for approximately 30 minutes.

Nutrition:

Calories 239

Total Fat 14 g

Saturated fat 3.8 g

Protein 27 g

## Stuffed Green Peppers

Preparation time: 10 minutes

Cooking Time: 40 minutes

Serving: 2

Ingredients:

- ½ tsp. oregano, dried
- 7 ½ oz. diced and canned tomatoes
- Two green peppers, halved and seeded
- 1 tbsp. Worcestershire sauce
- cheddar cheese, shredded
- 1 lb. ground beef

Directions:

1. Set water in pot and boil. While boiling, immerse the peppers and let sit for about 3 minutes. Drain using paper towels.
2. Set a skillet over medium heat. Add meat and cook until browned. Get rid of fat by draining. Add in salt, sauce, pepper, tomatoes, and oregano.
3. Boil the mixture. Set heat on low and simmer for about 15 minutes. Add in half the cheese and stir well.
4. Fill the meat mixture into the peppers and set in a baking dish.
5. Set oven to 375° F and bake for about 15 minutes.
6. Top with the rest of the cheese and allow it to sit for 2 minutes.
7. Serve and enjoy.

Nutrition:

Calories 386

Total Fat 3.4 g

Saturated fat 0.8 g

Protein 11 g

## Chicken With Olives

Preparation time: 15 minutes

Cooking Time: 30 minutes

Serving: 2

Ingredients:

- 1 tsp. chopped fresh thyme
- 4 tbsps. sliced olives
- 2 lbs. boneless chicken
- ½ c. chopped onion
- Salt.
- 1 c. chicken broth

Directions:

1. Set the skillet on heat and add olive oil.
2. Add chicken and season with salt.
3. Cook until browned and remove from heat.
4. To the skillet, add onions and cook to soften. Stir in thyme, broth, chicken, and olives.

5. Reduce the intensity of heat and simmer for about 25 minutes while covered.

Nutrition:

Calories 193

Total Fat 27 g

Saturated fat 6.8 g

Protein 2.5 g

## Turkey With Delicious Bacon

Preparation time: 10 minutes

Cooking Time: 25 minutes

Serving: 2

Ingredients:
- 1/2 c. chicken broth
- 2 bacon slices
- 1/2 c. sliced mushrooms
- 1 lbs. boneless turkey

Directions:
1. Over medium-high heat, cook the bacon slices until golden brown. Add in mushrooms and continue heating until the mushrooms become tender. Set aside.
2. Using the same pan, add in the turkey, and cook to browning. Mix in chicken broth and allow to boil.
3. Set heat to low and let simmer for approximately 20 minutes.

4. Re-add the bacon and mushrooms and cook until ready
5. Enjoy.

Nutrition:

Calories 541

Total Fat 42 g

Saturated fat 14 g

Protein 37 g

## Teriyaki Beef

Preparation time: 10 minutes

Cooking Time: 20 minutes

Serving: 2

Ingredients:
- 1 c. soy sauce
- One c. oil
- 1 tsp. Ginger
- ¼ c. sherry
- Four packets of artificial sweetener
- ¼ c. diced scallions
- One diced garlic cloves
- 1 lb. thinly sliced beef

Directions:
1. In a bowl, combine all the above ingredients, excluding the meat.
2. Add the meat to the sauce and allow it to marinate for some

hours. Remove from the sauce and stir fry.
3. Enjoy alongside buttered and steamed asparagus.

Nutrition:

Calories 250

Total Fat 15 g

Saturated fat 6 g

Protein 26 g

## Dijon Pork Chops With Grapes

Preparation time: 10 minutes

Cooking Time: 20 minutes

Serving: 2

Ingredients:
- ½ tbsp. yellow mustard
- Four pork chops
- ½ c. sliced grapes
- 1 tbsp. Of Dijon mustard
- ½ c. light cream

Directions:
1. Set a pan over medium heat. Add olive oil and heat.
2. Mix in the pork chops and allow cooking until lightly browned. Set on a serving plate.
3. Mix grapes, mustard, and cream and cook.
4. Top the pork chops with the sauce and enjoy the meal.

Nutrition:

Calories 231

Protein 24 g

## Chicken Stuffed With Sundried Tomatoes

Preparation time: 10 minutes

Cooking Time: 45 minutes

Serving: 2

Ingredients:
- Four chicken breast halves
- ¼ c. parmesan cheese
- 1 tsp. Basil
- ¼ c. sundried tomatoes, oil-packed

Directions:
1. Set your oven to 425° F.
2. Chop tomatoes and combine with parmesan, salt, basil, and pepper.
3. Make a small opening in the chicken breasts.
4. Fill the openings with the tomato mixture.
5. Season with pepper and some salt
6. Set in the oven to bake for about 40 minutes.

7. Serve and enjoy.

Nutrition:

Calories 213

Total Fat 14 g

Saturated fat 1.9 g

Protein 5 g

## Chicken Stuffed With Cheesy Bacon

Preparation time: 10 minutes

Cooking Time: 40 minutes

Serving: 2

Ingredients:

- ¼ c. mozzarella cheese
- Four halved chicken breasts
- ¼ c. ricotta cheese
- Eight cooked and crumbled bacon slices
- 1/8 c. spinach

Directions:

1. Set oven to 425° F.
2. In a mixing bowl, mix cheeses, spinach, and bacon.
3. Make a pocket opening into the chicken breasts. Fill in the bacon mixture.
4. Add a seasoning of pepper and salt.
5. Bake for about 40 minutes.

6. Serve and enjoy.

Nutrition:

Calories 213

Total Fat 14 g

Protein 5 g

## Stuffed Turkey Rolls

Preparation time: 10 minutes

Cooking Time: 25 minutes

Serving: 2

Ingredients:

- One garlic clove, crushed
- Four turkey breasts
- Salt.
- Four tips. Tomato paste
- ¼ c. fresh spinach
- Pepper.
- 1 tbsp. cream, light
- 4 Swiss cheese slices

Directions:

1. Use a rolling pin to ensure the turkey breasts are flattened.
2. Spread garlic, cheese, spinach, and tomato paste to each of the breasts. Add pepper and salt for seasoning. Roll and set using a toothpick.
3. Line a pan with a foil and lay the spirals in place. Set in the broiler

and broil for about 20 minutes. Turn after every 5 minutes.

4. Serve and enjoy.

Nutrition:

Calories 189

Total Fat 7 g

Saturated fat 2.2 g

Protein 29 g

## Grilled Spicy Sesame Chicken

Preparation time: 10 minutes

Cooking Time: 20 minutes

Serving: 2

Ingredients:

- ¼ c. green onion, chopped
- Pepper.
- One crushed garlic clove
- 1 tbsp. sesame seeds
- 2 lbs. sliced boneless chicken
- 1 tbsp. sesame oil
- Salt.
- Four tips. Ginger, fresh

Directions:

1. In a bowl, combine garlic, ginger, and one tablespoon oil.
2. Toast the chicken in the oil mixture, then coat with the sesame seeds. Set in a frying pan to stir fry to cook through.

3. Serve and enjoy.

Nutrition:

Calories 110

Protein 6 g

## Italian Style Pork Chops

Preparation time: 10 minutes

Cooking Time: 10 minutes

Serving: 2

Ingredients:

- 1/3 large green bell pepper cut six pieces
- 1/8 cup water, if needed
- 1/8 tsp. ground black pepper
- 1/8 tsp. salt
- 1/8 tsp. dried oregano
- 1/3 tsp. dried basil
- 1/3 14.5-oz can dice Italian tomatoes, undrained
- 1/8 cup chopped shallots
- 2/3 cloves garlic, crushed
- 2 pork loin chops, 3/4-inch thick
- 2/3 tbsp. + 1 tsp. olive oil, divided
- 2/3 cups sliced button mushrooms
- 1/8 cup scallions, sliced

Directions:

1. On medium fire, place a nonstick pan and heat 1 tsp. oil. Sauté mushrooms until soft, around 5 to 7 minutes. Once cooked, transfer to a plate.

2. In the same pan, heat the remaining oil.

3. Add pork chops, and for 5 minutes, brown each side of chops. Once done, transfer to a plate.

4. Leave at least a tablespoon of chop drippings and discard the rest. Continue heating and add shallots and garlic. Sauté for 5 minutes or until shallots are soft and translucent.

5. Add pepper, salt, oregano, basil, and tomatoes.

6. Return pork chops cover and simmer for at least 20 minutes or until chops are fully cooked. If needed, add water.

7. Return reserved mushrooms and add bell pepper. Continue simmering for another 10 minutes.

8. Add scallions and simmer for a minute or two before serving.

Nutrition:

Carbs (g): 7.8

Fiber (g): 2

Net Carb Grams: 5.8

Protein (g): 25.4

## Pollo Con Queso

Preparation time: 30 minutes

Cooking Time: 45 minutes

Serving: 2

Ingredients:

- 2 oz. Pepper Jack cheese, cut into pieces
- 2 oz. Monterey Jack cheese, grated
- 2 oz. cheddar cheese, grated
- 2 oz. American cheese slices, torn into pieces
- ¼ cup heavy cream
- ¼ tsp. garlic powder
- ¼ tsp. chili powder
- 1/3 cup chicken stock
- ½ can 10-oz Ro-tel tomatoes & chilies, drained solids
- 1 tbsp. butter
- One 3-lbs chicken

Directions:

1. Remove the chicken's neck, wings, and skin and make chicken soup by boiling in 3 cups water for 40 minutes.

2. Cut up chicken breasts into four equal sizes. The thighs and drumstick would make up an extra four more servings. Store in the freezer if not needed.

3. Pan Fry chicken breasts in a cast-iron skillet until all sides are

browned, around 3 minutes per side on medium-high fire. Once done browning, turn off the fire and stir in Ro-tel, chicken soup, and spices.

4. Add half of the cheeses over the chicken, cover the top with foil, and pop in a preheated 350-degree oven. Bake for 40 minutes.

5. Once done, remove from oven, stir in cream and sprinkle remaining cheese on top.

6. Return to oven uncovered and baked for an additional 5 minutes.

7. Serve immediately.

Nutrition:

Carbs (g): 3.48

Fiber (g): 0.48

Net Carb Grams: 3

Protein (g): 35

## Baked Chicken Lebanese Style

Preparation time: 10 minutes

Cooking Time: 30 minutes

Serving: 2

Ingredients:

- Pepper and Salt to taste
- Juice of 1 lemon
- ¼ tsp. oregano
- Ten garlic cloves, crushed
- 2 Roma tomatoes cut into wedges
- One medium onion, cut into wedges and layers separated
- Eight chicken pieces
- 4 tbsps. olive oil

Directions:

1. In a large baking pan, drizzle 1 tbsp. oil and grease the pan.

2. Add chicken in one layer without overlapping any piece.

3. In between chicken pieces, add garlic, onions, and tomatoes.

4. Squeeze lemon juice evenly on chicken and drizzle with remaining oil.

5. Season with pepper, salt, and oregano.

6. Pop in a preheated 500oF broiler for 30 minutes.

7. Remove chicken and lower oven temperature to 350oF. Baste chicken with juices.

8. Return pan to oven and continue baking for 20-30 minutes more or until chicken juices run clear.

9. Serve and enjoy.

Nutrition

Carbs (g): 7.98 Fiber (g): 1.1

Net Carb Grams: 6.88

Protein (g): 34.8

## Tilapia With Garlic Lemon Flavor

Preparation time: 15 minutes

Cooking Time: 30 minutes

Serving: 2

Ingredients:

- Pepper to taste
- 1 tsp. dried parsley flakes
- One clove garlic, finely chopped
- 1 tbsp. butter, melted
- 3 tbsps. fresh lemon juice
- Four tilapia filets

Directions:

1. Grease a large baking dish with cooking spray and preheat oven to 375oF.
2. Wash tilapia filets under tap water and dry with a paper towel. Place on the greased baking tray.
3. Pour lemon juice and butter on top.
4. Season with pepper, parsley, and garlic.
5. Pop in the oven and bake for 30 minutes or until flaky.

Nutrition

Carbs (g): 1.4

Fiber (g): 0.2

Net Carb Grams: 1.2

Protein (g): 23.1

## Shrimp Curry

Preparation time: 10 minutes

Cooking Time: 3-5 minutes

Serving: 2

Ingredients:

- Chopped fresh cilantro – optional
- 1/3 tsp. garam masala
- 1/8 cup of water
- 3/4 lbs. medium shrimp, peeled and deveined
- 1/3 tsp. ground red Chile pepper
- One tomato, finely chopped
- 1/4 tsp. ground turmeric
- 1/4 tsp. salt
- 1/3 tsp. ground coriander
- 1/3 tbsp. ginger garlic paste
- 4 fresh curry leaves
- 1/3 large onion, chopped
- 1/8 cup of vegetable oil

Directions:

1. On high fire, place a large saucepan and heat oil.
2. Sauté onions for 3-5 minutes or until lightly browned.
3. Add salt, coriander, ginger-garlic paste, and curry leaves. Fry for a minute.
4. Add water, shrimp, Chile powder, tomato, salt, and turmeric.
5. Lower fire to medium-high and continue sautéing shrimps until cooked, around 7 to 8 minutes

6. Season with garam masala, sauté for a minute, and turn off the fire.
7. Serve and enjoy.

Nutrition

Carbs (g): 5.3

Fiber (g): 1.5

Net Carb Grams: 3.8

Protein (g): 30.7

## Korean Beef Bulgogi

Preparation time: 10 minutes

Cooking Time: 10 minutes

Serving: 2

Ingredients:

- ½ tsp. ground black pepper
- 2 tbsp. sesame oil
- 2 tbsps. sesame seeds
- 2 tbsps. minced garlic
- ¼ cup chopped green onion
- 2 ½ tbsps. white sugar
- 5 tbsps. soy sauce
- 1 lb. flank steak thinly sliced
- 1 tbsp. oil

Directions:

1. In a shallow dish, marinate flank steak with black pepper, sesame oil, sesame seeds, garlic, green onion, sugar, and soy sauce. Leave in the ref for at least an hour. Overnight is best.
2. In a nonstick saucepan, place on high heat.
3. Once the pan is hot, add beef and marinade. Stir fry until meat is cooked and sauce is fully absorbed, around 7-10 minutes.
4. Add 1 tbsp. oil once the sauce is nearly dry. Continue stir-frying for 5 minutes more after the oil is added.
5. Serve and enjoy.

Nutrition:

Carbs (g): 12.4 Fiber (g): 1

Net Carb Grams: 11.4

Protein (g): 16.2

## Salmon With Basil Tomato

Preparation time: 10 minutes

Cooking Time: 20 minutes

Serving: 2

Ingredients:

- 2 tbsps. grated Parmesan cheese
- 1 tbsp. olive oil
- One tomato, sliced thinly
- 1 tbsp. dried basil
- Two 6-oz boneless salmon fillet
- Pepper and salt to taste

Directions:

1. Line a baking sheet with aluminum foil, grease with cooking spray, and preheat the oven to 375oF.
2. Place salmon on greased foil with skin side down.
3. Sprinkle with basil, top salmon with tomato slices, and season with pepper, salt, Olive oil, and Parmesan cheese.
4. Pop in the oven and bake for 20 minutes or until Parmesan cheese is lightly browned.

Nutrition:

Carbs (g): 4 Fiber (g): 1.6

Net Carb Grams: 2.4

Protein (g): 36.2

Directions:

1. Season steaks on both sides with pepper and salt.
2. On medium-high fire, place a nonstick skillet and once hot pan fry steaks for a minute per side or until browned.
3. Add red wine and balsamic vinegar while lowering fire to medium-low. Cover and simmer for 4 minutes per side.
4. Remove steaks from pan and serve with a drizzle of sauce.

Nutrition:

Carbs (g): 5.7

Fiber (g): 0.1

Net Carb Grams: 5.6

Protein (g): 20.3

## Rich Balsamic Glaze On Filets Mignon

Preparation time: 10 minutes

Cooking Time: 50 minutes

Serving: 2

Ingredients:

- ¼ cup dry red wine
- ¼ cup balsamic vinegar
- salt to taste
- ½ tsp. freshly ground black pepper
- Two 4-oz filets mignon steaks

## Beef London Broil

Preparation time: 5 minutes

Cooking Time: 7 minutes

Serving: 2

Ingredients:

- 1 lbs. flank steak
- 1/8 tsp. dried oregano
- 1/8 tsp. ground black pepper
- 1/4 tbsp. vegetable oil
- 1/4 tbsp. ketchup
- 3/4 tbsps. soy sauce
- 1/4 tsp. salt
- 1/4 clove garlic, minced

Directions:

1. Mix oregano, black pepper, vegetable oil, ketchup, soy sauce, salt, and garlic in a small bowl.
2. In both ends of the beef, score a 1/8-inch deep diamond shape. Rub within the cut and around the meat the sauce mixture above. Tightly wrap in aluminum foil and along with the remaining sauce.
3. For 5-6 hours, marinate meat in the ref (or up to overnight), flipping meat over every once in a while.
4. Preheat grill and grease grate. Once grate is hot, remove meat from foil and grill on medium-high fire for 7 minutes per side or to desired doneness.
5. Slice meat into strips, serve and enjoy.

Nutrition:

Carbs (g): 1.2 Fiber (g): 0.1

Net Carb Grams: 1.1 Protein (g): 48.6

## Crab Frittata

Preparation time: 10 minutes

Cooking Time: 3 minutes

Serving: 2

Ingredients:

- One green onion, chopped
- 1 cup crab meat, flaked
- ¼ cup grated Parmesan cheese
- 1 cup shredded Monterey Jack cheese
- Three dashes hot pepper sauce
- ½ tsp. black pepper
- ½ tsp. salt
- 1 cup heavy cream
- Four large eggs

Directions:

1. Grease a cast iron pan with cooking spray and place on medium fire. Preheat broiler to low and position rack nearest to the top.
2. On a large bowl, whisk okay eggs. Add hot sauce, pepper, and salt. Whisk well.
3. Add crab meat, onion, and cream. Whisk well.
4. Pour into a hot pan. Cover and cook for 3 minutes.
5. Slowly, with a spatula, insert into one side of the frittata and gently pull up. Allowing uncooked eggs from the top to flow underneath. Repeat process on the other four sides of the pan. Cover and cook for another 2 minutes.
6. Turn off the fire, uncover the pan, add chopped green onions and cover with cheese.
7. Pop in to the top rack of the oven and broil on low for 3-5

minutes or until cheese is melted, and the frittata is set.

8. Cut into four equal servings and enjoy.

Nutrition:

Carbs (g): 13

Fiber (g): 0

Net Carb Grams: 13

Protein (g): 33

## Yellow Squash Casserole

Preparation time: 20 minutes

Cooking Time: 30 minutes

Serving: 2

Ingredients:

- 1/8 cup coarsely chopped roasted, salted almonds
- 1 egg
- 1/8 cup heavy whipping cream
- 1/4 cup shredded Colby-Monterey Jack cheese, divided
- 1/8 cup finely chopped raw almonds
- 1/8 tsp. freshly ground black pepper
- 1/4 tsp. kosher salt
- 1 cups peeled and cubed yellow squash
- 1 cloves garlic, minced
- 1 small onion, chopped
- 1/4 tsp. butter
- 1/4 tbsp. olive oil

Directions:

1. Grease a 9 x 13 baking dish and preheat oven to 400oF.
2. On medium-high fire, place a skillet and heat butter and oil.
3. Sauté garlic and onions for 3 minutes or until onions are soft.
4. Stir in pepper, salt, and squash. Cover and cook for 5 minutes while stirring occasionally.
5. Pour squash into prepped baking dish.
6. In the dish, add ½ cup of cheese and ½ raw almonds. Mix well.
7. In a small bowl, whisk well the eggs and cream. Pour into the dish of squash and mix well.
8. Top the casserole with remaining almonds and cheese. Pop into the oven and bake for 25-30 minutes or until the hash's tops are golden brown.

Nutrition:

Carbs (g): 6.7

Fiber (g): 2.6

Net Carb Grams: 4.1

Protein (g): 8.

# CHAPTER 9:

# Mains

## Asparagus And Leek Soup

Preparation time: 40 minutes

Cooking Time: 30 minutes

Serving: 2

Ingredients:

- Unsalted butter, two tablespoons
- Leek x 1
- Asparagus, 0.75lb
- Garlic, one teaspoon
- Chicken broth, 14.5 oz.
- Heavy cream, 1/3 cup

Directions:

1. In a large pot, melt the butter before adding the leeks and cooking for around 3 minutes
2. Add the asparagus and cook for a further minute
3. Add the garlic and cook for half a minute
4. Add the broth and bring the pot to a boil
5. Turn the heat down and simmer for around 10 minutes
6. Add the cream, salt, and pepper
7. Blend the soup in a blender or food processor
8. Heat up if required
9. Season to taste

Nutrition:

Total carbs per serving 5.2g

## Chocolate And Hazelnut Mousse

Preparation time: 4hrs

Cooking Time: 3.5 hrs.

Serving: 2

Ingredients:

- Low carb chocolate, 2 oz.
- Unsalted butter, 2 tsp.
- Hazelnut syrup (sugar-free), 1 teaspoons
- Heavy cream, ½ cups
- The sugar substitute, 1teaspoons
- Chopped and toasted hazelnuts, 1 tablespoons
- Fresh raspberries, x2

Directions:

1. Into a small bowl, melt the chocolate, butter, and syrup over low heat
2. Transfer to a bowl and set to one side
3. Add the cream and sugar substitute to another bowl and whip together well
4. Fold 1/3 of the mixture into the chocolate and stir
5. Combine the rest and stir
6. Add the hazelnuts and raspberry as a garnish

Nutrition:

Total carbs per serving 3g

## Crispy, Spicy Cauliflower

Preparation time: 10 minutes

Cooking Time: 30 minutes

Serving: 2

Ingredients:

- Two eggs
- Cauliflower florets, 4 cups
- Almond flour, four tablespoons
- Chili powder, one teaspoon
- Canola oil
- Fish sauce, two teaspoons
- Lime juice, one tablespoon
- Scallions, chopped, one tablespoon

Directions:

1. Combine the eggs in a large bowl and toss in the cauliflower florets, coating completely.
2. Place the florets onto a plate
3. Add the almond flour and chili powder, sprinkling over the top
4. Using a wok or high sided frying pan, fill with canola oil and heat to 170°C
5. Fry the florets in the oil
6. Transfer to paper towels to absorb extra oil
7. Drizzle with fish sauce and lime juice
8. Add the chopped scallions as a garnish

Nutrition:

Total carbs per serving 5g

## Asian Vegetable Bowl

Preparation time: 10 minutes

Cooking Time: 20 minutes

Serving: 2

Ingredients:

- 1 cups Spring onions,
- 2/3 cups Mushrooms,
- 1 1/3 tablespoons tamari soybean sauce,
- 1 tsp Ginger,

- Garlic, one clove
- 1/3 Serrano pepper
- 1/3 cup Sliced red tomato
- 2 oz. Tofu, the firm variety,
- Carrot
- 1/8 oz. Cilantro,
- 2/3 cups Chinese cabbage, shredded,
- 2 cups Chicken broth,

Directions:
1. Heat the broth and tamari and bring to a boil
2. Turn down the heat and add the Chinese cabbage, mushrooms, ginger, garlic, and chili
3. Simmer for around 5 minutes
4. Add the tomatoes, onions, tofu, and carrot, cook for around 1 minute more
5. Stir in the cilantro and serve

Nutrition:

Total carbs per serving 4.6g

## Banana & Coconut Rum

Preparation time: 10 minutes

Cooking Time: 5 minutes

Serving: 1

Ingredients:

- Small banana, 1/3
- Coconut cream, 1/3 cup
- Rum, one fluid oz.
- Ice cubes, x2
- Sweetener, 0.75 teaspoon

Directions:
1. Combine the banana, coconut, rum, and sugar substitute in a blender, before adding the ice
2. Blend until totally combined
3. Serve in a glass and enjoy!

Nutrition:

Total carbs per serving 8.9g

## Breakfast Sausage Sauteed With Red & Green Peppers

Preparation time: 10 minutes

Cooking Time: 15 minutes

Serving: 1

Ingredients:

- Canola oil, one teaspoon
- Turkey breakfast sausage, four links (cooked)
- Red sweet pepper, one quarter
- Green sweet pepper, one quarter
- Monterey Jack cheese, 1 oz.

Directions:
1. Over medium heat, add the oil to a skillet pan and heat up
2. You can either crumble the sausage or slice after cooking, but add to the pan and brown for around 3 minutes

3. Add the red and green peppers
4. Cook for a further 5 minutes
5. Sprinkle on the cheese, allowing to melt
6. Serve

Nutrition:

Total carbs per serving 3g

## Cajun Pork Chops

Preparation time: 10 minutes

Cooking Time: 20 minutes

Serving: 2

Ingredients:

- Paprika, one tablespoon
- Cumin, 0.5 teaspoon
- Ground sage, 0.5 teaspoon
- Black pepper, 0.5 teaspoon
- Garlic powder, 0.5 teaspoon
- Cayenne pepper, 0.5 teaspoon
- Pork chops, 24oz
- Unsalted butter, 0.5 tablespoons
- Canola oil, 0.5 tablespoons

Directions:

1. In a bowl, combine all the spices
2. Season the pork chops on both sides
3. Over high heat, melt the butter and oil
4. Cook the chops in the skillet over medium heat for just under 10 minutes, turning halfway through
5. Serve

Nutrition:

Total carbs per serving 0.7g

## Key Lime Mousse

Preparation time: 1hr 30 minutes

Cooking Time: 1hr 20 minutes

Serving: 2

Ingredients:

- Mashed avocados, 2 cups
- Lime zest, 0.5 teaspoon
- Lime juice, 3 oz.
- Powdered xylitol, 0.25 cups
- Stevia crystals, 0.5 teaspoon
- Vanilla extract, two teaspoons
- Salt, one pinch
- The ground cinnamon, one pinch
- Ground nutmeg, one pinch
- Almond butter, two tablespoons
- Extract (your choice), 0.25 teaspoon
- Strawberries, 0.25 cup

Directions:

1. In a food processor, place all ingredients (except strawberries) and combine until creamy
2. Remove from the processor and allow it to rest for around 20 minutes at the very least
3. Add the strawberries as a garnish

Nutrition: Total carbs per serving 4g

## Cauliflower Potato Salad

Preparation time: 10 minutes

Cooking Time: 20 minutes

Serving: 2

Ingredients:

- 1 Spring onions
- 1 1/3 tbsp. Mayonnaise
- 1/3 fluid oz. Lemon juice,
- 1/3 teaspoon The sugar substitute,
- 1/8 teaspoon Ground mustard,
- 1/3 Cauliflower head
- 1/3 Jalapeno pepper
- 1/8 teaspoon Salt
- 1/8 teaspoon Black pepper

Directions:

1. Cook the cauliflower first of all in salted water, to your taste
2. Drain and pat dry the cauliflower
3. Mix the mayonnaise, lemon juice, sugar substitute, and mustard until well combined
4. Add the cauliflower, pepper, and onion
5. Mix until well coated
6. Add salt and pepper

Nutrition: Total carbs per serving 3.8g

## Greek Salad

Preparation time: 10 minutes

Cooking Time: 20 minutes

Serving: 2

Ingredients:

- 50 g Feta cheese, cut into chunks
- 2/3 tbsp. Feta brine,
- 1 tbsp. Fresh lime juice,
- 1 1/3 tbsp. Extra virgin olive oil
- 1/3 cup Plum tomatoes,
- 1/4 cup Cucumber
- 1/8 cup Red onion
- 1/4 cup Green bell pepper,
- 1/8 cup Black olives
- 2/3 cups Arugula
- 2/3 tbsp Dried oregano
- 1/3 tsp. Salt

Directions:

1. Blend up half of the feta cheese, brine, olive oil, and lemon juice in a blender or food processor
2. Mix the rest of the ingredients in a bowl (except the arugula)
3. Add the dressing and mix
4. Add the arugula and toss gently

Nutrition:

Total carbs per serving 5g

## Cheese Sauce

Preparation time: 10 minutes

Cooking Time: 15 minutes

Serving: 2

Ingredients:

- 1/4 cup Heavy cream
- 1/8 cup (crumbled) Roquefort cheese
- 1/2 oz. Jarlsberg cheese
- 1/8 cup Grated parmesan cheese
- 1/8 teaspoon Paprika

Directions:

1. Over low heat, heat the cream
2. Add the Roquefort until melted
3. Add the Jarlsberg until melted
4. Add the parmesan until melted
5. Add the paprika and continue to cook until hot and smooth, stirring regularly
6. Season with salt and pepper

Nutrition: Total carbs per serving 1.5g

## Cream Soup With Chicken And Mushrooms

Preparation time: 10 minutes

Cooking Time: 10 minutes

Serving: 2

Ingredients:

- Two chicken breasts on the bone with skin
- 2 cups chanterelles (freshly welded)
- One onion weighing 100g
- Cream of 33% 200 ml
- Dill (a little)
- Carrot 100g
- Celery stalks 100g.
- + Allspice
- + Bay leaf
- + Salt
- + Butter 1 tbsp.

Directions:

1. In 1.5 liters of cold water, we put onion, carrot, celery, chicken breast, pepper, bay leaf, salt a little, and cook on low heat for about an hour.
2. Pour broth into another saucepan through a colander, salt.
3. In melted butter, fry the mushrooms with salt and pepper for 10 minutes, transfer them to the broth.
4. We also put chicken meat, trimmed from the bones, divided into small fragments, poured in the cream, and cooked for 10 minutes.
5. Grind the dill and add to the soup directly to its readiness.

Nutrition:

(Carbohydrates on the soup pot - 10g)

## Cream Soup From Zucchini With Salmon

Preparation time: 20 minutes

Cooking Time: 10 minutes

Serving: 2

Ingredients:

- Zucchini weighing 1.4 kg (in the purified form will be 1 kg)
- Salmon steak weighing 470g
- Two bulb onions small 115g
- Vegetable broth 1.5 liters
- Cream of 20% 200 ml
- Butter 100g
- + Saffron 1 tsp.
- + Nutmeg 1/2 tsp.
- + Lemon pepper 1/3 tsp.
- + Salt
- + A pair of parsley and dill

Directions:

1. At the zucchini, cut the edges, cut along in half, clean the seeds, everything else are cut into a cube 1-3 cm.
2. Put the broth on the fire, put the zucchini in it, and cook until soft, try, and salt.
3. Cut the onion in half rings and pass in melted butter until golden brown.
4. Add all the spices and a soup spoon of boiling broth nearby, cook it a little until the saffron spreads, and put it in the pan to the zucchini.
5. Cook the soup for about 10 minutes; during this time, gently remove the skin from the steak and discard it, wash the steak under running cold water, and put it in the soup straight over the zucchini (the steak will sink into the water and lie still on the squash).
6. After 10 minutes, take out the steak and disassemble it into pieces, carefully choosing the bones.
7. Put the immersion blender into the saucepan with the soup, pour the contents, and add salt.
8. When the soup becomes more or less homogeneous - pour the cream in a thin stream, continuing to puree.
9. Slices of salmon can be put immediately into the saucepan with the soup, and you can first pour it into plates and then spread the salmon.
10. Put green twigs on top.

Nutrition:

(For the whole pot 40g of carbohydrates, salmon can take even more)

## Fried Chicken With Feta Inside, Baked With Mushroom Sauce And Cheese

Preparation time: 5 minutes

Cooking Time: 5 minutes

Serving: 2

Ingredients:

- 400g chicken mince
- 80g fantasy
- Two large champignons
- One small onion weighing 40g
- a small bunch of parsley
- 50g of Alterman or yellow mozzarella cheese
- Cream 20% 200ml
- Several leaves of fresh basil
- + Cooking oil for frying
- + Salt
- + Ground pepper

Directions:

1. Cheese cut into cubes 1x1cm.
2. Wrap the feta in minced meat, do not season with anything, layout on a plate or lodge.
3. Heat the pan greased with a thin layer of oil.
4. Quickly transfer the meatballs to the skillet and, over high heat, begin to shake .the skillet so that the meatballs roll and roast on it from all sides.
5. When they are browned - we shift them to the baking dish.
6. Crush the onion, pass in oil to transparency.
7. Mushrooms cut in half and cut into slices - add to the onion, fry until done.
8. Fill all with cream, salt, pepper, add chopped parsley and basil, quickly stir, and after 30 seconds, turn off the fire.
9. Shake the sauce from the pan into the baking dish, spreading it evenly over the meatballs.
10. Three pieces of cheese on a fine grater sprinkle everything on top.
11. We remove in the oven for 250g the upper heating for 2 minutes - it is ready.

Nutrition:

(Carbohydrates just 7g)

## Friends

Preparation time: 10 minutes

Cooking Time: 5 minutes

Serving: 2

Ingredients:

- Minced pork 600g
- Onion 100g

- 330% cream 150g
- Cranberries 100g (note that thawed cranberries weigh less than 150 - they are thawed)
- Sugar substitute 20 tablets
- Tablespoon of butter
- + Cooking oil
- + Salt
- + Ground pepper
- + Turmeric
- + Nutmeg

Directions:
1. Put the cranberries in a saucepan, slightly press with a spoon, and add half a glass of water and a sugar substitute boil to a state of jam).
2. Clean the onion, wrap it in foil, put it in the oven, and cook in it for 30 minutes.
3. We get an onion, put it in a saucepan, fill it with cream, grind it with a blender until smooth, and add salt, set on low fire.
4. When the sauce gurgles - try and add a few other spices.
5. Mince salt and pepper, sculpt meatballs.
6. Melt the butter on the vegetable in a large flat skillet; when intense heat comes from it - put the meatballs and move the frying pan back and forth so that they roll over and roast it on all sides).
7. When they turn brown, reduce the heat to a minimum and leave them under the lid for another 5 minutes.
8. Putting it all together - putting meatballs on a plate, pouring onion sauce, putting cranberry jam on top – ready.

Nutrition:

(Total Carbohydrates (2 servings here) 11g)

## Protein Variation "Cordon Blu"

Preparation time: 20 minutes

Cooking Time: 15 minutes

Serving: 2

Ingredients:
- Four chicken fillets
- Four slices of ham
- 80 grams of Alterman cheese
- 12 strips of bacon
- Four teaspoons of tomato puree
- + Salt
- + Ground pepper

Directions:
1. Beat the fillets to a thickness of 5mm.

2. Spread out in front of you, salt and pepper, place the ham in the center.

3. Cut the cheese into 4 bars, but one per ham.

4. Twist the chicken into a roll (turning along, along the length), put on the seam, and smear with tomato puree.

5. Wrap each roll with three strips of bacon in the overlap; fasten the bacon ends along the edges with a toothpick.

6. Remove in preheated oven for 180 minutes for 15 minutes (put on parchment is desirable).

7. Cut the finished cordon bleu into 1.5 cm wide slices.

Nutrition:

(Carbohydrates in all four rolls - 2g (due to mashed potatoes, there would be 0 without it)

## Chicken Fillets With Mozzarella And Tomatoes

Preparation time: 10 minutes

Cooking Time: 5 minutes

Serving: 2

Ingredients:

- Four chicken fillets
- One tomato 100g
- Two mozzarella balls 200g
- Extra virgin olive oil a little
- Fresh basil and dried a little
- olives are not required)
- + Salt
- + Ground pepper
- + Cooking oil
- + Liquid smoke (optional)
- + Paprika

Directions:

1. Cut the fillets from fats and films, rub them with salt, paprika, cooking oil, and liquid smoke, marinate in the refrigerator under the lid for an hour.

2. On a hot griddle, generously greased with frying oil (preferably olive), fry the fillet on both sides for 2 minutes on high heat on each side.

3. We shift the fillets on napkins so that the fat flows, then on the parchment

4. Preheat oven to 220gr top heated.

5. Put 1.5 mozzarella circles in a chicken and one tomato circle, pour-over EV olive oil, sprinkle with salt, basil, and ground pepper. We clean in the oven for 2-3 minutes.

6. Sprinkle the finished dish with fresh sliced basil.

Nutrition:(Carbohydrates in 1 fillet - 1.2g!)

## Basturma With Creative Cheese

Preparation time: 10 minutes

Cooking Time: 0 minutes

Serving: 2

Ingredients:

- Package of chopped basturma
- Almette cheese with greens (it contains 3g of carbohydrates, and in the usual, without additives, much more) 200g
- Salad leaves 15g
- + Parsley
- + Sesame
- + Extra virgin olive oil

Directions:

1. Spread basturma pieces in front of you (I had oblong ones, similar to 8).
2. At the edge of each place, a teaspoon of cheese.
3. Cover the second half of a piece of basturma, flatten her cheese.
4. Salad leaves can be partially cut (coarser parts); put basturma with cheese on them.
5. Drizzle with oil, sprinkle with sesame, and greens.

Nutrition:

(Total Carbohydrate 6.2g)

## 9greek Type Salad

Preparation time: 10 minutes

Cooking Time: 0 minutes

Serving: 2

The most crucial thing in this salad is more feta, fewer vegetables, and especially olives! You can add paprika, paprika, lettuce leaves, etc., at will) if you put onions, quite a bit ... and most importantly! NO VINEGAR !!!

Ingredients:

- Cucumber 100g
- Tomato 100g
- Feta 150g
- Olives 20g
- + Extra Virgin Olive Oil
- + Salt
- + Pepper

Direction:

1. All cut and refuel.

Nutrition:

(Carbohydrate 7g)

## Boiled Lobster + Sauce

Preparation time: 10 minutes

Cooking Time: 50 minutes

Serving: 2

Ingredients:

- Lobsters 2kg

- Dried dill (we have our sticks) a LOT
- Bay leaf
- Allspice
- Salt

Sauce:
- Protein mayonnaise
- Sour cream 4 tbsp.
- Parsley and dill on a small bunch without stems 10 grams
- A pair of lemon slices

Directions:
2. Put all ingredients from 2 to 5 points into a saucepan and pour 4 liters of water, bringing to a boil (water should be salty and green).
3. Lobsters can be pre-put in the fridge/freezer to fall asleep, throw in boiling water, cover and cook for 5 minutes.
4. Water, cover, and cook for 5 minutes.
5. For the sauce - chop the greens; mix with sour cream and mayonnaise).
6. Serve with lemon wedges.

Nutrition:

(Carbohydrate lobster 0, 6g sauce)

# Boiled Point Kyiv In Dietary Interpretation

Preparation time: 10 minutes

Cooking Time: 10 minutes

Serving: 2

Ingredients:
- Chicken minced 600g.
- Butter 150g
- Dill 15g
- Lemon juice 10g (1/3 lemon)
- Salad leaves 20g.
- Tomato 1pc 50g
- + Cooking oil
- + Dried basil
- + Black pepper
- + Paprika
- + Salt

Directions:
1. In a stuffing package, add 1 tsp. without a hill of salt, paprika, basil, mix, form 8 balls.
2. Put the butter in a bowl, add lemon juice, a little pepper, chopped dill, mix it, and divide it into eight oblong parts.
3. Spread each ball of minced meat in the palm of your hand, put butter in the middle, wrap in minced beef, and form a flat patty.

4. Heat the pan greased.
5. Put the burgers on it, leave it on high heat for 1.5-2 minutes, and then turn it over as much.
6. We clean in the oven heated to 200gr for 8-10 minutes.
7. During this time, we cut lettuce and tomatoes, which will be a side dish for cutlets.

Nutrition:

(5.5g of carbs)

# Delicious Sausage And Egg Casserole

Preparation time: 3hrs 30 minutes

Cooking Time: 3 minutes

Serving: 2

Ingredients:

- 1/3 head, chopped broccoli
- 1/8 oz., low carb, cooked and sliced sausages
- 1/3 cup, shredded, divided cheddar cheese
- 3 eggs
- 2/3 cloves, minced garlic
- 1/8 teaspoons salt
- 1/8 teaspoons pepper
- 1/4 cup whipping cream

Directions:

1. Grease stoneware insert with cooking oil or ghee.
2. Now add these ingredients in layers, ½ of broccoli, cheese, and sausage. Repeat with the remaining ingredients.
3. Combine whipping cream, garlic, eggs, pepper, and salt in a large bowl and whisk.
4. Pour egg mixture over layered ingredients.
5. Secure and cook on for 3 hours on high. The casserole is finished when the edges are fully browned and is set in the center. Enjoy!

Nutrition:

Protein: 13.2 g, Fat: 15.4 g, Carbohydrate: 7.6 g, Fiber: 0.6 g Total Calories: 223.6

# Satisfying Pork Stew

Preparation time: 10hrs and 30 minutes

Cooking Time: 10hrs

Serving: 2

Ingredients:

- onion (1 small, thinly sliced)
- cabbage (½ small, cut into four wedges)
- garlic (3 cloves, smashed)
- carrots (¼ lb., baby)
- pork shoulder (1 ½ lb., cut into 1-inch cubes)
- seasoning blend (½ tablespoons)
- fish sauce (½ tablespoons)
- marinara sauce (½ low carb)

- vinegar (½ tablespoons)
- salt and pepper (to taste)

Directions:

1. Slice the onions, carrots, and garlic and place in the slow cooker.
2. Season pork with your favorite seasoning blends and layer pork cubes over the vegetables in the cooker.
3. Add cabbage wedges and top with marinara and fish sauce.
4. Let cook on low for 10 hours. Season with pepper, salt, vinegar, and herbs before serving.

Nutrition:

Protein: 24 g, Fat: 7 g, Carbohydrate: 2 g, Fiber: 3 g Total Calories: 272

## Tempting Breakfast Casserole With Tomato And Spinach

Preparation time: 5hrs

Cooking Time: 4hrs 30 minutes

Serving: 2

Want an exciting breakfast? Try this Breakfast Casserole filled with Tomato and Spinach!

Ingredients:

- quinoa (¼ cup, uncooked)
- milk (½ cup)
- eggs (3 large)
- salt and pepper (to taste)
- spinach (handful)
- tomatoes (½ cup)
- cheese of choice (⅛ cup, shredded)
- parmesan cheese (⅛ cup)

Directions:

1. Combine the quinoa, milk, pepper, salt, and eggs and stir in a mixing bowl.
2. Add the tomatoes, spinach, and half of the cheese and stir.
3. Grease stoneware insert and then pour in the mixture
4. Sprinkle with parmesan cheese on top.
5. Secure and cook for 4 hours until edges are fully browned, and eggs are set in the center.

Nutrition:

Protein: 16.2 g, Fat: 9.3 g, Carbohydrate: 2.2 g, Fiber: 3.7 g, Total Calories: 188.2

## Slow-Cooker Lemon And Olive Chicken

Preparation time: 7hrs

Cooking Time: 7hrs

Serving: 2

Ingredients:

- 4 large, stuffed green olives
- 1/4 tablespoon lemon juice
- zest lemon, grated

- 1/2 ribs, chopped celery
- 1 cloves, crushed garlic
- 1/2 bay leaves
- 1/8 cup all-purpose flour
- 1/4 onion
- 1/4 bulb, cored and chopped fennel
- 3 boneless, skinless chicken thighs
- 1/4 cup chicken broth
- 1/8 cup, chopped parsley
- 1/8 teaspoons, dried oregano
- salt and pepper to taste
- 1/2 chopped carrots

Directions:

1. Place all ingredients except for the flour and lemon juice into the slow cooker and cook for 6 hours on medium heat. Leave a few herbs for garnishing.
2. Mix flour and lemon juice in a little water for flavor, then add to mixture in a slow cooker and stir. Let cook for a further for 15 minutes.
3. Garnish and serve.

Nutrition:

Protein: 18 g, Fat: 17 g, Carbohydrate: 10 g, Fiber: 32 g, Total Calories: 176

## Scrumptious Breakfast Pie

Preparation time: 8hrs

Cooking Time: 7hrs 30 minutes

Serving: 2

Ingredients:

- eggs (4)
- sweet potato (1 small, shredded)
- sausage (½ lb., pork, broken up)
- onion (1 little, yellow, diced)
- garlic powder (½ tablespoons)
- basil (1 teaspoon, dried)
- salt and pepper (to taste)
- bell peppers (chopped)

Directions:

1. Grease inside of stoneware inserts.
2. Use a box grater and shred sweet potato, and place it in a slow cooker.
3. Add the remaining ingredients and stir well.
4. Cook for 7 hours on Low. Ensure that pork sausages are cooked thoroughly. Enjoy!

Nutrition:

Protein: 7.8 g, Fat: 10.8 g, Carbohydrate: 2.8 g, Fiber: 4.1 g Total Calories: 234.2

## Chicken Fajita Soup

Preparation time: 8 hrs.

Cooking Time: 7hrs 45 minutes

Serving: 2

Ingredients:

- taco Seasoning (2 tablespoons)
- garlic (2 large cloves, minced)

- chicken stock (16 Oz)
- salt (to taste)
- tomatoes (7 ½ oz., diced)
- onion (1 small, diced)
- cilantro (1 tablespoon, chopped)
- Chicken breast (1 lb.)
- mushrooms (3 oz., thinly sliced)
- bell pepper (1 small, yellow, diced)
- bell pepper (1 small, orange, diced)

Directions:

1. Place all ingredients; chicken stock, chicken, cilantro, seasoning, and all vegetables into the slow cooker. Cook on low for 5-6 hours.
2. Use two forks to shred the chicken and cook for one additional hour.

Nutrition Protein: 7 g, Fat: 9 g, Carbohydrate: 4 g, Fiber: 2 g, Total Calories: 200

## Tender Autumn Oxtail Stew

Preparation time: 5hrs 30 minutes

Cooking Time: 5hrs 30 minutes

Serving: 2

Ingredients:

- 7 1/3 lbs. Oxtail
- 1/3 tablespoon butter
- 1/3 cup beef stock
- 1/3 small, red onion
- 1/3 head garlic
- 1/3 carrot
- 1/3 celery stalk
- orange juice (splash)
- 1/3 cinnamon stick
- nutmeg (pinch)
- 1 2/3 cloves
- bay leaf (dried)
- black pepper and salt (to taste)
- 2/3 heads, small lettuce

Directions:

1. Season oxtail with pepper and salt, place on a baking sheet, and bake at 300 degrees Fahrenheit for a minimum of 30 minutes, until it becomes brown. You can brown the oxtail alternately in a frying pan.
2. Peel carrot, garlic, and onion. Chop the carrot and mince the garlic and onion.
3. Place the beef stock, orange juice, and spices in a small pot; boil, let simmer for 7 minutes, turn off the heat, and put aside.
4. Place browned oxtail in a slow cooker; add remaining ingredients and cook for 4 hours on Low. Oxtail is finished when it's fork-tender.
5. Turn off the slow cooker and remove oxtail, discard all the vegetables and spices.
6. Use two forks and shred meat; serve on a bed of lettuce. Enjoy!

Nutrition: Net Carbohydrates 4g, fiber 1.4g, protein 54.4g, fat 49.5g Total Calories: 693

## Delightful Carnitas & Paleo Nachos

Preparation time: 12hrs 45 minutes

Cooking Time: 12hrs

Serving: 2

This Delightful Carnitas and Paleo Nachos are sure to leave you craving.

Ingredients:

- chicken broth (1/4 cup)
- olive oil (for frying)
- bay leaves (1)
- thyme leaves (½ tablespoon)
- Pork shoulder (1 lb.)
- sea salt and pepper

Directions:

1. Use salt and pepper to rub the pork shoulder. Heat olive oil in a frying pan over medium heat and lightly brown on all sides.
2. Place pork, bay leaves, thyme, and chicken broth in the slow cooker.
3. Cook on low for 12 hours.
4. Use two forks to shred meat and serve.

Nutrition:

Protein: 35 g, Fat: 63 g, Carbohydrate: 37 g, Fiber: 16 g Total Calories: 1,080

## Tasty Tarragon Lamb Shanks With Cannellini Beans

Preparation time: 7hrs

Cooking Time: 6hrs 30minutes

Serving: 2

Topped with beans and tomatoes and, when combined, makes a great meal.

Ingredients:

- 1 bone-in, lamb shanks
- 1/8 teaspoons ground black pepper
- 1/4 28 oz., diced tomatoes
- 1/4 cup, chopped celery
- 1/4 cup, chopped onion
- 1/2 teaspoons, dried tarragon
- 1/3 cup, diced and peeled carrot
- 1/8 teaspoons salt
- 4 3/4 oz. can cannellini beans

Directions:

1. Place tarragon, beans, tomatoes, salt, and pepper into a slow cooker. Position lamb shanks among mixture and cooks for 6 hours on Low.
2. Remove lamb shanks to a plate and remove bones.
3. Spoon bean mixture into serving dish and top with the lamb shanks.

Nutrition:

Protein: 36 g, Fat: 21 g, Carbohydrate: 9 g, Fiber: 7 g Total Calories: 470

## Mouthwatering Chicken And Kale Soup

Preparation time: 7hrs 30 minutes

Cooking Time: 6hrs minutes

Serving: 2

All in one healthy Mouth-Watering Chicken and Kale Soup.

Ingredients:

- chicken (2 boneless, thighs or breasts)
- chicken broth (1 cups)
- onion (1/4 large, chopped)
- garlic (1 cloves, smashed)
- carrots (½ cups, shredded)
- kale (1 cups, chopped)
- parsley (½ teaspoon, dried)
- salt and pepper (to taste)

Directions

1. Place the chicken broth, chicken, onion, and garlic into a slow cooker.
2. Cover with lid and cook for about 6 hours on low until the chicken is tender and starts to fall apart.
3. Add remaining ingredients and use two forks to shred the chicken. Let cook for another hour. Enjoy your hearty meal!

Nutrition: Protein: 7 g, Fat: 12 g, Carbohydrate: 7 g, Fiber: 1 g, Total Calories: 69

## Slow Cooker Frittata

Preparation time: 3hrs 20mins

Cooking Time: 3hrs

Serving: 2

Nutritious Slow Cooked Frittata filled with veggies and spices.

Ingredients:

- spike Seasoning (½ teaspoons)
- feta (1 oz., crumbled)
- kale (2 oz., chopped)
- red pepper (2 oz., roasted)
- spray (non-sticking)
- eggs (3, well beaten)
- onion (1/8 cup, sliced, green)
- olive oil (1 teaspoons)
- black pepper (ground)

Directions:

1. Over medium heat, heat oil in a frying pan and sauté kale for 4 minutes.
2. Add the fried kale, eggs, red pepper, and green onion to the slow cooker and season with the Spike Seasoning.
3. Sprinkle feta on top and cook for 3 hours on Low.

Nutrition:

Protein: 26 g, Fat: 47 g, Carbohydrate: 11 g, Fiber: 1 g, Total Calories: 590

## Appetizing Orange Chicken

Preparation time: 6 hours 20 minutes.

Cooking Time: 6 hrs.

Serving: 2

This Appetizing Orange Chicken is overwhelmingly delicious and makes a good meal.

Ingredients:

- butter (¼ cup, melted)
- coconut milk (¼ cup)
- swerve Confectioners (2 tablespoons)
- sesame oil (1 teaspoon, toasted)
- soy sauce (1 teaspoon, organic)
- ginger (½ teaspoons, grated)
- sesame seeds (½ teaspoons)
- orange extract (½ teaspoons)
- fish sauce (¼ teaspoons)
- chicken (1 ½lbs. thighs or breasts)
- sesame seeds (1 tablespoon, black)
- onions (4 spring, sliced)

Directions:

1. Combine all ingredients except for the chicken in a small bowl and whisk until smooth.
2. Cook chicken in a slow cooker on low for 5 hours until it becomes soft but not falling apart.
3. Pour in the sauce, cover with the lid and cook for another 40-60 minutes.
4. Garnish with back sesame and spring onions.

Nutrition:

Protein: 34g, Fat: 32g, Carbohydrate: 1.1g, Fiber: 0 g, Total Calories: 491

## Simple And Delicious Chicken Enchiladas

Preparation time: 30 minutes

Cooking Time: 4-5 hrs.

Serving: 2

Ingredients:

- 10 ½ oz. Cream of Chicken soup (reduced fat)
- 1 lb. boneless chicken breasts, skinless and cut in half
- 1/2 cup salsa
- Diced green chilies to taste (they're hot!)
- One teaspoon chili powder
- 1/2 teaspoon ground cumin
- 4 cups packaged baby lettuce mix
- 2-4 warmed corn tortillas (warm in the microwave and wrap in a towel until serving)
- 1/2 cup shredded cheese blend

Directions:

1. Place chicken in the slow cooker.
2. In a small bowl, combine the soup, salsa, chilies, and cumin. Mix well and pour the mixture over the chicken.
3. Cover the cooker and cook on the Low setting for 4- 5 hours.
4. Remove the chicken breasts and shred with two forks. Add some of the sauce from the cooker until you have a saucy enchilada filling. Cover a large serving plate with the lettuce mix. Place a few spoonfuls of chicken mixture into the center of a tortilla; top with lettuce, roll up and place on the platter. Repeat with remaining tortillas. Spoon the remaining sauce over the enchiladas and sprinkle cheese on top. Serve.

Nutrition:

Protein: 36.2 g, Fat: 19.8 g, Carbohydrate: 3.4 g, Fiber: 5.0g Total Calories: 351.3

## Easy Heart-Warming Caramel Rolls

Preparation time: 10 minutes

Cooking Time: 3 minutes

Serving: 2

Ingredients:

- One package of refrigerated cinnamon rolls
- 4 Tbsp. butter
- 1/2 cup brown sugar

Directions:

1. Spray the inside of the stoneware insert with cooking spray.
2. In a small saucepan over low-to-medium heat, melt the butter. Add the brown sugar. Let cook, stirring the caramel sauce occasionally until its thick and smooth - about 3 minutes.
3. Open the package of cinnamon rolls, separate, and form the rolls according to manufacturer instructions. Place the rolls into the bottom of the slow cooker and pour the caramel sauce over them. Cover and cook for an hour on High. Enjoy these warm and tender caramel rolls.

Nutrition:

Protein: 2g, Fat: 15g, Carbohydrate: 6g, Fiber: 0g Total Calories: 245

## Creamy Reuben Soup

Preparation time: 20 minutes

Cooking Time: 4-5 hours

Serving: 2

Ingredients

- 1 small onion, diced
- 1 rib celery, diced
- 1 large cloves garlic, minced

- 1 ½ Tbsp. butter
- 1/2 lb. corned beef, chopped
- 2 cups homemade or 'clean' beef stock
- ½ cup sauerkraut
- ½ tsp. sea salt
- ½ tsp. caraway seeds
- ½ tsp. black pepper
- 1 cup heavy cream
- 1 ½ cups Swiss cheese, shredded

Directions

1. Start heating the slow cooker on High.
2. In a large sauté pan, add onions, celery, butter and garlic and cook over low-medium heat until soft and translucent. Transfer to slow cooker.
3. Add corned beef, sauerkraut, sea salt, beef stock, caraway seed and black pepper to the slow cooker.
4. Cover and cook on High for 4-5 hours.
5. When the beef is almost done, add heavy cream and Swiss cheese and cook 1 additional hour.

Nutrition:

Protein: 11.5g, Fat: 18.5g, Carbohydrate: 4g, Fiber: 0 g, Total Calories: 225

## Tasty Slow-Cooked Pesto Chicken Salad

Preparation time: 10 minutes

Cooking Time: 4-5hours

Serving: 2

Ingredients

- 3 or 4 chicken breasts
- 1 garlic clove, chopped
- 1 small sized white onion, chopped
- 1 cup organic preferably homemade chicken broth
- 1/4 teaspoon garlic powder
- Pinch of salt and ground pepper to taste
- ¼ cup pine nuts for garnishing
- 1/2 cup cashews, walnuts, or nuts of choice
- 1 cup basil
- 1 1/2 cup spinach
- 1 Tbsp. virgin olive oil
- 1 garlic clove
- 1/2 lemon, juiced
- Salt and pepper to taste

Directions:

1. Place the chicken, garlic, onion, broth and seasoning into the slow cooker and cook on High for 4-5 hours.
2. Meanwhile, prepare the pesto sauce. Place the nuts, basil, spinach, olive

oil, garlic clove, lemon juice, salt and pepper in a food processor and process until smooth.

3. Shred the chicken with two forks; place in a bowl, add the pesto sauce and stir to combine.

4. In a small pan, toast the pine nuts for 3-4 minutes, constantly stirring to avoid burning.

5. Garnish the pesto chicken salad with the pine nuts and serve.

Nutrition:

Protein: 10.1 g, Fat: 6.9 g, Carbohydrate: 1.4 g, Fiber: 1.7 g Total Calories: 144.4

## Delicious Stuffed Poblano Peppers

Preparation time: 20 minutes

Cooking Time: 4 hours

Serving: 2

Ingredients

- 1 poblano pepper
- 1 Tbsp. chopped onion
- 1 cup tomato juice
- 3 Tbsp. tomato sauce
- 1/3 cup finely chopped cauliflower
- 1/3 lb. ground beef

Directions

1. In a medium bowl, combine the beef, onion, and cauliflower and tomato sauce.

2. Place 1/2 inch of tomato juice in the slow cooker.

3. Stuff the peppers with the beef mixture and carefully place the stuffed peppers into the cooker.

4. Cook on Low for about 4 hours or until the meat is cooked and tender.

Nutrition:

Protein: 21.7 g, Fat: 13.7 g, Carbohydrate: 6.8 g, Fiber: 5.2 g, Total Calories: 314.6

## Yummy Cheesy Roasted Brussels Dip

Preparation time: 20 minutes

Cooking Time: 1-2 hours

Serving: 2

Ingredients

- ½ lb. Brussels sprouts, chopped
- ½ Tbsp. olive oil
- 1 clove of peeled and crushed garlic
- ¼ tsp fresh thyme, chopped
- 2 ounces cream cheese
- 1/8 cup sour cream
- 1/8 cup mayonnaise
- ½ cup mozzarella cheese, shredded
- 1/8 cup parmesan cheese, grated
- salt and pepper to taste

Directions

1. Literally toss all the ingredients into the cooker (trust us!).
2. Cover the cooker and cook for 1-2 hours on Low. It's done when the cheese is nice and melted.

Nutrition:

Protein: 13 g, Fat: 33g, Carbohydrate: 12g, Fiber: 4 g, Total Calories: 396

## Delicious Slow-Cooked Italian Beef

Preparation time: 10 minutes

Cooking Time: 50 minutes

Serving: 2

Ingredients:

- 2 lbs. beef roast
- ½ cup chopped carrots
- One small white or yellow onion, sliced
- 3-4 cloves garlic, chopped
- ½tsp. kosher salt
- ½tsp. garlic powder
- ½tsp. dried basil
- ½tsp. dried oregano
- ¼tsp. dried thyme
- Pinch of ground cinnamon
- Pinch of red chili flakes
- 1 cup organic crushed tomatoes
- 1 cup beef stock
- 1 cup tomato paste

Directions:

1. Cut the beef into 1" pieces, trimming any extra fat, and place in the slow cooker.
2. Wash, peel, and slice the vegetables; add all remaining ingredients to the slow cooker. Stir to dissolve the tomato paste into the beef stock.
3. Cover and cook on High for 5-6 hours or until the beef is fork-tender.
4. Serve with a side of roasted vegetables or legumes.

Nutrition:

Net Carbohydrates 1.2 g, Fiber 0g, Protein 32.4 g, fat 5.9 g, Total Calories: 197.0

## Delightful Garlic Butter Chicken With Cream Cheese Sauce

Preparation time: 7 hrs.

Cooking Time: 6hrs

Serving: 2

Ingredients:

- 2 lbs. boneless chicken breasts or thighs
- ½ stick of butter
- Four garlic cloves, sliced

- 1 tsp. salt or to taste
- One small onion, sliced
- 4 oz. cream cheese
- ½ cup of chicken stock. (You can also use the liquid left in the slow cooker after the chicken is cooked)
- salt to taste

Directions:

For the garlic chicken:

1. Place the chicken in the slow cooker.
2. Add in the butter, garlic, and salt, distributing evenly in the cooker.
3. Cover and cook on Low for 6 hours.
4. Once the chicken is done, take it out and place it on a serving dish.

For the cream cheese sauce:

1. Put the chicken stock or the liquid from the cooker into a medium saucepan.
2. Add in the cream cheese and salt.
3. Cook on medium heat until the sauce is creamy and well combined. Serve hot with the chicken.

Nutrition: Protein: 28.2 g, Fat: 21.3 g, Carbohydrate: 7.9 g, Fiber: 1.1 g Total Calories: 169.3

## Slow-Cooked Brats

Preparation time: 2hrs

Cooking Time: 6hrs

Serving: 2

Ingredients:

- One package of Bison Brats
- One medium onion, sliced
- 1 cup bell pepper, cut into strips
- 1 cup homemade chicken or beef broth
- Dried herbs of your choice, such as thyme, basil, parsley
- Any hot sauce, to taste
- Salt to taste

Directions:

1. Place the sliced onions and peppers in the bottom of the slow cooker.
2. Layer the brats overtop.
3. Add the broth, spices, and hot sauce.
4. Cover and cook on Low for 4-6 hours, or on High for 30 minutes
5. Serve with organic cooked rice

Nutrition: Protein: 26 g, Fat: 50 g, Carbohydrate: 5 g, Fiber: 2 g Total Calories: 733

## Low-Carb Slow-Cooked Pizza

Preparation time: 2hrs

Cooking Time: 6hrs

Serving: 2

Ingredients

- ¾ lb. ground beef, cooked
- 3/4 lb. Italian sausage, cooked
- 3 cups mozzarella cheese, shredded
- 16 slices of low-carb pepperoni
- 1 15-oz. can pizza sauce
- 3 cups fresh spinach
- Any favorite topping like olives, mushrooms or herbs

Directions:

1. Slice the sausage, chop the onions and combine them with the pizza sauce. Divide the mixture in half and put one half into the slow cooker
2. Layer half of the fresh spinach on top of the sauce mixture
3. Layer half of the pepperoni and the remaining toppings on top.
4. Top with half of the cheese.
5. Repeat layers and cook for 6 hours. Let cool slightly before cutting and serving.

Nutrition Value: Protein: 14.3 g, Fat: 11.9 g, Carbohydrate: 5.4 g, Fiber: 0.5 gTotal Calories: 186.4

## Easy Italian Zucchini Meatloaf

Preparation time: 10 minutes

Cooking Time: 30 minutes

Serving: 2

Ingredients

- 2 lbs. extra lean ground beef
- 2 large eggs
- 1 cup shredded zucchini
- 1/2 cup grated Parmesan cheese
- 1/2 cup finely chopped parsley
- 4 crushed garlic cloves
- 2 tbsp. balsamic vinegar
- 1 tbsp. dry oregano
- 2 tbsp. minced dry onion or onion powder
- Salt to taste
- 1/2 tsp. ground black pepper
- Cooking coconut oil spray

Directions:

1. Place all the ingredients in a large bowl and mix thoroughly.
2. Prepare the slow cooker by lining with aluminum foil with flaps on the outside, to make it easier to remove the meatloaf later. Spray the lining with coconut oil spray.
3. Put the mixture in cooker. Cover and cook on Low for about 6 hours, or on High for 2-2.5 hours.

Nutrition Value: Protein: 20.7g, Fat: 9 g, Carbohydrate: 3.4 g, Fiber: 0.1 gTotal Calories: 97.5

## Easy Slow-Cooker Chicken Roast

Preparation time: 10 minutes

Cooking Time: 30 minutes

Serving: 2

Ingredients

- 3-4 pound whole organic chicken
- 2 Tbsp. homemade ghee
- 2 medium sized chopped onions
- 1 clove of peeled garlic
- 1 tsp tomato paste
- ¼ cup chicken stock
- ¼ cup white wine
- 1 tbsp. freshly ground black pepper
- Kosher salt to taste
- 1 tsp. dried mixed Italian herbs

Directions:

1. In a hot cast iron pan, sauté all the vegetables in ghee. Add the tomato paste and season with salt and pepper. Cook for 5-7 minutes until the vegetables are slightly softened.
2. Deglaze the pan with wine or chicken stock. Add all the vegetables into the slow cooker. Season the chicken with salt and pepper and place it breast side down in the slow cooker.
3. Cook the chicken for 3-4 hours on Low.

Nutrition Value: Protein: 30.1 g, Fat: 4.1 g, Carbohydrate: 1.4 g, Fiber: 0.6 g, Total Calories: 169.6

## Canneloni with Meat And Mushrooms

Preparation time: 10 minutes

Cooking Time: 30 minutes

Serving: 2

Ingredients:

- ½ cup soy flour
- 1/3 cup of water
- 9 oz. cream
- Two eggs
- ½ Tbsp. olive oil
- One onion
- Six mushrooms
- 10 oz. halves of chicken breasts
- ½ lb. sirloin
- 1 ½ cups of tomato sauce
- 1/cup Parmesan
- ¼ cup parsley
- Salt

Directions:

1. To start with, you will need to blend the salt, eggs, water, cream,

and soy flour in a blender and then let sit for 15 minutes.

2. Heat a sauté pan and spray with cooking spray. Add 2 Tbsp. Of the batter to the pan for each crepe, you want to make, cook for about 1 minute, loosen with the spatula, and flip to cook for another 30 seconds. Let the crepes cool.

3. To do the filling, you will want to season the chicken and then cook for around 5 minutes on each side. Once it is cooked, you will want to cut it up and transfer it to a bowl. Add the onion and cook for around 5 minutes before adding the mushroom and cooking for another 5 minutes. Lastly, add the beef to the skillet and cook for another 5 minutes before adding the chicken mixture.

4. Stir in half the cream, the parsley, and the Parmesan and let it cool. In the baking dish, you will need toad ½ cup of the tomato dish and then heat the oven to 400 degrees. Scoop about ¼ of the filling and use it to form a cylinder and place it in the middle of the crespelle that you made at the beginning. Fold over the filling and flatten a little bit, and place in the pan. Bake all of this for about 20 to 30 minutes and serve with extra Parmesan.

Nutrition:

Calories 243

Protein 22.5 grams

Fat 27 grams

## Eggplant Lasagna

Preparation time: 10 minutes

Cooking Time: 20 minutes

Serving: 2

Ingredients:

- 1 ½ lb. eggplant
- 1 cup tomato sauce
- 1 lb. beef chuck
- ¼ cup olive oil
- 2 cups ricotta cheese
- Four mushroom caps
- 10 oz. spinach
- Two eggs
- 1 lb. mozzarella cheese
- ¼ cup Parmesan
- Salt
- Pepper

Directions:

1. Trim and cut up the eggplant, layer it in the colander, make sure to salt between each layer and then let it stand for about 15 minutes.

2. While this is happening, you can cook up the beef, making sure to break it into smaller pieces and

then drain out the grease before adding the tomato sauce. Once mixed, you can set aside to cool.

3. Brush some olive oil onto the mushrooms and cook for about 4 minutes on each side before slicing and setting aside. Heat the broiler, and then, after patting the eggplants dry and brushing both sides with olive oil, cook up the eggplant for 3 minutes on each side. Combine the Parmesan, eggs, spinach, and ricotta in a food processor and mix. Arrange the eggplant slices in a layer in the baking dish and top with the mushrooms and half of the mozzarella before spooning on half of the meat sauce and spreading the ricotta mixture over it. Make another layer of eggplant and repeat the process.

4. Bake all of it for about 20 minutes and then let it cool before serving.

Nutrition:

Calories: 264.2

Total Fat: 9.4 g

Dietary Fiber: 6.5 g

Saturated Fat: 4.7 g

## Hot Wings

Preparation time: 10 minutes

Cooking Time: 50 minutes

Serving: 2

Ingredients:

- One bag chicken wings
- One bottle Wing Sauce
- Celery oil
- ½ stick of butter
- Salt
- Pepper

Directions:

1. Heat the oil in a pot or fryer before seasoning the wings in salt and pepper. You will then need to fry up the winds until they are crispy and brown. Remove all the attachments from the oil and set it on a cooling rack. Do this process with all of the wings.

2. You can meet all of the butter and add in the wing sauce while you are doing this. Place the finished wing in a bowl and mix them with the sauce. When ready to serve, they had a side of celery and some dressing.

Nutrition:

Calories734.4---

Total Carbs 0.6g1.

Net Carbs info.3g

## Beef Veggie

Preparation time: 20 minutes

Cooking Time: 1hour 30 minutes

Serving: 2

Ingredients:

- 2 Tbsp. olive oil
- 1.5 lbs. stew beef
- One onion
- 2 Tbsp. beef base
- 2 cups celery
- 4 cups of water
- Two garlic cloves
- 1 cup cabbage
- One tomato, diced
- ½ cup carrots, chopped

Directions:

1. Heat some oil in a skillet and then cook the onion and garlic together until they are tender and then set the mix aside.
2. Add some more of the oil to the skillet before adding the beef and browning it. Drain out the grease with the meat before adding the beef base and the celery, cloves, cabbage, carrots, and tomato.
3. Cook the mixture on the low setting for an hour to an hour and a half.

Nutrition:

Calories 250

Protein 18 grams

Fat 12 grams

## Sausage, Bell Pepper, And Onion Pizza

Preparation time: 10 minutes

Cooking Time: 15 minutes

Serving: 2

Ingredients:

- 1 cups baking mix, all-purpose
- 1 ½ tsp. baking powder
- One packet sugar substitute
- 1 1/8 cup water
- 3 Tbsp. olive oil
- 1 cup mozzarella cheese
- ½ of a red pepper
- ½ cup tomato sauce
- One sausage link
- ½ green pepper
- One red onion

Directions:

1. Heat the oven to 425 degrees and then blend the sugar substitute, salt, baking powder, and baking mix in a bowl before adding the oil and the water.
2. Combine all of these ingredients into dough and then place it on a clean surface.

3. Use a rolling pin to roll out the dough to fit onto your pizza pan, and then bake this crust for about 10 minutes. Remove from the oven and then spread out the tomato sauce, sprinkle on the mozzarella along with the onions, red pepper, green pepper, and sausage links.

4. Place all of this back in the oven for another 10 to 15 minutes, cut into slices and serve.

Nutrition:

Calories 273.8

Cholesterol 12.5 mg

Total Carbohydrate 39.5 g

## Beef Fajitas

Preparation time: 10 minutes

Cooking Time: 5 minutes

Serving: 2

Ingredients:

- Three garlic cloves
- 2 Tbsp. lime juice
- One jalapeno pepper
- 2 lbs. steak
- 2 tsp. cumin, grounded
- 1 Tbsp. canola oil
- One green pepper
- One red pepper
- 2 Tbsp. olive oil
- One red onion
- 12 tortillas
- ¾ c. sour cream
- ¾ c. green salsa
- ¼ cup cilantro

Directions:

1. Start by preparing the marinade; you can do this by combining the olive oil, cumin, jalapeno, lime juice, salt, and garlic in a large bowl.

2. Once that is done, you can marinade the steak by letting it sit in the juices for no less than an hour. Heat the oven to 350 degrees and warm up the tortillas for about 15 minutes.

3. After the hour has passed, take the steak out of the marinade and grill for about 3 to 4 minutes on each side. You will need to heat the canola oil on a skillet to cook the onion and bell peppers for about 5 minutes.

4. After the steak has been grilled, you need to slice into thin pieces. Take the tortillas out of the oven and spread the vegetables, cilantro, sour cream, steak, and salsa over them. Fold the tortilla over and then enjoy.

Nutrition:

Calories 165 Fat 15 grams

## Baked Quesadillas

Preparation time: 10 minutes

Cooking Time: 5 minutes

Serving: 2

Ingredients:

- 2 Tbsp. olive oil
- 1 lb. pork loin
- 8 oz. Monterey Jack cheese
- 2 Tbsp. onion
- One jalapeno pepper
- ¼ cup green salsa
- ¼ cilantro leaves
- Salt
- Pepper
- 16 tortillas

Directions:

1. Heat the oven to 450 degrees. While that is heating up, you can heat 1 Tbsp. Of oil in a skillet and cook the onion for about 5 minutes.
2. Transfer the onion over to a bowl and then add the salt, pepper, cilantro, jalapeno, green salsa, cheese, and pork. With the remaining oil, brush each tortilla on just one side before spooning on the pork mixture and fold the tortilla in half.
3. Place the tortillas on the baking sheet and let bake for about 5 minutes before serving.

Nutrition:

Calories 383

Protein 17.7 grams

Fat 10.6 grams

# CHAPTER 10:

# Sides

## Red Beans Grill For 1

Preparation Time: 15 minutes

Cooking Time: 30 minutes

Servings: 2

INGREDIENTS:

- 4 - 5 pieces of red mullet,
- Two pieces of pepper
- One piece of tomato
- Sauce:
- One tablespoon of olive oil
- One tablespoon of lemon juice
- Salt

DIRECTIONS:

1. As prep, cut the fish bellies to clean the inside. After removing the internal organs, wash the fish in plenty of water. Clean the washers with a sharp knife. Cook for 10 minutes on the grill and place on a serving plate.

2. Cook the tomatoes and peppers on the grill. For the sauce, mix one tablespoon of olive oil, one tablespoon of lemon, and salt. Serve the fish after pouring the sauce on the fish.

3. Note: You can cook red beans in a pan as well as the grill. However, to ensure that the fish is delicious after shaking, it is useful to shake thoroughly. The taste of the fried fish, together with excess flour, can be distorted.

NUTRITION: Carbs: (g): 8 Fiber (g): 0.7 Net Carb Grams: 1 Protein (g): 29

## Vegetable Skewers And Grilled Cheese

Preparation Time: 15 min

Cooking Time: 10 minutes

Servings: 2

INGREDIENTS:

- Two colored peppers, seeded and cut into cubes
- 340 g (3/4 lb.) Haloumi type grilled cheese, cubed
- 225 g (1/2 lb.) whole white mushrooms
- 30 ml (2 tablespoons) of olive oil

- 10 ml (2 teaspoons) balsamic vinegar
- 5ml (1/2 teaspoon) of dried oregano

DIRECTIONS:
1. Preheat the barbecue to medium-high power. Oil the grill.
2. In a bowl, mix all the ingredients. Salt and pepper.
3. Thread the vegetables alternately on skewers. Thread the cheese on other skewers. Reserve on a large plate.
4. Grill the vegetable skewers for 10 minutes, turning them a few times during cooking with tongs. Oil the grate again. Grill the cheese skewers on both sides, turning them over as soon as the cheese begins to grill, about 1 minute on each side.
5. Serve immediately. Serve with pita bread, if desired.

Note:

A little advice when you prepare your mushrooms: keep their foot. Not only do they grill well, but they also give more stability to this vegetable on the skewer.

NUTRITION:

Calories: 1067 kcal

Protein: 61.58 g

Fat: 73.33 g

Carbohydrates: 45.84 g

## Mustard Sauce

Preparation Time: 5 min

Cooking Time: 10 minutes

Servings: 125 ml (½ cup)

INGREDIENTS:
- 1/4 cup (60 mL) yellow mustard
- 30 ml (2 tablespoons) old-fashioned mustard
- 30 ml (2 tablespoons) brown sugar
- 15 ml (1 tablespoon) of cider vinegar
- 15 ml (1 tablespoon) Worcestershire sauce

DIRECTIONS:
1. Inside a small saucepan, bring to the boil all the ingredients stirring with a whisk. Pepper. Simmer 5 minutes.
2. The mustard sauce can be stored for ten days in an airtight container in the refrigerator.

NUTRITION: 520 calories 36g Protein 39gCarbohydrates 25g Fat

## Quiche with Spinach, Mushrooms & Feta

Preparation Time: 20 minutes

Cooking Time: 55 minutes

Servings: 2

INGREDIENTS:
- 150 grams of mushrooms

- Two cloves of garlic
- 200 grams of spinach
- Three eggs
- 150 ml unsweetened almond milk 50 grams of feta cheese
- Three tablespoons of Parmesan
- One teaspoon salt
- One teaspoon of black pepper 50 grams of mozzarella

DIRECTIONS:
1. Preheat the oven. Slice the mushrooms and garlic into thin slices.
2. Put them together with salt & pepper in a greased frying pan and sweat for about 5 minutes until soft.
3. Grease a baking dish, add the spinach to the baking dish, and then add the mushrooms and feta cheese.
4. Then add the eggs, milk, and Parmesan together in a bowl.
5. Season something with pepper.
6. Pour the egg mixture into the mold and sprinkle with the grated mozzarella.
7. Bake, the quiche for 45 - 55 minutes or until the cheese, is golden brown

NUTRITION: Carbohydrates: 3g

## Eggs Baked In Avocado

Preparation Time: 5 minutes

Cooking Time: 25 minutes

Servings: 2

INGREDIENTS:
- Two eggs
- One avocado
- One teaspoon salt
- One teaspoon of black pepper
- One tablespoon of fresh chives

DIRECTIONS:
1. Preheat the oven. Halve the avocado and remove the core. Pick up about two tablespoons of the meat from the middle of the avocado, just enough to make the egg fit right in the middle. Then put them in a small baking dish.
2. Make an egg in each avocado half. Try to put the yolk in the cavity first, and then add the egg whites to fill in the rest.
3. Put in the oven and bake for 15 to 20 minutes. The cooking time depends on the size of the eggs and avocados. Make sure that the
4. Protein has enough time to sit down. Remove from the oven and season with salt, pepper, and chives.

NUTRITION: Carbohydrates: 2g

## Crunchy Chocolate Covered Strawberries

Preparation Time: 10 minutes.

Cooking Time: 10 minutes.

Servings: 2

INGREDIENTS:

- Ten fresh strawberries
- 1 Atkins crispy milk chocolate bar

DIRECTIONS:

1. Place the baking tray with baking paper. Break the Atkins bar into even pieces and place it in a heat-resistant bowl (take one that fits your pot).
2. Fill a pot 1/3 with water; bring the water to a boil. Once cooked, reduce the heat. Place the bowl over the pool - make sure the bowl does not contact the water. Stir the chocolate with a metal spoon until completely melted and smooth.
3. Dip each strawberry about 2/3 into the melted chocolate, keeping it at the top, then place it on the baking paper. Repeat for all strawberries.
4. Put the strawberries in the fridge to cool.
5. Use the remaining chocolate to decorate your platter.

NUTRITION: Carbohydrates: 12g

## Fish Pie

Preparation Time: 10 minutes

Cooking Time: 60 minutes

Servings: 2

INGREDIENTS:

- One tablespoon of olive oil 50 grams of white onion
- Two cloves of garlic
- 400 grams of canned tomatoes
- One tablespoon of fresh ginger
- One teaspoon of cinnamon powder
- One teaspoon salt
- One teaspoon of black pepper
- 150 grams of salmon fillet
- 150 grams of white fish fillet
- Two tablespoons butter
- 100 grams of celery

DIRECTIONS:

1. Preheat the oven to gas level 3 or 175 ° C. Chop the celery and cook for 7 - 10 minutes in salted water. Pass, purée, and mix in the butter.
2. Taste it with salt and pepper.
3. Put the fish in a pot of boiling water, with just enough water to cover it. Cook for 5 minutes. The fish should be dark and quickly disintegrate.
4. Drain the fish and put it in a bowl. Put the oil in a pan over

medium heat and sweat the onion and garlic for 5 minutes. Stir in the boiled fish, chopped tomatoes, cinnamon, ginger, salt, and pepper.

5. Let it simmer over medium heat to allow the flavors to develop. Put the mass in a small frying pan and cover with the puree. Cook everything in the oven for 20 minutes, until the puree is crispy.

NUTRITION: Carbohydrates: 5g

## Pancakes With Berries & Whipped Cream

Preparation Time: 5 minutes

Cooking Time: 5 minutes

Servings: 1

INGREDIENTS:

- Two eggs
- Two tablespoons cream cheese
- ¼ teaspoon sweetener
- One pinch of cinnamon
- 40 g blueberries
- 20 ml of cream double

DIRECTIONS:

1. Mix the eggs, cream cheese, sweetener, and cinnamon to the dough.
2. Stir the ingredients till you have smooth dough. Let the mass rest for 2 minutes to allow the bubbles to settle.
3. Put half of the dough in a hot non-stick skillet that has been greased with butter. Fry the dough for 3 - 4 minutes over medium heat until it is golden brown, then turn over and fry for 3 minutes on the other side.
4. Repeat this with the remaining dough. Beat the crème double until it is firm and serve the pancakes with the crème and blueberries.

NUTRITION: Carbohydrates: 3g

## Sausages Stuffed Mushrooms

Preparation Time: 10 minutes

Cooking Time: 25 minutes

Servings: 1

INGREDIENTS:

- Two sausages
- One clove of garlic
- Two tablespoons cream cheese
- One tablespoon of ground flaxseed
- 1/2 onion
- Share page

DIRECTIONS:

1. Remove the intestines and fry the link with the pressed garlic. Then place it on the page. Then

remove the stems of mushrooms and chop them small.

2. Mix the finely chopped champignon stems with the cream cheese, and then add the cooled sausage meat.

3. Finally, add the ground flax seeds and fill the mushrooms with the mixture. Place the mushrooms in a large casserole dish and bake at 160 ° C for 25 minutes.

NUTRITION: Carbohydrates: 6g

## Salmon With Avocado Salsa

Preparation Time: 10 minutes

Cooking Time: 15 minutes

Servings: 1

INGREDIENTS:

- 0.5 tablespoon olive oil
- 0.25 teaspoon salt
- 0.5 teaspoon black pepper
- 0.5 teaspoon paprika powder
- 115 grams of salmon fillet
- 0.5 Avocado
- 0.25 red onions
- One tablespoon of fresh lime juice
- One tablespoon of fresh coriander
- Three cherry tomatoes

DIRECTIONS:

1. Mix the oil, salt, pepper, including paprika into a bowl. Coat the salmon fillet, including the marinade, and put it in the fridge for 30 minutes. Grate the salmon on both sides for two minutes over high heat.

2. Mix the avocado, chopped tomatoes, 1/4 red onion, lime juice, one tablespoon of olive oil, and salt to taste in a separate bowl. Serve the salmon on the avocado salsa and garnish with chopped cilantro. Serve with a mixed green salad.

NUTRITION: Carbohydrates: 5g

## Brie & Caramelized Onion Burger

Preparation Time: 10 minutes

Cooking Time: 20 minutes

Servings: 1

INGREDIENTS:

- One tablespoon of olive oil 50 grams of white onion
- One teaspoon salt
- One tablespoon butter
- Three mushrooms
- 120 grams of ground beef
- One teaspoon of black pepper
- 30 grams of Brie

DIRECTIONS:

1. Preheat the grill to medium oven heat. Heat the olive oil on a large pan and fry the onions with a pinch of salt for 5 minutes until they are soft and golden brown.

2. Do not let them get too crispy! Put the onions upon a plate and keep the pan handy to fry the mushrooms.

3. Put the ground beef, salt, and pepper for the burgers in a large bowl. Knead the mass well by hand and form 2 patties.

4. Cover one half with a bit of brie and onions, then put the second half on top of the cheese plus onions to form the burger!

5. Put the burgers under a preheated grill and grill each side for 4-5 minutes. While the burgers are grilling, fry the mushrooms in a little butter for 2 - 3 minutes.

6. Once the burgers are cooked, take them off the grill.

NUTRITION: Carbohydrates: 5g

## Baked Meatballs And Green Beans

Preparation time: 10 minutes

Cooking Time: 45 minutes

Serving: 2

Ingredients:

- 6 oz. Green String Beans
- One fruit (2-1/8" dia) Lemon
- One large Young Green Onion
- One clove Garlic
- One large Egg
- 8 oz. Ground Pork
- 8 oz. Ground Beef (85% Lean / 15% Fat)
- 1 1/2 tbsp. Olive Oil
- 1/4 cup Parmesan Cheese (Grated)
- 1/4 tsp. Salt
- 1/4 tsp. Black Pepper

Directions:

1. Preheat the oven to 375°F. Remove the ends from the greens beans and discard; set the green beans aside. Zest the lemon; set zest aside. Juice the lemon into a small bowl, discarding seeds. Slice the green onions into ¼-inch diced pieces; set aside. Finely chop the garlic clove and set aside. Crack the egg into another small bowl and whisk with a fork; set aside.

2. Heat ½ tablespoon of olive oil in a large sauté pan over medium-high heat. When the oil is hot, add the green onion and cook for 5 minutes, stirring, until softened. Add the garlic and cook for 1 minute more. Transfer to a large bowl and let cool slightly.

3. Pat dries the ground pork and the ground beef with paper towels. Place in the large bowl with the green

onions and garlic; add the Parmesan cheese, egg, and ⅛ teaspoon salt, and ⅛ teaspoon black pepper. Mix until all ingredients are well combined

4. Form the beef/ pork mixture into golf-ball-size meatballs and place them on a sheet pan lined with foil. Bake for 20 to 25 minutes until browned and cooked through.

5. Heat 1 tablespoon of olive oil in a medium sauté pan over medium-high heat. Add the green beans and sauté for 3 to 5 minutes, until crisp-tender. Add the lemon juice, lemon zest, and ¼ teaspoon each of salt and pepper. Toss to combine.

6. Divide the green beans between two plates, place the meatballs to the green beans and enjoy!

Nutrition:

Protein: 50.2g

Fat: 57.2g

Fiber: 4.2g

Calories: 762

## Balsamic And Thyme Pearl Onions

Preparation time: 5 minutes

Cooking Time: 25 minutes

Serving: 2

Ingredients:

- 1/2 tbsps. Olive Oil
- 4 oz. Cooked Pearl Onions (from Frozen)
- 1/4 tsp. Xylitol
- 1/8 tbsp. Balsamic Vinegar
- 1/3 tsp. thyme

Directions:

1. Heat oil over medium-high heat in a medium skillet. Add thawed onions (be sure to pat them dry after thawing), season with salt and freshly ground black pepper, and sauté until they begin to brown.

2. Sprinkle the onions with xylitol and the balsamic vinegar. Stir and continue to cook for 1 minute.

3. Add 2/3 cup water and thyme. Continue to cook over low heat until the onions are tender and the liquid has evaporated; about 20 minutes. Serve immediately. One serving is about 1/8 cup (5-6 onions).

Nutrition:

Protein: 0.4g Fat: 1.1g

Fiber: 1.3g Calories: 28

## Broccoli Florets With Lemon Butter Sauce

Preparation time: 10 minutes

Cooking Time: 15 minutes

Serving: 2

Ingredients:

- 1/4 lb. Broccoli Flower Clusters
- 1/2 tbsps. chopped Shallots
- 1/4 FL oz. Sauvignon Blanc Wine

- 1/4 tbsp. Fresh Lemon Juice
- 1 tbsps. Unsalted Butter Stick
- 1/8 tsp. Salt
- 1/8 tsp. White Pepper

Directions:

1. Cook florets in a large pot of lightly salted water for 5-7 minutes, until tender. Drain; return to pot to keep warm while you prepare the sauce.

2. Place shallots, 2 tbsps. Wine and one tablespoon lemon juice in a small saucepan over medium heat. Simmer until reduced to 1 tablespoon. Reduce heat to very low; stir in a few small butter pieces, swirling with a wire whisk until mostly melted.

3. Gradually add the remaining butter, continually whisking until sauce is smooth. Season with 1/8 tsp. Salt, 1/8 tsp. White pepper and remaining lemon juice to taste. Do not allow the sauce to boil. Pour sauce over broccoli. Enjoy!

Nutrition:

Protein: 3.7g Fat: 11.9g

Fiber: 3.4g Calories: 144

## Broccoli Rabe Parmigiano

Preparation time: 15 minutes

Cooking Time: 10 minutes

Serving: 2

Ingredients:

- 2 tbsps. Extra Virgin Olive Oil
- Two cloves Garlic
- 1/4 tsp. Crushed Red Pepper Flakes
- 2 lbs. Broccoli
- 1/4 cup Tap Water
- 2 tbsps. Fresh Lemon Juice
- 2 tbsps.' Lemon Peel
- 1/8 tsp. Salt
- 1/8 tsp. Black Pepper
- 1/2 cup Parmesan Cheese (Grated)

Directions:

1. Broccoli rabe has 6- to 9-inch stalks and scattered clusters of tiny broccoli-like buds. It has a more bitter taste than its more familiar cousin. It takes beautifully to sautéing or braising. Feel free to substitute broccoli in this recipe if you prefer. Cut a 2-pound head of broccoli into small florets, peel the stems and cut into 1/2-inch pieces.

2. Heat oil over medium-high heat in a large deep skillet, t. Add garlic and pepper flakes; sauté 30 seconds.

3. Add broccoli rabe, water, lemon juice, and lemon zest; mix well. Cover skillet and cook over medium heat 8 minutes or until broccoli rabe is crisp-tender.

4. Season to taste with salt and freshly ground black pepper.
5. Transfer to a serving dish and sprinkle with Parmesan.

Nutrition:

Protein: 7.2g

Fat: 7g

Fiber: 4.7g

Calories: 114

## Browned Pumpkin With Maple And Sage

Preparation time: 10 minutes

Cooking Time: 15 minutes

Serving: 2

Ingredients:
- 1/4 lb. Pumpkin
- 1/8 cup chopped Shallots
- 1/4 tbsp. Unsalted Butter Stick
- 1/8 cup Bouillon Vegetable Broth
- 1/8 cup Sugar-Free Syrup
- 1/8 tsp. Sage (Ground)

Directions:

Use fresh sage for this recipe, if possible. You will need 7-8 leaves.

1. Heat butter in a medium skillet over medium-high heat. Cube pumpkin into 3/4-inch chunks.
2. Add pumpkin and shallots to pan and season with salt and freshly ground black pepper. Sauté until pumpkin is lightly browned and the shallots are translucent; 5-6 minutes.
3. Turn heat to low, add 1/4 cup vegetable broth, and simmer covered for 8-10 minutes until the pumpkin is tender.
4. Add maple syrup and sage. Tossing to combine. Serve immediately. The serving size is about 1/4 cup.

Nutrition:

Protein: 0.6g

Fat: 1.2g

Fiber: 0.4g

Calories: 26

## Brussels Sprouts With Bacon And Parmesan

Preparation time: 10 minutes

Cooking Time: 20 minutes

Serving: 2

Ingredients:
- 1 1/4 medium slices (yield after cooking) Bacon
- 1/3 lbs. Brussels Sprouts
- 1/8 tsp. Salt
- 1/8 tsp. Black Pepper
- 1/8 cup Heavy Cream
- 1/8 cup Parmesan Cheese (Grated)

Directions:

1. Wash, trim, and cut Brussels sprouts in half.

2. Heat a medium skillet over medium-high heat. Brown bacon, transferring to a paper towel when done and set aside to cool. Once cool, cut or break into bite-sized pieces. Set aside and remove all but 1-2 Tbsp. Bacon grease from the pan.

3. Add Brussels sprouts, salt, and pepper to the pan. Sauté over medium-high heat, occasionally stirring until lightly golden and cooked through; about 15 minutes.

4. Add cream and Parmesan cheese. Stir to heat through another 1 minute. Transfer to a serving platter and sprinkle bacon over the top. Serve immediately.

Nutrition:

Protein: 6.3g Fat: 7.8g

Fiber: 3.1g

Calories: 120

## Brussels Sprouts With Lemon And Parmesan

Preparation time: 5 minutes

Cooking Time: 15 minutes

Serving: 2

Ingredients:

- 1/4 tbsp. Olive Oil
- 1/4 lb. Brussels Sprouts
- 1/4 tbsp. Fresh Lemon Juice
- 1/4 oz. Parmesan Cheese (Hard)

Directions:

1. Heat oil in a large skillet over medium-high heat. Add Brussels sprouts, season with salt and freshly ground black pepper, and sauté until browned; about 5-8 minutes.

2. Add 1/3 cup water and 1 tsp. lemon zest (optional). Continue to cook until the water has cooked off, and the sprouts are tender; about 5 minutes.

3. Toss with 1 tbsp. Lemon juice, place in a serving bowl and top with shaved Parmesan.

Nutrition:

Protein: 3.2g

Fat: 2.8g

Fiber: 2.2g

Calories: 54

## Buffalo Chicken Salad

Preparation time: 10 minutes

Cooking Time: 45 minutes

Serving: 2

Ingredients:

- 1/2 fruit (2-1/8" dia) Lemon
- One medium (4-1/8" long) Young Green Onions
- One head Cos or Romaine Lettuce

- 2 stalk medium (7-1/2" - 8" long) Celery
- One medium (approx. 2-3/4" long, 2-1/2" dia) Red Sweet Pepper
- One medium Tomato
- One large Egg
- 5 1/3 tbsps. Apple Cider Vinegar
- 1/8 tsp. Celery Salt
- 1/8 tsp. Red or Cayenne Pepper
- Two thighs, bone removed Chicken Thigh Meat and Skin (Broilers or Fryers)
- 1/4 cup Real Mayonnaise
- 2 tbsp. Sour Cream
- 2/3 oz. Blue Cheese
- 1/8 tsp. Garlic Powder
- 1/3 tsp. Salt
- 1/4 tsp. Black Pepper

Directions:

1. Preheat oven to 450ºF. Juice the lemon into a large bowl discarding any seeds. Finely chop the green onions and add to the bowl; set aside. The lemon juice and green onions add the mayonnaise, sour cream, blue cheese, and garlic powder and stir to combine to the bowl with the lemon juice and green onions.
2. Cut the romaine lettuce into 1-inch pieces and place it into the large bowl with the dressing. Cut the celery into ½-inch pieces on a bias and add to the romaine. Remove the stem, pith, and seeds from the red bell pepper and discard. Cut the bell pepper into ¼-inch thin strips. Cut the tomato into 1" inch diced pieces and add to the bowl. Set in the refrigerator until step 5.
3. Using a fork beat the egg in another medium bowl. Add the apple cider vinegar, ¼ cup canola oil, ¼ teaspoon of black pepper, ⅓ teaspoon of salt, the celery salt, and cayenne pepper stir until well combined.
4. Pat the chicken thighs with paper towels and add to the marinade, then place on a sheet pan lined with foil. Bake for 18 to 20 minutes, turning the thighs and brushing with the marinade several times until cooked through and crisp. Cut the chicken thighs into ½-inch diced pieces and set aside for step 6.
5. Remove the salad from the refrigerator and toss to combine.
6. Divide the salad between two plates and place the chicken in the center. Enjoy!

Nutrition:

Protein: 27.2g

Fat: 44.1g

Fiber: 9.1g

Calories: 576

## Buffalo Hot Wing Cauliflower

Preparation time: 10 minutes

Cooking Time: 45 minutes

Serving: 2

Ingredients:

- One head large (6-7" dia) Cauliflower
- 2 tbsps. Light Olive Oil
- 4 tbsps. Red Hot Buffalo Wing Sauce
- Three tips Sriracha Hot Chili Sauce
- 2 tbsp. Unsalted Butter Stick
- 1 1/2 oz. Blue or Roquefort Cheese

Directions:

1. Preheat oven to 375°F.
2. Cut cauliflower into smaller florets and sprinkle with one tablespoon olive oil. Roast on a baking sheet for 35-40 minutes or until tender.
3. While cauliflower is roasting, put hot wing sauce and siracha into a small saucepan and heat until boiling. Lower heat and simmer for 10 minutes. Add butter, stir until melted, and allow cooling to room temperature. Heat a large sauté pan with remaining oil. Add the cauliflower and sauté until heated through add the hot sauce and continue to cook for 1 minute, tossing continuously until fully coated. Serve immediately with blue cheese sprinkled on top.

Nutrition:

Protein: 5.3g

Fat: 14.9g

Fiber: 4.2g

Calories: 177

## Caesar Salad Dressing

Preparation time: 20 minutes

Cooking Time: 0 minutes

Serving: 2

Ingredients:

- 1 cup mayonnaise
- ¼ cup parmesan cheese - grated
- Two tablespoons olive oil
- ¼ cup egg substitute
- Two tablespoons water
- One tablespoon anchovy paste
- One tablespoon lemon juice
- Two cloves garlic – crushed
- ¼ teaspoon dried parsley – crushed fine
- ½ teaspoon pepper - coarsely ground
- ¼ teaspoon salt
- Two teaspoons sugar

Directions:

1. Start with combining all the ingredients required for the dish in a medium glass bowl.

2. With the help of an electric mixer, beat the ingredients above for just about 1 minute.
3. With the covered lid, refrigerate this for several hours.
4. That will increase the flavors of the dish.

Nutrition:

You can keep the dressing in the fridge for several days in a covered container. The dish is having Carbs per Serving as 17g total.

## Peanut Cole Slaw

Preparation time: 10 minutes

Cooking Time: 0 minutes

Serving: 2

Ingredients:

- 1 Medium Head Cabbage
- 1 cup Sour Cream
- ½ Cup peanuts
- 1/2 cup mayonnaise Sweetener

Directions:

1. Start with chopping the cabbage semi-fine. Now process peanuts.
2. Add sour cream, mayo, and the sweetener into the mix.
3. Combine with cabbage and peanuts.
4. Keep it for several hours in the fridge to blend flavors. You can also garnish it with a few whole peanuts.

Nutrition:

The dish will be having a total Carbs per Serving of 26g. The effort needed to make the recipe is low. The word contains an assortment of healthier and more effective veggies as well, which enhances the taste.

## Pecan and Gorganzola Salad

Preparation time: 10 minutes

Cooking Time: 0 minutes

Serving: 2

Ingredients:

- lettuce leaf
- Gorgonzola cheese
- Pecan pieces
- Olive oil/balsamic vinegar
- Salt to taste
- Pepper to taste

Directions:

1. Start with toasting the Pecan pieces with some amount of butter.
2. Ensure that the toast will not get burn as it is very soft.
3. Now combine all the other ingredients with the toasted Pecan pieces and toss well.

4. Add the seasoning of Olive oil, salt, and pepper and toss it again. The dish is ready for serving.

Nutrition:

Calories 110 Saturated fat 0.8 g

Total Carbohydrate 16 g

Sugar 3 g Protein 6 g

## Pepper Ranch Salad Dressing

Preparation time: 10 minutes

Cooking Time: 0 minutes

Serving: 2

Ingredients:

- Two tablespoons sour cream
- Two teaspoons heavy cream
- One tablespoon parmesan cheese – grated
- Pepper to taste - freshly ground
- One teaspoon ranch dressing

Directions:

1. Combine all the required ingredients all together in a big bowl and chill for several hours to set before serving.

Nutrition:

The count of Carbs per Serving is 2g total. The preparation process is easy. You will find a great taste of salad with the touch of Pepper.

## Philly Cheesesteak Salad

Preparation time: 10 minutes

Cooking Time: 0 minutes

Serving: 2

Ingredients:

- Four thin chip steaks – cut into strips
- 4 slices Provolone cheese
- Onion
- Green Pepper
- Olive Oil
- Tomato
- Lettuce
- Mayo

Directions:

1. Take a pan. Put some oil into it. Now fry green pepper and onion on low flame.
2. Combine steak strips and cook them until done.
3. Put slices of Provolone cheese into the mix and continue cooking until melted.
4. Position the mix on a bed of lettuce in a servicing plate.
5. Season and top with sliced tomatoes and mayo. The recipe is ready to eat.

Nutrition:

Energy (calories): 477 kca Protein: 31.84 g

Fat: 30.26 Carbohydrates: 21.71 g

## Pineapple Slaw

Preparation time: 10 minutes

Cooking Time: 0 minutes

Serving: 2

Ingredients:

- 2 cups cabbage - shredded finely
- ¼ cup green peppers – diced finely
- ½ cup pineapple in juice – crushed drained
- Two tablespoons onion
- Two tablespoons mayonnaise
- One teaspoon finely chopped Stevia
- ¼ teaspoon celery seed salt to taste
- Sugar
- Pepper to taste

Directions:

1. Combine pineapple with all types of veggies ingredients required for the dish. Toss well and Mix the remaining ingredients all together.
2. Again toss and mix them well. Chill for several hours and Mix also and serve cold.

Nutrition:

Energy (calories): 638 kcal

Protein: 47.6 g

Fat: 29.21 g

Carbohydrates: 50.28 g

## Quick Fixin Taco Salad

Preparation time: 10 minutes

Cooking Time: 5 minutes

Serving: 2

Ingredients:

- 1 Can Shredded Roast Beef
- 3 Tablespoons sour cream
- 1 cup shredded cheddar cheese
- 2 Tablespoons black olives
- 2 Cups Iceberg Lettuce
- 3 Tablespoons low carb salsa

Directions:

Start with draining gravy juice from the can. Now microwave the Beef. Take a serving plate place lettuce over it. Then position Roast beef over it. Top with sour cream, cheese, black olives, and salsa.

Nutrition:

The count of Carbs per Serving for the dish is 7g. A minimum effort is needed for the preparation. It's an energy-giving healthy alkaline diet loaded with good dietary value.

## Ranch Dressing With Blue Cheese Variation

Preparation time: 20 minutes

Cooking Time: 0 minutes

Serving: 2

Ingredients:

- ¾ cup sour cream

- ¼ cup mayonnaise
- ¼ cup heavy cream
- ½ teaspoon salt
- ½ teaspoon black pepper
- 1 tsp. garlic powder
- 1 tsp. onion powder
- 1 tsp dried parsley
- 2 tbsp. red wine vinegar
- 3 ounces gorgonzola cheese – crumbled

Directions:

1. To prepare ranch dressing, just combine all the ingredients in the list required for the dish and whisk well.
2. You can add more cream and mayonnaise.
3. For Blue cheese, combine all the ingredients in the list required for the dish with extra vinegar and 1 oz. Of the cheese.
4. Now make a perfect blend by combining with remaining crumbled blue cheese. Blend until smooth, stir well and serve.

Nutrition:

Carbs per Serving of the dish is 19g total. Less effort is required to make the dish. That is a good alternative for lunch for calorie conscious people.

## Sante Fe Beef And Hot Pepper Salad

Preparation time: 10 minutes

Cooking Time: 0 minutes

Serving: 2

Ingredients:

Dressing:

- ½ cup salsa – chunky and thick
- ½ teaspoon chili - powder
- ½ cup sour cream

Salad:

- 8 ounces lettuce
- ½ cup pitted ripe olives
- 8 ounces deli roast beef
- Two medium tomatoes – cut into pieces
- 4 ounces hot pepper cheese
- Two thin onion slices – separated into rings

Directions:

1. Take a small bowl. Combine the salsa all together with sour cream and chili powder.
2. Mix them well to coat all the ingredients evenly.
3. Now take all salad ingredients into a large bowl, combine with this mix, and give a light toss. Serve with proper seasoning and dressing.

Benefits:

Less effort is required to make the dish. Carbs per Serving of the plate is 6.5g total. The healthy plate is extremely rich in digestible energy. It is packed with bioavailable vitamins.

Nutrition:

Carbs per Serving of the dish is 6.5g total

## Asme (Tahini) Dressing

Preparation time: 5 minutes

Cooking Time: 0 minutes

Serving: 2

Ingredients:

- ¼ cup Tahini
- 2 tbsp. lemon juice
- ½ cup of water
- ½ clove garlic- crushed

Directions:

1. To prepare Tahini Dressing, Blend all ingredients required for the recipe to a smooth mix. As per your taste, you can use thicker dressing by decreasing the water requirement.
2. The dressing is delicious. Combine it with any type of salad you like and enjoy.

Nutrition:

The dish can serve four persons. Carbs per Serving is 1-2 per serving. It needs only 5 minutes Effort to make the dish. Green vegetables, salad, and beans are the core ingredients of this dish. A touch of Sesame (Tahini) Dressing over it makes this dish delicious and highly nutritious and healthy.

## Butternut Squash And Escarole Gratin

Preparation time: 30 minutes

Cooking Time: 60 minutes

Serving: 2

Ingredients

- 3/4 tbsps. Unsalted Butter Stick
- 4 oz. Escarole
- 2/3 lbs. Butternut Winter Squash
- 1/8 tsp. Salt
- 1/8 tsp. Black Pepper
- 3/4 leeks Leeks
- 1/4 fl. oz. Water
- 1/4 cup Heavy Cream
- 1/8 cup Chicken Broth, Bouillon or Consommé
- 1/2 tsps. Thick-It-Up
- 1/4 cup shredded Gruyere Cheese
- 1/2 tbsps. Parmesan Cheese (Grated)

Directions

1. Butter a 2- to 4-cup baking dish. Set oven rack in upper third of oven and heat oven to 400F.
2. Bring 3 inches of water to boil in a large saucepan. Add escarole and cook, stirring, until tender, 3 to 5 minutes. Drain in a colander and rinse under cold running water. Gently squeeze to remove as much moisture as possible.

3. Melt 1 tablespoon of the butter in a medium nonstick skillet over medium-high heat. Add half of the squash and season with 1/4 teaspoon of the salt and 1/8 teaspoon of the pepper; cook, turning occasionally, until lightly browned and nearly tender, about 8 minutes. Transfer to baking dish. Repeat and reserve.

4. Melt remaining tablespoon butter in skillet over medium-low heat. Add leeks and season with remaining 1/8 teaspoons salt; cook, stirring, 3 minutes. Add water, cover and cook, stirring occasionally, until tender, about 3 minutes. Stir in escarole and cook until heated through; spoon over squash in baking dish.

5. Top with reserved squash.

6. Wipe out skillet. Combine cream, broth and thickener in skillet, whisking until blended. Cook over medium heat, stirring, until thickened, about 2 minutes. Remove from heat and stir in Gruyere until melted.

7. Pour sauce over vegetables, spreading evenly. Sprinkle Parmesan on top and bake until bubbly and golden brown on top, about 30 minutes. Let stand 10 minutes before serving.

Nutrition:

Protein: 7.9g

Fat: 20.5g

Fiber: 5.7g

Calories: 300

# CHAPTER 11:

# Seafoods

## Tuna Salad

Preparation time: 15 minutes

Cooking Time: 10 minutes

Serving: 2

Ingredients:

- 7 Containers = Tuna in Water Strained
- ¾ Cup = Mayo
- 25 g = Green Onion
- 160 g = Celery
- ¾ Cup = Sugar-Free Relish
- 3 = Hardboiled Eggs
- 140 g = Green Pepper

Directions:

1. Hard boil the eggs. Open tuna and pull out the water.
2. Crumble tuna in a basin. Include all ingredients and mix as well.

Nutrition:

Calories: 363

Fat: 27

Carbohydrates: 2

Fiber: 1

Protein: 29

## Stuffed And Wrapped Shrimp

Preparation time: 20 minutes

Cooking Time: 10 minutes

Serving: 2

Ingredients:

- Lbs. = Large, (cooked and peeled shrimp)
- 15 slices = Bacon
- 1 Tbsp. = Pepper
- 15 = Jalapeno Slices
- ¼ tsp. = Cayenne Pepper
- 5 Slices = Cheddar Cheese
- 1 Tbsp. = Garlic Powder
- 1 Tbsp. = Paprika

Directions:

1. If your shrimp is frozen, melt them in water.
2. Combine the four dry ingredients in a basin.

3. Dry the thawed and peeled shrimp and combine it with ¾ of the spice mixture.
4. Slice the shrimp and put half a jalapeno slice and a little cheese into the opening.
5. Slice bacon in half and wrap the shrimp; try and cover it such that the start and end both are close to a center.
6. Skewer the shrimp. Grill till the bacon is crunchy.

Nutrition:

Calories: 252

Fat: 15

Carbohydrates: 3

Fiber: 1

Protein: 28

## Quick Steamed Red Snapper

Preparation time: 20 minutes

Cooking Time: 10 minutes

Serving: 2

Ingredients:

- 1 lb. = red snapper fillet
- 1 = garlic clove (minced)
- 1 tablespoon = light soy sauce
- 1/8 teaspoon = black pepper
- 1 tablespoon = sugar
- 1 teaspoon = fresh ginger, finely grated
- 1/8 teaspoon = salt

Directions:

1. Mix up ginger, soy sauce, sugar, garlic, salt, and pepper.
2. Place fish on a hot stand. Cover fish with soy-ginger mixture. Put perspective over boiling water and co
3. Steam it for 10 minutes. Brush occasionally with soy-ginger mixture.

Nutrition:

Calories 161

Fat 1

Carbohydrate 3

Protein 30

## Simple Shrimp Dip

Preparation time: 10 minutes

Cooking Time: 10 minutes

Serving: 2

Ingredients:

- 2 = green onions
- 4 ounces = seafood cocktail sauce
- 8 ounces = light cream cheese (soften)
- 8 ounces = mayonnaise
- 1/2 lb. = baby shrimp

Directions:

1. Cut up green onions and keep aside.
2. Combine cream cheese and mayonnaise and set in serving dish.
3. Wash off shrimp and put over mixture.
4. On top of shrimp, add the cocktail sauce. Garnish with green onions.

Nutrition:

Calories 170

Fat 13

Carbohydrate 6

Protein 9

## Iceberg Salad with Shrimp

Preparation time: 10 minutes

Cooking Time: 10 minutes

Serving: 2

Ingredients:

- 1 cup = small shrimp
- 1 head = iceberg lettuce
- 2 tablespoons = lemon zest
- 1/2 cup = seafood cocktail sauce, prepared
- 3 tablespoons = chives (chopped)
- 3 drops = hot sauce
- 1 = lemon (juiced)
- 1/4 cup = mayonnaise
- 1/2 teaspoon = salt
- 1/4 teaspoon = pepper

Directions:

1. Take away core out of lettuce head. Cut up the head of lettuce end-to-end. Mix lemon juice, cocktail sauce, mayo, hot sauce, and zest.
2. Mix shrimp into the dressing and spread it lightly down over quartered lettuce.
3. Add salt and pepper to salads and spread chives over the salads, and eat.

Nutrition:

Calories 84

Fat 0.7

Carbohydrate 11

Protein 1

## Shrimp and Mushroom Cowder

Preparation time: 20 minutes

Cooking Time: 5 minutes

Serving: 2

Ingredients:

- 1/2 cup = whipping cream
- 1/4 cup = all-purpose flour
- 1/2 lb. = shrimp (cooked)

- 1/2 lb. = mushroom (sliced)
- 1/2 cup = wine (dry white)
- 1/2 = thyme leaves (dried)
- 1/2 teaspoon = dill
- 1 = onion (chopped)
- 2 tablespoons = butter
- 2 cups = fish stock
- 1/4 tsp. = salt
- 1/4 tsp = mace

Directions:
1. Buy cleaned shrimp and drain well.
2. Fry mushrooms and onion in butter for almost 2 minutes or till onion is soft. Mix in flour.
3. Fry for 1 minute additionally on medium heat.
4. Mix in the broth juice. Put in the wine and let it boil. Put in thyme, mace, salt, dill, and weed and mix them well. Put in shrimp.
5. Cook till heated throughout. Whisk in cream just before serving.
6. Top soup, if needed, with some slim slices of mushroom and fresh parsley.

Nutrition:

Calories 311 Fat 19

Carbohydrate 12

Protein 17

## Cod With Oregano

Preparation time: 20 minutes

Cooking Time: 10 minutes

Serving: 2

Ingredients:
- 1 tbsp. = fresh oregano (chopped)
- 1 tbsp. = orange juice
- 1 tbsp. = olive oil
- 1 1/2 lbs. = cod fish fillets
- 1 tbsp. = lemon juice
- 1/2 tsp. = salt

Directions:
1. Preheat the oven to 450 degrees. In a basin, combine the lemon juice, orange juice, oregano, olive oil, and Salt jointly.
2. Put the fillets on the baking sheet. Cover the fish with the dressing. Bake the cod for 10 minutes. Serve right away.

Nutrition: Protein 30

Calories 173 Fat 4 Carbohydrate 0.8

## Ritz Fish

Preparation time: 35 minutes

Cooking Time: 30 minutes

Serving: 2

Ingredients:
- 1/2 cup = butter

- 4 = fish fillets
- 32 = Ritz crackers

Directions:

1. Rinse fish filets and dry them. Place fillets in a baking tray. Keep aside. Place Ritz crackers in a baggie and break the crackers to a slight crush.
2. Put in butter to the Ritz and mix up well. Put the Ritz mixture on the top of all the filets. Cook in the oven at 350 degrees for 25 - 30 minutes.
3. Check by placing a fork in the fish. The fish should be crunchy, and the Ritz crackers should be well browned. Eat instantly.

Nutrition:

Calories 522

Fat 30

Carbohydrate 16

Protein 43

## Lori's Oil Poached Fish

Preparation time: 25 minutes

Cooking Time: 14 minutes

Serving: 2

Ingredients:

- Olive oil
- 4 = firm-fleshed fish fillets
- 2 = garlic cloves (minced)
- 3 tbsp. = parsley
- Lemon wedges
- Fresh ground pepper
- Salt

Directions:

1. Wash and dry the fish. Transfer sufficient oil in a deep pan.
2. Include the garlic and parsley as well.
3. Let it fry and add fish into it. Simmer over low heat for almost 14 minutes.
4. Take away fish. Remove excess oil, if any. Put it on plates. Season it. Dish up with lemons.

Nutrition:

Calories 241

Fat 1

Carbohydrate 0.6

Protein 51

## Catfish In Creamy Shallot Sauce

Preparation time: 2 minutes

Cooking Time: 1 minute

Serving: 1

Ingredients:

- One catfish fillet
- 1 T olive oil (or coconut oil)
- 2 T butter

- One shallot sliced into small pieces
- Approximately ¼ cup lemon juice
- ¼ cup unsweetened coconut milk

Directions:

1. Lift fillet, pat, and let it dry.
2. Sauté sliced shallot for 30 seconds.
3. Add 2 T butter.
4. Melt butter, then add fillet.
5. Fry on either side for a few minutes, then turn it over.
6. Remove fillets from the pan and add lemon juice over it.
7. Add coconut milk into the pan and heat for a minute or two before putting the fillet back, and then stir.
8. In about 3 minutes, the catfish fillet will be ready to serve.

Nutrition's:

(555.25 calories per serving, 51g fat, 14.21 carbs, 16.73g protein)

## Grilled Fish In Grape Tomato Sauce

Preparation time: 10 minutes

Cooking Time: 20 minutes

Serving: 2

That is an excellent Atkins fish recipe for those who love tomato sauce. Depending on your carbohydrate limit, you can have it without brown rice or pasta. Without brown rice or pasta, this meal has less than 10 grams of carbohydrates.

Ingredients:

- 15oz can tomato sauce
- Six ground garlic cloves
- 1 T of olive oil
- One fresh pepper
- Salt for taste
- Four tilapia pieces
- Fresh basil chopped

Directions:

1. Use a large pan and add olive oil. Heat before adding garlic.
2. Fry garlic until golden brown.
3. Reduce heat, add tomato sauce and pepper.
4. Simmer sauce, and then add salt. Add basil for 15 minutes.
5. After another 5 minutes, add fish. Let it simmer for a while. Grill fish until golden brown.

Nutrition:

(159.8 calories per serving, 5.9g fat, 2.1g carbs, 23.6g protein)

## Baked Tilapia

Preparation time: 5 minutes

Cooking Time: 15 minutes

Serving: 1

Ingredients:

- 7oz tilapia
- 1 tsp. chili pepper
- 1 tsp. oregano
- 2 tsp. lemon juice
- 1 T cayenne pepper

Directions

1. Mix chili pepper, cayenne, oregano, and salt in one small container.
2. Melt butter and pour it into a shallow pan. Add lemon to the butter.
3. Add spice mixture with the butter and lemon.
4. Add fillets into the mixing bowl. Ensure the mixture is massaged and spread evenly on all the fillets.
5. Transfer it into a casserole.
6. Preheat the oven to 450F. In about 15 minutes, the fillets should be flaky, soft, and ready to serve.

Nutrition:

(287.3 calories per serving, 6.2g fat, 6g carbs, 52.8g protein)

## Crispy Baked Fish

Preparation time: 10 minutes

Cooking Time: 50 minutes

Serving: 2

Ingredients:

- 16oz fish fillets (about four fillets 4oz each)
- ¼ cup skim milk
- 2 tsp. vinegar
- 1 T honey mustard
- 1 tsp. salt
- 1 tsp. garlic
- 1 tsp. pepper
- ½ tsp. thyme
- 1 tsp. cayenne pepper
- 1 tsp. paprika

Directions

1. Add vinegar and honey mustard to the skim milk. Mix it thoroughly and let it rest for 15 minutes.
2. Mix cornmeal chopped onions, paprika, cayenne, and all other spices.
3. In a sizeable bowl, add milk and then fillets. After a few seconds, remove and place the fillets into the cornmeal and spice mixture.
4. Apply some olive oil on the pan you will be using to avoid the mixture sticking when baking.

5. Place pan on moderate heat and let it cook for about 5 minutes as you turn. The fish will be ready once it's flaky and soft. You may serve after squeezing the lemon.

Nutrition:

(247.5 calories per serving, 13.7g fat, 1.9g carb, 26.23g protein)

## Crusted Salmon with Herbs

Preparation time: 10 minutes

Cooking Time: 15 minutes

Serving: 1

Ingredients:

- 6oz salmon fillets
- 2 T dried parsley
- 1 T coconut flour
- 1 T pepper
- 1 T salt
- 1 T olive oil
- 1 tsp. Dijon mustard cream

Directions:

1. Place fillet on a foil.
2. Preheat the oven to 450F.
3. Add olive oil to the fillet, and then add mustard and massage.
4. Create a mixture of dried parsley, salt, and pepper.
5. Now add the mixture onto the salmon and pat.
6. Place salmon into the oven for 12-15 minutes.
7. Make a vegetable salad and top the crusted salmon.

Nutrition:

(529 calories per serving, 37.3g fat, 9.1g carbs, 36g protein)

## Sautéed Salmon

Preparation time: 2 minutes

Cooking Time: 10 minutes

Serving: 2

Ingredients:

- Four 6oz salmon fillets
- ¼ cup butter
- 1 tsp. lemon juice
- 1 T of pepper
- Salt for taste
- ¼ cup cream

Directions:

1. Use a pan to melt ¼ cup butter.
2. Place salmon on the pan and sauté for 10 minutes, turning to ensure it's cooked evenly.
3. Add salt and pepper for taste.
4. Use a spoon to sprinkle some lemon juice on the salmon.
5. After a minute or so, remove and place on a plate.

6. Add butter and cream.
7. Place salmon back onto the pan and cook for about 2 minutes.
8. Once cooked, you may serve the salmon with several slices of lemon.

Nutrition:

(512 calories per serving, 39.6g fat, 1.9g carbs, 34.5g protein)

## Spiced Tilapia

Preparation time: 10 minutes

Cooking Time: 20 minutes

Serving: 2

Ingredients:

- Two 4oz tilapia fillets
- 3 T olive oil
- Three garlic cloves cut into small pieces
- Salt for taste
- 1 tsp. pepper
- 1 T lemon juice
- ½ cup chopped parsley

Directions:

1. Mix salt and pepper.
2. Apply the mixture onto fillets.
3. Place oil in a pan and heat moderately.
4. Heat the pan before placing the fillets.
5. Turn fillets from time to time until they begin to change color.
6. Add some garlic to the fillets.
7. Continue frying the fish in the pan. When cooked, it should peel easily. Poke the fillets with a knife or fork.
8. Also, for better tasting garlic tilapia, continue frying fillets slowly until garlic is golden brown. However, you should ensure that the garlic doesn't turn black, i.e., get burned.
9. You may now squeeze some lemon juice over the fillets and serve.

Nutrition:

(343 calories per serving, 24.1g fat, 3g carbs, 30.9g protein)

# CHAPTER 12:

# Poultry

## Flavorful Fried Chicken

Preparation time: 10 minutes

Cooking Time: 30 minutes

Serving: 2

Ingredients:

- Four small chicken thighs
- 1 cup of flour
- 1 cup of breadcrumbs
- Two beaten eggs
- 1 tsp. of salt
- 1 tbsp. of Cajun seasoning

Directions

1. Preheat your air fryer to 390 degrees Fahrenheit.
2. Using three bowls, add the flour to the first bowl. In the second bowl, add the eggs and beat it properly, and in the third bowl, add the breadcrumbs, salt, Cajun seasoning, and mix properly.
3. Dredge the chicken thighs in the flour, immerse it into the egg mixture, and cover it with the breadcrumbs.
4. Grease your air fryer basket with a nonstick cooking spray and put in the four chicken thighs inside.
5. Cook it for 25 minutes until the chicken is crispy and turns golden brown.
6. Serve and enjoy!

Nutrition:

Calories: 200, Fat: 22g, Protein: 19g, Carbohydrates: 19g

## Delectable Whole Roast Chicken

Preparation time: 20 minutes

Cooking Time: 50 minutes

Serving: 1

Ingredients:

- 1 (4-pound) whole chicken
- One tablespoon of olive oil
- One teaspoon of salt
- One teaspoon of black pepper
- One teaspoon of paprika
- One teaspoon of onion powder
- One teaspoon of garlic powder

- One teaspoon of Italian seasoning
- One teaspoon of brown sugar
- One tablespoon of dried thyme
- One tablespoon of dried oregano
- One tablespoon of cayenne pepper

Directions

1. Preheat your air fryer to 340 degrees Fahrenheit.
2. Sprinkle the whole chicken with olive oil and rub the seasoning all over.
3. Grease your air fryer basket with a nonstick cooking spray and add the chicken to it.
4. Cook the chicken inside your air fryer for 30 minutes at 340 degrees Fahrenheit.
5. After 30 minutes, flip the chicken and cook it for 20 minutes or until it is done. Serve and enjoy!

Nutrition:

Calories: 155, Fat: 3.8g, Dietary Fiber: 0g, Carbohydrates: 0g, Protein: 28g

## Divine Buffalo Wings

Preparation time: 10 minutes

Cooking Time: 25 minutes

Serving: 2

Ingredients:

- 2 pounds of chicken wings
- Three tablespoons of melted butter
- ¼ cup of hot sauce
- One teaspoon of paprika
- One teaspoon of cayenne pepper
- One teaspoon of salt
- One teaspoon of black pepper

Buffalo Sauce Ingredients:

- Three tablespoons of melted butter
- ¼ cup of hot sauce

Directions:

1. Using a separate bowl, add three tablespoons of melted butter, ¼ cup of hot sauce, paprika, cayenne pepper, salt, black pepper, chicken wings, and allow it to marinate for 4 hours or overnight.
2. Preheat your air fryer to 390 degrees Fahrenheit.
3. Lubricate your air fryer basket with a nonstick cooking spray and add half of the chicken wings.
4. Cook the chicken wings for 14 minutes, shake it 7 minutes after, and repeat this with the other batch.
5. Using another bowl, add three tablespoons of melted butter and ¼ cup of hot sauce.

6. Remove the chicken wings from your air fryer and combine it with the buffalo sauce.

7. Serve and enjoy!

Nutrition:

Calories: 240, Fat: 15.5g, Protein: 8g, Carbohydrates: 5g, Dietary Fiber: 6g

## Flavorsome Honey Lime Chicken Wings

Preparation time: 10 minutes

Cooking Time: 30 minutes

Serving: 2

Ingredients:

- 2 pounds of chicken wings
- ¼ cup of honey
- Two tablespoons of lime juice
- One tablespoon of lime
- 1 pressed clove of garlic
- One teaspoon of salt
- One teaspoon of black pepper

Directions:

1. Preheat your air fryer to 360 degrees Fahrenheit.

2. Using a bowl, mix the honey, lime juice, lime zest, garlic clove, salt, and black pepper.

3. Add the chicken wings and toss it until it is well covered with the honey-lime mixture.

4. Working in batches, add half of the chicken wings into the air fryer.

5. Cook it for 25 to 30 minutes or until it turns golden brown and crispy while shaking it every 8 minutes.

6. Serve and enjoy!

Nutrition:

Calories: 280, Fat: 25g, Dietary Fiber: 0.2g, Carbohydrates: 3.6g, Protein: 23g

## Delightful Coconut Crusted Chicken Tenders

Preparation time: 5 minutes

Cooking Time: 30 minutes

Serving: 2

Ingredients:

- 1 pound of chicken tender
- Three beaten eggs
- 2 cups of sweetened shredded coconut
- 1 cup of cornstarch
- One teaspoon of salt
- One teaspoon of black pepper
- One teaspoon of cayenne pepper

Directions:

1. Preheat your air fryer to 360 degrees Fahrenheit.

2. Using three bowls, add the cornstarch, salt, black pepper, and cayenne pepper into the first bowl. Then in the second bowl, add the eggs and beat it until it mixes properly. While in the third bowl, add the shredded coconut.

3. Dredge each chicken tender in the cornstarch mixture, then dip it into the egg wash, and then cover it with the shredded coconut.

4. Grease your air fryer with a non-stick cooking spray and add the chicken tenders.

5. Cook for 8 minutes at 360 degrees Fahrenheit or until it turns golden brown.

6. Serve and enjoy!

Nutrition:

Calories: 345, Fat: 11g, Protein: 32g, Carbohydrates: 9g, Dietary Fiber: 2.4g

## Well-Tasted Popcorn Chicken

Preparation time: 10 minutes

Cooking Time: 20 minutes

Serving: 2

Ingredients:

- Two boneless, skinless chicken breasts
- 1 cup of breadcrumbs
- Two beaten eggs
- 1 cup of flour
- One teaspoon of salt
- One teaspoon of black pepper
- One teaspoon of onion powder
- One teaspoon of garlic powder

Directions:

1. Preheat your air fryer to 390 degrees Fahrenheit.

2. Using a food processor, add the chicken breasts and beat it until it minced adequately.

3. Using two bowls add the flour, the eggs and mix it properly into the first bowl, then in the second bowl, add the breadcrumbs, seasonings and mix it properly.

4. Mold the minced chicken into small balls.

5. Cover the minced chicken in the flour, dip it into the egg wash, and then cover it with the seasoned breadcrumbs.

6. Place it inside your air fryer and cook it for 10 minutes at 390 degrees Fahrenheit or until it is entirely done.

7. Serve and enjoy!

Nutrition:

Calories: 170, Fat: 17g, Protein: 14g, Dietary fiber: 0g, Carbohydrates: 13g

## Easy Chicken Strips

Preparation time: 10 minutes

Cooking Time: 20 minutes

Serving: 2

Ingredients:

- Two boneless, skinless chicken breasts, sliced into strips
- ½ cup of shredded coconut
- ½ cup of oats
- 1 cup of panko breadcrumbs
- 1 cup of flour
- Two beaten eggs
- One teaspoon of salt
- One teaspoon of black pepper
- One teaspoon of onion powder
- ½ teaspoon of garlic powder
- One teaspoon of smoked paprika

Directions:

1. Preheat your air fryer to 360 degrees Fahrenheit.
2. Firstly, slice the chicken breasts into thin strips.
3. Using a bowl, add the oats, shredded coconut, breadcrumbs, seasonings, and mix properly.
4. Pick a second bowl, add the egg and mix properly, then pick another bowl, add the flour and place it aside.
5. Dredge the strips in the flour, dip the strips into the egg wash, and cover it with the coconut breadcrumb mixture.
6. Grease your air fryer basket with a nonstick cooking spray.
7. Place the chicken breasts inside your air fryer and cook it for 8 minutes at 360 degrees Fahrenheit.
8. Reduce the heat to 340 degrees Fahrenheit and cook it for an additional 5 minutes until it is done.
9. Serve and enjoy!

Nutrition:

Calories: 130, Fat: 12g, Protein: 14g, Carbohydrates: 8g, Dietary Fiber: 0.9g

## Savory Sriracha Chicken Drumsticks

Preparation time: 10 minutes

Cooking Time: 1 hour

Serving: 2

Ingredients:

- 2 drumsticks
- 1/3 cup of sriracha
- 1/8 cup of honey
- 1/8 cup of melted butter
- 1/3 tablespoon of soy sauce
- 1 1/3 cloves of minced garlic
- 1/3 teaspoon of salt
- 1/3 teaspoon of black pepper

Directions:

1. Preheat your air fryer to 390 degrees Fahrenheit.
2. Grease your air fryer basket with a nonstick cooking spray and add the chicken drumsticks.
3. Cook it inside your air fryer for 10 minutes at 390 degrees Fahrenheit.
4. While still doing that, using a small bowl, add and mix the remaining ingredients.
5. After 10 minutes, remove the chicken drumsticks and brush it with the sriracha sauce.
6. Lower the heat to 360 degrees Fahrenheit and cook the drumsticks for an additional 10 minutes.
7. With the remaining sauce, microwave it inside your air fryer for 30 seconds or at most 1 minute.
8. Carefully remove the chicken drumsticks from your air fryer and cover it with the sriracha sauce again.
9. Serve and enjoy!

Nutrition:

Calories: 290, Fat: 36g, Protein: 13g, Dietary Fiber: 0g, Carbohydrates: 22g

## Chinese-Style Honey Garlic Chicken

Preparation time: 10 minutes

Cooking Time: 35 minutes

Serving: 2

Ingredients:

- 1 pound of chicken wings
- One tablespoon of olive oil
- ¼ cup of soy sauce
- Three cloves of minced garlic
- 1/3 cup of honey
- One teaspoon of white vinegar
- One teaspoon of garlic salt
- Green onions (for garnishing purpose)
- Sesame seeds (for garnishing purpose)

Directions:

1. Using a bowl, add and mix the olive oil, soy sauce, garlic cloves, honey, white vinegar, and the garlic salt properly.
2. Add the chicken breasts and toss it until it gets appropriately covered.
3. Using a Ziploc bag, add the chicken wings, honey-garlic mixture, and allow it to marinate for 4 hours or overnight.
4. Preheat your air fryer to 390 degrees Fahrenheit.

5. Using your baking accessory, add the chicken wings and honey-garlic mixture.
6. Place it inside your air fryer and cook it for 8 minutes at 390 degrees Fahrenheit.
7. After 8 minutes, stir the chicken wings inside your baking accessory, cook it for an additional 10 minutes, and then increase the temperature to 400 degrees Fahrenheit.
8. Garnish it with the green onions and the sesame seeds.
9. Serve and enjoy!

Nutrition:

Calories: 200, Fat: 25g, Dietary Fiber: 0.1g, Carbohydrates: 8g, Protein: 27g

## Rich Parmesan Crusted Chicken Breasts

Preparation time: 10 minutes

Cooking Time: 30 minutes

Serving: 2

Ingredients:

- Four small boneless, skinless chicken breasts
- 1 cup of panko bread crumbs
- ½ cup of Parmesan cheese
- Three tablespoons of freshly chopped parsley
- One teaspoon of black pepper
- Three tablespoons of melted butter
- Three tablespoons of fresh lime juice
- Two garlic pressed cloves

Directions:

1. Preheat your air fryer to 360 degrees Fahrenheit.
2. Using a bowl, add and mix the panko breadcrumbs, Parmesan cheese, parsley, salt, and black pepper properly.
3. Pick another bowl, and mix the melted butter, fresh lime juice, and garlic.
4. Soak the chicken breasts into the butter mixture and cover it with the panko breadcrumb mixture until it is adequately protected.
5. Grease your air fryer basket with a nonstick cooking spray and place the chicken breasts inside.
6. Cook it for 20 to 25 minutes inside your air fryer under 360 degrees Fahrenheit of heat or until it turns golden brown and has a crispy texture.
7. Serve and enjoy!

Nutrition:

Calories: 290, Fat: 16g, Protein: 59g, Dietary Fiber: 0.5g, Carbohydrates: 2.6g

## Chicken Low Carb Meal Prep Bowls

Preparation time: 10 minutes

Cooking Time: 10 minutes

Serving: 2

Ingredients:

- Cilantro Lime Cauliflower Rice
- four cups cauliflower (riced)
- One tablespoon olive oil
- 1/four teaspoon salt
- 1/4 teaspoon garlic powder
- One lime, zested
- 1/four cup cilantro leaves (packed)
- Veggies
- Two bell peppers sliced
- half of the crimson onion sliced
- 30
- One tablespoon olive oil
- Chicken
- Two big hen breasts (sliced in half horizontally; roughly 14 oz.)
- One tablespoon olive oil
- Two tablespoons taco seasoning
- To serve
- 1/4 cup cheese (shredded)
- Two avocados

Directions:

1. Heat olive oil in a non-stick pan over medium heat.
2. Add the rice cauliflower, salt, garlic powder, and lime zest. Cook 5
3. Or so minutes, until cauliflower rice is slightly softened (you need it to hold a few crunches).
4. Remove from heat, stir in the cilantro, and divide among four meal 31 prep bins.
5. Add any other tablespoon of olive oil to the pan. Add bell peppers and onion, and cook dinner for five or so minutes, until slightly softened.
6. Remove from heat and divide among meal prep packing containers.
7. Prepare the fowl: slice horizontally to make two thin portions from each hen breast. Brush with olive oil and sprinkle with taco seasoning.
8. Add hen to the pan and cook dinner 4-5 minutes per facet. Remove from warmness, cover, and permit relaxation in the pan for 5 minutes
9. Divide chook among meal prep boxes, alongside cheese (1 tablespoon consistent with bowl).
10. Storage. Store in a sealed box inside the refrigerator for up to 4 days.

11. To Serve. Heat within the microwave till steaming warm, and cheese is melted over the chicken. Add sliced avocado fresh, if desired.

Notes:

Adding 1/2 an avocado to a meal prep bowl brings net carb count to 9 g with 30 g protein

Nutrition: Calories: 303kcal | Carbohydrates: 11g | Protein: 28g | Fat: 16g | Saturated Fat: 3g |

Cholesterol: 79mg

## This Tasty Low Carb Soup Recipe Is Loaded With Healthy Vegetables And Hen.

Preparation time: 10 minutes

Cooking Time: 20 minutes

Serving: 2

Ingredients:

- four slices bacon, chopped
- 1 Tbsp. olive oil
- ¼ cup onion, chopped
- 1 Tbsp. sparkling garlic, minced
- ¼ cup sundried tomatoes, chopped
- 1 cup sliced white mushrooms
- eight cups chook inventory
- three cups water
- 2 cups celery root, peeled and chopped into ½ inch cubes (or cauliflower, jicama, radish, turnip)
- four cups cooked chook breast, chopped 2 cups yellow squash, sliced and quartered
- 1 cup green beans, cut into 1-inch portions
- four cups Swiss chard, chopped (or collards – NOT KALE)
- 2 Tbsp. red wine vinegar
- ¼ cup fresh basil, chopped
- Salt and pepper to flavor

Directions:

1. In a massive soup pot, cook the bacon and olive oil over medium warmness for 2 minutes.

2. Add the onions, garlic, sundried tomatoes, and mushrooms. Cook for 5 minutes.

3. Pour in the fowl stock and water, and then add the celery root and fowl.

4. Simmer for 15 minutes. Add the squash, green beans, and Swiss chard and simmer for 10 minutes. Add the pink wine vinegar and season with salt and pepper to taste. Stir in the fresh basil only before serving. Approx. vitamins information in keeping with 1.5 cup serving: 136

Nutrition:Calories, 4g fat, 4g internet carbs, 19g protein

## Pecan Chocolate Cake

Ingredients:

- 2 cups pecans (finely floor)
- 1/three cup unsweetened cocoa powder
- One half of tsp. baking powder
- 1/4 teaspoon salt
- Four eggs
- half of cup (I stick) butter, melted
- 1 tsp. vanilla
- 1 cup of Splenda
- half of cup water
- Frosting:
- Eight ounces cream cheese
- 1 cup Splenda
- 1 tsp. Vanilla extract
- One tbs. Unsweetened cocoa powder
- Two tbs. Butter (softened)

Directions:

1. Heat oven to 350 F.
2. Grease two eight or nine" round pans.
3. Process pecans in the food processor -
4. pulse till their meal - but they may not get relatively as small as corn
5. Meal (I used a nut grinder).
6. Add the rest of the dry ingredients and pulse once more.
7. Add the wet components and
8. Method until properly-combined.
9. Pour into pans and bake for 15
10. Minutes, or till a toothpick inserted in the middle comes out smooth.
11. Remove from the oven and funky before frosting.
12. Mix all components properly to spreading consistency, and frost the cake.

## Low-Carb Chicken Alfredo with Baron Verulam

Preparation time: 5 minutes

Cooking Time: 10 minutes

Serving: 2

Spicy, soft bird breast is blended with broccoli, blanketed with Alfredo sauce, and sprinkled with bacon for a satisfying, low carb meal.

Ingredients:

- 1/three lb. chook breast
- Salt and pepper
- 1/8 teaspoon ancho chili powder
- Pinch of cayenne
- pinch of garlic powder

- Olive oil for sautéing ideally chipotle infused
- 1/four cup Alfredo Sauce
- 3/4 cup broccoli
- One slice bacon cooked crisp

Directions:

1. Steam the broccoli till tender.
2. Cut the fowl breast into chew sized portions or leave entire
3. Season on each facet with salt, pepper, ancho, cayenne, and garlic.
4. Heat the olive oil in a heavy pan until it shimmers and then carefully
5. Lay the meat down in it.
6. Cook until golden brown and caramelized on one aspect.
7. Flip and cook dinner on the other facet till it's far done, approximately 160 on a meat thermometer.
8. Let stand for a few minutes for the juices to be absorbed into the meat. It will end cooking to 165F during this time.
9. Heat the Alfredo sauce.
10. Mix the hen and broccoli lightly and then pour the sauce over it and mix it in well. Crumble bacon on the pinnacle.
11. If using the hen breast complete, then arrange the broccoli at the plate and add the chicken breast carefully. Add the bacon for garnish.

## Low Carb Whole Grain Pie Crust

Preparation time: 10 minutes

Cooking Time: 50 minutes

Serving: 2

Ingredients:

- 1/three cup (45g) whole-wheat flour
- 1/3 cup (28g) soy flour
- 2 oz. (57g) critical wheat gluten flour three tbsps. wheat bran
- ½ tsp. salt
- Eight tbsps. unsalted butter (bloodless, ½."
- diced)
- 1 tbsp. cold water

Directions:

1. Process all elements (besides cold water) in a meals processor until you have an aggregate resembling a coarse meal.
2. Gradually upload in cold water and maintain pulsing till dough is fashioned.
3. Wrap a dough ball with plastic, then flatten to 7-inch thick and hold in a freezer for 15 minutes.
4. Sprinkle the bloodless dough with some wheat gluten flour and

roll out among plastic sheets to make a 12-inch circle.

5. Transfer the flattened dough into a nine-inch pie plate and press onto the bottom of the plate's perimeters.
6. Remove the more excellent dough and chill for 15 minutes
7. Preheat oven to 405 levels centigrade
8. Prick the cold pie crust with a fork and cowl with a foil, 43 with the pie weight.
9. Bake within the preheated oven for sixteen minutes.
10. Remove the weights, cowl loosely with foil, and bake for every other 5-6 minutes, until golden brown.
11. Cool the baked pie crust for 15-20 minutes on a rack earlier than using.

Nutrition:

Each serving: five.8g Net Carbs

## Low Carb Satay Beef Meal

Preparation time: 20 minutes

Cooking Time: 40 minutes

Serving: 2

Ingredients:

- Low Carb Beef Satay
- 3/4 lb. flank steak (sliced into 1/4 inch strips)
- one hundred sixty mL coconut milk (five.4
- ounces)
- 1/four cup peanut butter (herbal)
- One tablespoon lime juice
- Two teaspoons reduced-sodium soy sauce (or liquid amino)
- One teaspoon granulated monk fruit
- sweetener
- Two tablespoons Thai pink curry paste
- half of teaspoon floor ginger Meal Prep Bowls
- One tablespoon olive oil
- 4 cups riced cauliflower
- salt & pepper
- eight ounces green beans

Directions:

1. Shake together the coconut milk, peanut butter, lime juice, soy sauce, monk fruit sweetener, purple curry paste, and floor ginger.
2. In a large bowl, fire ups the sliced flank steak with 1/2 of the coconut sauce. Portion the last 1/2 of the sauce out into small storage packing containers.

3. Allow pork to marinate for 30 minutes

4. While beef is marinating, prepare the cauliflower rice and inexperienced beans. Cauliflower rice- heat oil over medium heat in a non-stick skillet. Add the rice cauliflower, season with salt & pepper, and cook for 5 minutes, or until cooked to your liking. Divide up among four 3 cup meal prep boxes.

5. Green beans- add another tablespoon of oil to the pan and prepare dinner the inexperienced beans for five minutes, till shiny green and barely softened. Divide among the meal prep bins.

6. Heat an indoor grill. Working in batches, cook the strips of beef for two-three minutes, until cooked thru.

7. You can also cook dinner on an outdoor grill and desire to apply for a grilling plate or skewer the red meat.

8. Divide beef out between the meal prep boxes. Cool absolutely, then seal and save in the fridge for up to four days.

9. To serve, Remove the sauce, and then reheat inside the microwave till steaming warm. Spoon the sauce over the red meat and vegetables, and enjoy!

Notes

\* I used granulated monk fruit sweetener; if you are powdered or liquid, begin with half of and taste. You also can change for one tablespoon brown sugar or maple syrup if you aren't Sugar: 4g

Nutrition:

Calories: 333kcal

The low carb beef meal prep has a creamy Thai peanut sauce that serves as a marinade for the pork and a dipping sauce. Serve with cauliflower rice and inexperienced beans for four lunches.

## Low Carb Meatball Burrito

Preparation time: 10 minutes

Cooking Time: 20-25 minutes

Serving: 2

Ingredients:

- Taco Meatballs
- 1 lb. lean ground red meat
- One teaspoon Worcestershire sauce
- half of teaspoon salt
- Two tablespoons low carb taco seasoning one egg
- Lime Cauliflower Rice
- One tablespoon olive oil (or coconut oil) 3 cups riced cauliflower (\*\* see observe) half of teaspoon salt half of teaspoon garlic powder

- One lime (zested)
- Pico De Gallo
- 1 cup cherry tomatoes (quartered)
- One jalapeno (minced)
- half lime (juiced)
- 1/eight teaspoon salt
- Low Carb Burrito Bowls
- 1/2 cup shredded cheese
- 1/four cup sour cream salsa (elective)
- avocado or guacamole
- (optionally available)

Directions:
1. Heat oven to 375°F. Stir all components collectively. Roll into 1. Five tablespoon balls, set up on a baking sheet.
2. Bake for 20-25 minutes, or until cooked via. Lime Cauliflower Rice
3. While meatballs are baking, warmness oil in a massive non-stick pan over medium heat
4. Add all substances to the pan and cook dinner for 3-five minutes, stirring continuously, till softened barely (however not mushy!). Set aside to cool.

Nutrition:

Calories: 347kcal

Low carb meatball burrito bowls with taco-pro meatballs, cauliflower rice, and % de Gallo, cheese, and sour cream with best 5 g net carbs in line with serving.

## Yummy Chicken Pot Pie

Preparation time: 40 to 45 minutes

Cooking Time: 4 hours

Serving: 2

Ingredients:
- 1/3 cup celery (Sliced)
- About 1/4 tsp. pepper
- 2/3 cup frozen mixed vegetables
- 1 cup chicken broth
- 1/4 tsp. poultry seasoning
- About 1/2 tsp. dried thyme
- 10 oz. chicken thighs, boneless and skinless
- 1/4 cup onion (Chopped)

Directions:
1. First of all, please make sure you've all the ingredients available. Please use the "Slow Cooker" setting on your Instant Pot.
2. Now quickly add all ingredients except frozen vegetables into the slow cooker & mix well.
3. Cover and cook properly on low for about 3 to 4 hours.

4. One thing remains to be done. Then add frozen vegetables and cook properly on high for another 30 to 35 minutes.

5. Finally, serve & enjoy.

Nutrition:

Calories 338

Fat 11.3 g

Carbohydrates 10.5 g

Sugar 3.1 g

Protein 45.5 g

Cholesterol 126 mg

## Tasty Classic Spiced Chicken Breasts

Preparation time: 10 to 15 min.

Cooking Time: 15 to 20 minutes.

Serving: 2

Ingredients:

- 1/8 teaspoon oregano (Dried)
- 1 cup of water
- About 1/4 teaspoon dried basil
- Three chicken breasts, boneless and skinless
- One tablespoon olive oil
- 1/4 teaspoon garlic powder
- About 1/4 teaspoon black pepper
- 1/2 teaspoon salt

Directions:

1. First of all, please make sure you've all the ingredients available. In a mixing bowl of medium size, combine the garlic powder, oregano, salt, black pepper, and basil.

2. Now rinse the chicken, pat dry, and season one side with the 1/2 portion of the prepared mix.

3. Place your Instant Pot on a flat kitchen surface; plug it & turn it on.

4. To start making the recipe, press the "Sauté" button.

5. This step is essential. Add the oil & chicken, seasoned side down, season the second side, and use remaining seasoning mix; cook appropriately for about 2 to 5 minutes per side to soften the ingredients.

6. Remove from the pot. Pour the water into the pool.

7. Then arrange the trivet in the pot & add the chicken over the trivet.

8. Carefully close its lid and firmly lock it. Then, seal the valve too.

9. To start making the recipe, press the "Manual" button.

10. Then you have to set cooking time; set the timer for about 5 to 10 minutes.

11. Allow the pot to cook the mixture until the timer goes off.

12. Turn off the pot & press "Cancel."
13. Now allow the built-up pressure to vent out naturally; it will take 5 to 10 minutes to release inside force completely.
14. One thing remains to be done. Open its lid and transfer the cooked mixture into serving container/containers.
15. Finally, serve warm!

Nutrition:

Calories – 324

Fat – 9.3g

Carbohydrates – 19.5g

Fiber – 2g

Protein – 42.3g

## Titanic Tomato Chicken Stew

Preparation time: 10 minutes

Cooking Time: 50 minutes

Serving: 2

Ingredients:

- One tablespoon sugar
- 3 ounces sweet potato
- About 1.5 teaspoon salt
- 1 pound boneless chicken breast
- One tablespoon oregano
- One teaspoon cilantro
- Two tablespoons olive oil
- About 1.5 teaspoons fresh ginger
- Two carrots
- Three red onion
- 3 ounces scallions
- 5 ounces shallot
- About 1.5 tablespoons ground black pepper
- 1/2 cup cream
- 1/2 cup tomato juice
- 3 cups chicken stock

Directions:

1. First of all, please make sure you've all the ingredients available. Combine the tomato juice with the salt, cilantro, oregano, ground black pepper, & cream in a mixing bowl and stir.
2. Now peel the onions, sweet potato, and carrots.
3. Chop the vegetables into medium-sized pieces.
4. This step is essential. Set the Instant Pot to the" Sauté" mode.
5. Place the chopped vegetables into the Instant Pot and sprinkle them with the olive oil. Sauté the vegetables for about 5 to 10 minutes.
6. Then add the tomato juice mixture and stir. Chop the shallot & scallions.

7. Add the chopped ingredients into the Instant Pot.
8. Now chop the boneless chicken breast roughly & add it into the Instant Pot, then add the chicken stock.
9. Stir well using a spoon and close the Instant Pot lid.
10. One thing remains to be done. Cook the dish on the" Meat/Stew" mode for about 30 to 35 minutes.
11. Finally, when the stew is cooked, remove it from the Instant Pot & transfer it to serving bowls.

Nutrition:

Calories 349

Fat 19.1  Fiber 5

Carbs 34.85

Protein 11

Directions:
1. First of all, please make sure you've all the ingredients available. Throw everything into your Instant Pot pressure cooker.
2. Now select "Manual" & then 25 to 30 minutes at "High" pressure.
3. When the timer goes off, quick-release the pressure.
4. One thing remains to be done. Carefully open the cooker & shred the chicken.
5. Finally, serve & enjoy.

Nutrition:

Calories: - 340

Fat: - 7

Fiber: - 0

Carbs: - 6

Protein: - 59

## Rich Chicken Salsa.

Preparation time: 25 minutes

Cooking Time: 30 minutes

Serving: 2

Ingredients:
- 5 1/3 oz. of salsa verde
- 1/3 tsp. smoked paprika
- 1/2 tsp. cumin
- 1/3 tsp. salt
- 2/3 and 1/2 lb. of boneless chicken breasts

## Elegant Orange Spice Chicken

Preparation time: 15 to 20 minutes

Cooking Time: 15 to 20 minutes

Serving: 2

Ingredients:
- 2/3 tablespoons vegetable oil
- 1 1/3 green onions and orange zest
- 3/4 garlic heads (Minced)
- 1/3 cup tomato sauce
- Salt and pepper to taste
- 1/3 cup of orange juice

- 1/8 cup soy sauce
- 1 1/2 tablespoons corn starch
- 1/8 cup granulated sugar
- 2/3 lb. chicken breast cut into two-inch pieces
- 1/8 cup brown sugar

Directions:

1. First of all, please make sure you've all the ingredients available. Dry the chicken pieces with a paper towel.
2. Now add oil and chicken to the pot of the cooker.
3. Press the 'sauté' key, & cook the chicken properly on medium-high heat for about 2 to 5 minutes, stirring constantly.
4. This step is essential. When the chicken turns golden brown, add the rest of the ingredients to the pot.
5. Then mix all the ingredients well.
6. Cover and lock the cooker lid.
7. Select the 'poultry' option and set the timer for about 5 to 10 minutes.
8. After the completion beep, use 'natural release' to vent the steam for about 10 to 15 minutes. Then open the lid.
9. Mix the corn-starch with the orange juice in a separate bowl and add it to the pot.
10. Then select the 'sauté' function & cook the chicken properly in the sauce for about 5 to 10 minutes.
11. One thing remains to be done. Stir it constantly until it thickens.
12. Finally, garnish with chopped green onions & orange zest on top.

Nutrition:

Calories: 818 Carbohydrate: 23.7g

Protein: 128.2g Fat: 19.6g

Sugar: 19.6g

Sodium: 1120g

## Excellent Chicken And Potatoes Dish

Preparation time: 15 to 20 minutes

Cooking Time: 15 to 20 minutes

Serving: 2

Ingredients:

- 2 pounds chicken thighs, skinless and boneless
- Salt and black pepper to the taste
- 3/4 cup chicken stock
- 1/4 cup lemon juice
- About 2.5 tablespoons Italian seasoning
- About 2 pounds red potatoes, peeled and cut into quarters
- Two tablespoons olive oil
- About 3.5 tablespoons Dijon mustard

Directions:

1. First of all, please make sure you've all the ingredients available. Now set your instant pot on sauté mode, add the oil, heat it up, add chicken thighs, salt, pepper, stir & brown for about 2 to 5 minutes.

2. One thing remains to be done. In a bowl, mix stock with mustard, Italian seasoning, and lemon juice, stir well, pour over chicken, add potatoes, cover and cook properly on High for about 15 to 20 minutes.

3. Finally, divide among plates and serve. Enjoy!

Nutrition:

Calories 190

Fat 6

Fiber 3.3

Carbs 23

Protein 18

## Quick Spicy Chicken Curry

Preparation time: 6 hours

Cooking Time: 20 to 25 minutes

Serving: 2

Ingredients:

- 3 tbsp. flour
- 1 tbsp. vegetable oil
- About 2.5 tsp. ground coriander
- 14 oz. canned tomatoes (Chopped)
- 2 tsp. garam masala
- 2 tsp. turmeric
- Two green chilies (Chopped)
- About 2.5 tsp. ground cumin
- 1 tsp. ginger (Grated)
- Two onion (Chopped)
- 1/2 lemon juice
- Four garlic cloves, crushed
- Four chicken thighs, boneless and cut into chunks

Directions:

1. First of all, please make sure you've all the ingredients available. Now please use the "Slow Cooker" setting on your Instant Pot.

2. Now add ginger, garlic, chilies, & onion into the blender and blend until smooth.

3. Now quickly heat oil in the pan over medium heat.

4. This step is essential. Add blended puree into the pan & sauté for about 2 to 5 minutes.

5. Then add spices and sauté for about 2 to 5 minutes.

6. Add flour and tomatoes into the pan and stir well.

7. Refill tomato can get halfway with water & adds in the pan. Stir well.
8. Now add chicken into the Instant Pot and season with pepper & salt.
9. Pour pan mixture over the chicken with lemon juice.
10. One thing remains to be done. Cover and cook properly on low for about 5 to 6 hours.
11. Finally, serve & enjoy.

Nutrition:

Calories 387

Fat 14.8 g

Carbohydrates 17.3 g

Sugar 6 g

Protein 44.9 g

Cholesterol 130 mg

## Excellent Eggplant Thai Style Chicken

Preparation time: 5 to 10 min.

Cooking Time: 10 to 15 minutes

Serving: 2

Ingredients:

- 2 boneless, skinless chicken thighs make small pieces
- 1/2 tablespoon oil
- 1/3 can of coconut milk
- 1 tablespoon red curry paste
- 2 basil leaves, julienned
- 3/4 tablespoons sugar
- 4 eggplants, make halves
- 1/8 cup chicken stock
- 2/3 tablespoons fish sauce

Directions:

1. First of all, please make sure you've all the ingredients available. Place your Instant Pot on a flat kitchen surface; plug it & turn it on.
2. Now to start making the recipe, press the "Sauté" button.
3. Add the curry paste, chicken, and two tablespoons of coconut milk; cook appropriately for about 2 to 5 minutes to soften the ingredients.
4. This step is essential. Now add the fish sauce, eggplants, the rest of the coconut milk, and stock.
5. Then carefully close its lid & firmly lock it. Then, seal the valve too.
6. To start making the recipe, press the "Manual" button. Now you have to set cooking time; set the timer for about 5 to 10 minutes.
7. Allow the pot to cook the mixture until the timer goes off.
8. Now turn off the pot & press "Cancel."
9. Allow the built-up pressure to vent out naturally; it will take 5 to 10 minutes to release inside force completely.

10. One thing remains to be done. Open its lid & transfer the cooked mixture into serving container/containers.

11. Finally, top with basil leaves. Serve with your favorite rice or salad.

Nutrition:

Calories - 388

Fat – 13g

Carbohydrates – 55.2g

Fiber – 25g

Protein – 13g

# CHAPTER 13:

# Meat

## Jamaican Jerk Pork Roast

Preparation time: 10 minutes

Cooking Time: 45 minutes

Serving: 2

Ingredients:

- 1 pounds of pork shoulder
- 1/8 cup Jamaican Jerk spice blend
- 1/8 cup olive oil
- 1/4 cup beef broth

Directions:

1. Drizzle the pork shoulder with the olive oil; reserve one tablespoon.
2. Rub the pork shoulder all over with the Jamaican Jerk spice blend.
3. Press the Sauté button and add one tablespoon of olive oil.
4. Once the oil is hot, add the pork shoulder and brown on all sides.
5. Add the beef broth; close and seal the lid.
6. Cook at high pressure for 45 minutes.
7. When the cooking is done, naturally release the pressure and remove the lid.
8. Remove the pork shoulder to a plate or cutting board and shred using two forks.
9. Serve and enjoy!

## Chinese-Style Pulled Pork

Preparation time: 25 minutes

Cooking Time: 1 hour and 30 minutes

Serving: 2

Ingredients:

- 1 pounds of pork shoulder
- 1/2 cups chicken stock
- 1/4 tablespoon Chinese five-spice seasoning
- 1/8 cup butter
- 1/8 cup coconut amino
- 1/4 tablespoon toasted sesame oil
- 1/4 teaspoon ground ginger
- 1/8 teaspoon red pepper flakes
- 1/4 teaspoon onion powder
- 1/4 teaspoon garlic powder
- 1/4 teaspoon black pepper
- 1/2 teaspoons salt

Directions:

1. na small bowl, combine the five-spice, ground ginger, red pepper flakes, onion powder, garlic powder, black pepper, and salt. Rub the pork shoulder all over the seasoning mixture.
2. Press the Sauté button and add the butter.
3. Once the butter has melted, add the pork shoulder and cook until brown on all sides. Turn off the Sauté function and remove the pork shoulder to a plate.
4. Add the chicken stock and remaining ingredients to the Instant Pot.
5. Add the pork shoulder and close the lid. Cook at high pressure for 90 minutes.
6. When the cooking is done, naturally release the pressure and remove the lid. Remove the pork shoulder to a plate and shred using two forks.
7. Return the pulled pork to the Instant Pot and stir in with the sauce. Serve!

## Fantastically Delicious Pork Stew With Poblano Peppers

Preparation time: 20 minutes

Cooking Time: 45 minutes

Serving: 2

Ingredients:

- 3/4 pounds pork shoulder, cut into bite-sized pieces
- 3/4 tablespoons olive oil
- 1/2 onions, chopped
- 1 1/2 garlic cloves, minced
- 2 tablespoons chili powder
- 1/4 tablespoon dried oregano
- 1 poblano Chile peppers, diced
- 1/4 (28-ounce) can diced tomatoes
- 1/4 lime, juiced
- 1 1/4 cups chicken broth
- 1/4 tablespoon paprika
- 1/4 teaspoon ground cumin
- 1/4 teaspoon oregano
- 1/2 teaspoons salt
- 1/2 teaspoons black pepper

Directions:

1. Press the Sauté button and add the olive oil.
2. Add the pork and cook until brown on all sides. Set aside.
3. Add the onions and garlic cloves and cook until translucent, stirring frequently.
4. Return the pork to the Instant Pot with the remaining ingredients.
5. Close and seal the lid; cook at high pressure for 30 minutes.
6. When the cooking is done, naturally release the pressure and remove the lid.
7. Stir the stew again and adjust the seasoning as needed.
8. Serve and enjoy!

## Chili-Lime Pork Spare Ribs

Preparation time: 10 minutes

Cooking Time: 30 minutes

Serving: 2

Ingredients:

- One rack baby back ribs
- One tablespoon avocado oil
- One tablespoon chili powder
- One teaspoon paprika
- One teaspoon garlic powder
- One teaspoon onion powder
- One teaspoon salt
- One teaspoon black pepper
- ½ teaspoon cayenne pepper
- Two limes, juice, and zest

Directions:

1. Drizzle the avocado oil over the ribs.
2. In a small bowl, combine the lime juice, lime zest, and seasonings. Stir until well incorporated.
3. Sprinkle the mixture over the ribs and rub it in.
4. Place 1 cup of water and a trivet into the Instant Pot.
5. Place the ribs on top of the trivet and lock the lid.
6. Cook at high pressure for 20 minutes.
7. When the cooking is done, naturally release the pressure, open and remove the lid. Serve and enjoy!

## Kalua Pork And Cabbage

Preparation time: 45 minutes

Cooking Time: 1hour and 40 minutes

Serving: 2

Ingredients:

- 4-pound bone-in pork shoulder roast
- 1/2 tablespoons salt
- 1/4 tablespoon black pepper
- 1/8 cup liquid smoke
- 1/4 cup of water
- 1/4 cabbage, chopped

Directions:

1. Sprinkle the salt and black pepper over the pork roast.
2. Pour the liquid smoke over the pork roast.
3. Place the pork roast and 1 cup of water inside your Instant Pot.
4. Lock the lid and cook at high pressure for 90 minutes.
5. When the cooking is done, naturally release the pressure and remove the lid.
6. Check if the pork is tender. Cook longer if necessary.
7. Transfer the cooked pork to a large bowl and shred using two

forks. Taste and adjust the seasoning as needed.

8. Place the chopped cabbage in the Instant Pot and cook at high pressure for 4 minutes.

9. After, quick-release the pressure and remove the lid.

10. In a large bowl, stir together the cooked pork and cabbage. Serve & enjoy!

## Very Famous Cider-Glazed Pork

Preparation time: 330 minutes

Cooking Time: 1hour and 20 minutes

Serving: 2

Ingredients:

- 2 pounds pork loin, sliced
- Four bacon slices, cooked and crumbled
- ¼ cup apple cider vinegar
- One tablespoon Dijon mustard
- Two tablespoons olive oil
- One onion, sliced
- One teaspoon garlic powder
- One teaspoon onion powder
- One teaspoon salt
- One teaspoon black pepper
- 2 cups chicken stock

Directions:

1. Press the Sauté button and add the olive oil.

2. Once the oil is hot, add the pork loin and cook until brown on all sides. Turn off the Sauté function.

3. In a bowl, stir together the apple cider, Dijon mustard, onion slices, seasonings, and chicken stock.

4. Pour over the pork loin and top with the crumbled bacon.

5. Lock on the lid and cook at high pressure for 40 minutes.

6. When the cooking is done, release the pressure for 20 minutes; open and remove the lid.

7. Place the pork slices onto plates and spoon the sauce over.

8. Serve and enjoy!

## Phenomenal Baby Back Pork Ribs

Preparation time: 10 minutes

Cooking Time: 35 minutes

Serving: 2

Ingredients:

- One rack of baby back pork ribs
- Two tablespoons olive oil
- One teaspoon garlic powder

- One teaspoon onion powder
- One teaspoon cumin
- One tablespoon parsley, freshly chopped
- One tablespoon chili powder
- One teaspoon salt
- One teaspoon black pepper
- ¼ teaspoon cayenne pepper

Barbecue Sauce Ingredients:

- ½ cup sugar-free ketchup
- One tablespoon hot sauce
- Two teaspoons yellow mustard
- One teaspoon liquid smoke
- One teaspoon Worcestershire
- ½ teaspoon chili powder
- ½ teaspoon cumin
- ¼ teaspoon cayenne pepper

Directions:
1. Drizzle the olive oil over the ribs.
2. In a small bowl, stir together all of the seasonings and parsley until well combined.
3. Sprinkle the mixture over the ribs and rub it in until well coated.
4. Place 1 cup of water and a trivet in the Instant Pot.
5. Place the ribs on top of the trivet.
6. Lock the lid and cook at high pressure for 25 minutes.
7. When the cooking is done, naturally release the pressure and remove the lid.
8. In a small bowl, add all the barbecue sauce ingredients and stir together until well combined.
9. Remove the ribs from the Instant Pot and set on a foil-lined baking sheet.
10. Brush the barbecue sauce over the ribs and place under your oven broiler for 5 minutes.
11. Serve and enjoy!

## Sky-High Garlic And Lime Pork Chops

Preparation time: 10 minutes

Cooking Time: 20 minutes

Serving: 2

Ingredients:

- Four boneless pork chops
- 2 tbsp. olive oil
- 3 tsp. coconut amino
- Four garlic cloves, minced
- 1 tsp. cumin
- 1 tsp. chili powder
- 1 tsp. paprika
- One lime, juice, and zest
- One teaspoon salt
- One teaspoon black pepper

Directions:

1. In a bowl, combine the garlic, cumin, chili powder, paprika, lime juice, lime zest, coconut amino, salt, and black pepper.

2. Place the pork chops on a plate; drizzle the marinade over both sides, rub in to make sure the chops are well-coated, and allow marinating for 20 minutes.

3. Press the Sauté button and add the olive oil.

4. Working in batches, add the pork chops and brown on both sides.

5. Place all the pork chops inside the Instant Pot and lock the lid.

6. Cook at high pressure for 15 minutes.

7. When the cooking is done, naturally release the pressure for 5 minutes and then quick-release the remaining pressure.

8. Serve and enjoy!

## Generous Ranch Pork Chops

Preparation time: 15 minutes

Cooking Time: 30 minutes

Serving: 2

Ingredients:

- 2/3 pounds boneless pork chops
- 1/3 (10.5-ounce) cream of chicken soup
- 1/3 cup of water
- 1/3 cup mayonnaise
- 1/8 cup sour cream
- 2tsp. lemon juice
- 2/3 tsp. parsley
- 1/3 teaspoon dill
- 1/8 teaspoon garlic powder
- 1/8 teaspoon onion powder
- 1/8 teaspoon salt
- 1/8 teaspoon black pepper
- 1/8 cup non-dairy milk

Directions:

1. Place all the ingredients except for the pork chops inside the Instant Pot. Stir together until well blended.

2. Add the pork chops and lock the lid.

3. Cook at high pressure for 15 minutes.

4. When the cooking is done, naturally release the pressure for 5 minutes and quick-release the remaining tension.

5. Serve and enjoy!

## Steak Pizzaiola

Preparation time: 10 minutes

Cooking Time: 20 minutes

Serving: 2

Ingredients

- 12 oz. flank steak
- One sweet bell pepper, de-seeded and sliced

- Two tablespoons Italian seasoning
- 12 oz. pasta sauce, sugar-free
- 4 oz. shredded mozzarella cheese

Directions:
1. Grease a 4-quart slow-cooker with a non-stick cooking spray.
2. Season the beef with salt, ground black pepper, and Italian seasoning, place in the slow cooker, then pour in the pasta sauce.
3. Top with peppers and cover the slow-cooker with its lid.
4. Set the cooking timer for 6 to 8 hours and cook at a low heat setting.
5. Remove the beef, and keep warm. Add the mozzarella to the slow-cooker, allowing melting, but cooking for a further 20 minutes.
6. To serve, slice the beef, and serve alongside the tomato mixture.

Nutrition:

Energy: 211 Kcal

Carbohydrates: 4 g

Net Carbs: 3.6 g

Fats: 9.4 g

Protein: 26.3 g

## Sweet And Spicy Meatballs

Preparation time: 10 minutes

Cooking Time: 8hrs

Serving: 2

Ingredients
- 12 oz. meatballs
- 14 oz. chili sauce, sugar-free
- 12 oz. raspberry jam, sugar-free

Direction:
1. Grease a 4-quart slow-cooker with a non-stick cooking spray, and place the meatballs inside.
2. Stir the chili sauce and the jam together in a bowl, and then add to the slow-cooker.
3. Cover the slow-cooker with its lid, and set the cooking timer for 8 hours, allowing cooking at a low heat setting.
4. Serve with cauliflower rice.

Nutrition:

Energy: 92 Kcal

Carbohydrates: 4.5 g

Net Carbs: 3.9 g

Fats: 5.1 g

Protein: 7 g

## Beef Ragu

Preparation time: 30 minutes

Cooking Time: 8hrs

Serving: 2

Ingredients

- 3 oz. beef short ribs, trimmed and cut into chunks
- 1/4 cup white onion, peeled and sliced
- 1 cup chopped tomatoes
- 3/4 tablespoons tomato paste, sugar-free
- 1/4 teaspoon dried basil and dried oregano

Directions:

1. Season the beef with salt and ground black pepper.
2. Place a large skillet over medium heat, add a tablespoon of olive oil, and then add the beef pieces.
3. Allow cooking for 4 to 5 minutes, turning until all sides are seared.
4. Grease a 4-quart slow-cooker with a non-stick cooking spray and add the remaining ingredients, mixing well.
5. Add the seared beef pieces, and place the lid on the slow-cooker.
6. Allow cooking for 6 to 8 hours at a low heat setting.
7. Shred the beef with forks, and return it to the cooking liquid. Allow it to sit for 15 minutes.
8. Garnish with grated cheese, and serve with zucchini noodles.

## Corned Beef And Cabbage

Preparation time: 30 minutes

Cooking Time: 6hrs

Serving: 2

Ingredients

- 1 lb. corned beef brisket
- 2/3 medium-sized carrot, peeled and cut into bite-size pieces
- 1 1/3 cups shredded cabbage
- 1/8 corned beef spiced packet
- 1/4 cup of water

Directions:

1. Rub the meat with the corned beef spice packet.
2. Grease a 4-quart slow-cooker with a non-stick cooking spray and add the carrots and the cabbage.
3. Pour in water, and then top with the seasoned beef.
4. Cover the slow-cooker with its lid, and set the cooking timer for 6 hours, allowing cooking at low heat. Serve the meat immediately, with the vegetables alongside.

Nutrition:

Energy: 334 Kcal Carbohydrates: 8.1 g

Net Carbs: 5.5 g Fats: 22.8 g

Protein: 24.7 g

## Ancho-Beef Stew

Preparation time: 40 minutes

Cooking Time: 8-10 minutes

Serving: 2

Ingredients

- 8 oz. boneless beef chuck pot roast, trimmed
- 16 oz. low-carb vegetables
- One tablespoon ground ancho-chile pepper
- 12 oz. tomato salsa, sugar-free
- 1 1/2 cups of beef broth

Directions:

1. Cut meat into bite-size pieces and season on all sides with the ancho-chile pepper.
2. Place a large non-stick skillet pan over medium-high heat; add one tablespoon olive oil and seasoned beef.
3. Allow cooking for 5 to 7 minutes, or until browned on all sides. Depending on the size of your pan, you can cook the beef chunks in batches.
4. Grease a 4-quart slow-cooker with a non-stick cooking spray and add the vegetables.
5. Top with the browned meat and season with salt and ground black pepper.
6. Stir in the tomato salsa and the beef broth, and then cover the slow-cooker with its lid.
7. Set the cooking timer for 8 to 10 hours, allowing the meat to cook at a low heat setting or until beef is cooked through.
8. Serve the meat warm, with the vegetables alongside.

Nutrition:

Energy: 288 Kcal

Carbohydrates: 8 g

Net Carbs: 6 g

Fats: 20 g

Protein: 20 g

## Cider Braised Beef Pot Roast

Preparation time: 30 minutes

Cooking Time: 8hrs

Serving: 2

Ingredients

- 8 oz. boneless chuck pot roast, trimmed
- 1/2 cup chopped white onion
- One teaspoon garlic powder
- 1/4 cup apple cider vinegar
- 1/4 teaspoon xanthan gum

Directions:

1. Season the chuck roast with the garlic powder, salt, and ground black pepper.
2. Place a large non-stick skillet pan over medium-high heat, add a tablespoon of olive oil, and then add the meat.
3. Allow cooking for 7 to 10 minutes, turning until it has browned on all sides.
4. Grease a 4-quart slow-cooker with a non-stick cooking spray and add the browned meat.
5. Top with the onion and pour in the vinegar and 1 1/2 cups of water.
6. Cover the slow-cooker with its lid, and set the cooking timer for 8 hours, allowing the meat to cook at a low heat setting.
7. Place the meat on a plate, then shred using forks, and keep warm.
8. Transfer the remaining mixture to a saucepan, add the xanthan gum, and bring to boil, allowing cooking until sauce reduces to the desired thickness.
9. Serve the meat with the sauce alongside.

Nutrition:

Energy: 393 Kcal

Carbohydrates: 4 g

Net Carbs: 3 g

Fats: 28 g

Protein: 30 g

## Cajun Pot Roast

Preparation time: 45 minutes

Cooking Time: 6-8hrs

Serving: 2

Ingredients:

- 4 1/2 oz. boneless beef chuck roast, trimmed
- 1/4 white onion, peeled and chopped
- 3 1/2 oz. diced tomatoes with garlic,
- 1/4 tablespoon Cajun seasoning,
- 1/4 teaspoon Tabasco sauce

Directions:

1. Season the beef on all sides with the Cajun seasoning mix.
2. Grease a 4-quart slow-cooker with a non-stick cooking spray, add the seasoned beef, and top with the onion.
3. In a bowl, stir together the tomato with garlic, the Tabasco sauce, and a pinch of salt and ground black pepper.
4. Pour the tomato mixture over the vegetables and beef, and then cover the slow-cooker with its lid.
5. Set the cooking timer for 6 to 8 hours and cook at a low heat setting.

6. To serve, transfer the beef to a serving platter, then top with onion and tomato mixture.

Nutrition:

Energy: 314 Kcal

Carbohydrates: 10.4 g

Net Carbs: 8.2 g

Fats: 15.1 g

Protein: 38 g

## Sloppy Joes

Preparation time: 30 minutes

Cooking Time: 6-8hrs

Serving: 2

Ingredients:

- 1/3 lb. ground beef
- 2/3 tablespoon Worcestershire sauce
- 1/3 tablespoon Dijon mustard
- 1/3 cup Picante Sauce, sugar-free
- 1/4 cup hot barbecue sauce, sugar-free

Directions:

1. Place a large non-stick skillet pan over medium-high heat, and add the beef.
2. Cook for 8 to 10 minutes, stirring regularly until the meat is no longer pink.
3. Drain the fat from the mixture, and transfer to a 4-quart slow-cooker.
4. Stir in the remaining ingredients, and season with salt and black pepper.
5. Seal the slow-cooker with its lid, then set the cooking timer for 6 to 8 hours, allow the mixture to cook at a low heat setting.
6. To serve, place a generous helping of the mixture on roasted Portobello mushroom caps and top with a second Portobello mushroom cap.

Nutrition:

Energy: 162.5 Kcal

Carbohydrates: 2.5 g

Net Carbs: 2.5 g

Fats: 4.5 g

Protein: 24 g

## Moroccan Beef Lettuce Wraps

Preparation time: 30minutes

Cooking Time: 10hrs

Serving: 2

Ingredients:

- 12 oz. beef roast, trimmed and cut into bite-size pieces
- 1 cup sliced white onions
- One teaspoon sea salt
- Four tablespoons garam masala,
- Ten large lettuce leaves, for wrapping

Directions:

1. Grease a 4-quart slow-cooker and add all the ingredients apart from the lettuce.
2. Cover and seal slow-cooker with its lid.
3. Set the cooking timer for 8 hours and allow you to cook at a low heat setting.
4. Remove the beef, and shred it using forks. Place the meat back in the slow-cooker, and continue cooking for another 2 hours.
5. Serve warm, wrapped in the lettuce leaves.

Nutrition:

Energy: 209 Kcal

Carbohydrates: 0.7 g

Net Carbs: 0.7 g

Fats: 9.5 g

Protein: 30.4 g

## Steak Fajitas

Preparation time: 10 minutes

Cooking Time: 50 minutes

Servings: 2

Ingredients

- 16 oz. flank steak
- One red and one green bell pepper, de-seeded and sliced
- One white onion, peeled and sliced
- Two tablespoons fajita seasoning,
- 20 oz. tomato salsa, sugar-free

Directions:

1. Grease a 4-quart slow-cooker with a non-stick cooking spray and then pour the salsa in.
2. Place the peppers and onion on top, and sprinkle with the fajita seasoning.
3. Stir until mixed well, then cover and seal the slow-cooker with its lid.
4. Set the cooking timer for 3 to 4 hours and cook at a high heat setting.
5. Serve with shredded cheese and sour cream.

Nutrition:

Energy: 222 Kcal  Carbohydrates: 5 g

Net Carbs: 4 g  Fats: 12 g

Protein: 23 g

## Beef And Eggplant

Preparation time: 30 minutes

Cooking Time: 4.5hrs

Serving: 2

Ingredients:

- 2/3 lb. ground beef

- 1 can of chopped tomatoes
- 2/3 medium-sized eggplant, de-stemmed
- 1 tablespoon Lebanese Spice Blend
- 2/3 cup shredded mozzarella cheese

Directions:
1. Cut the eggplant into large chunks and add to a 4-quart slow-cooker, greased with non-stick cooking spray.
2. Stir together the ground beef and the spice blend, and season with salt and ground black pepper. Place this over the eggplant.
3. Pour over the chopped tomato, and then place the lid on the slow-cooker.
4. Set the cooking timer for 4 hours and allow you to cook at a low heat setting.
5. Add the shredded mozzarella and cook for a further 30 minutes, until the cheese is melted.
6. Garnish with parsley to serve.

Nutrition:

Energy: 209 Kcal  Carbohydrates: 8.1 g

Net Carbs: 7.4 g Fats: 12.8 g

Protein: 15.9 g

## Barbecue Pulled Beef

Preparation time: 30 minutes

Cooking Time: 4hrs

Serving: 2

Ingredients
- 12 oz. beef pot roast, trimmed and cut into bite-sized pieces
- One teaspoon minced garlic
- One teaspoon onion powder
- 1/4 cup apple cider vinegar
- 3/4 cup tomato ketchup, sugar-free

Directions:
1. Grease a 4-quart slow-cooker with a non-stick cooking spray.
2. Mix all of the ingredients, apart from the beef, and place the mixture in the slow-cooker.
3. Add the beef pieces and season with a pinch of salt and ground black pepper.
4. Cover and seal the slow-cooker with its lid, setting the cooking timer for 4 hours, and allowing cooking at a high heat setting.
5. Shred the meat with forks, and serve between roasted Portobello mushroom caps.

Nutrition:

Energy: 380 Kcal

Carbohydrates: 6 g

Net Carbs: 5.2 g

Fats: 15 g

Protein: 49 g

## Chili With Beef

Preparation time: 35 minutes

Cooking Time: 6-8hrs

Serving: 2

Ingredients

- 1/3 lb. ground beef
- 2/3 cans diced tomatoes with green chilies
- 2/3 white onions, diced
- 1 1/3 garlic cloves, minced
- 1/2 tablespoon Mexican seasoning
- 2 oz. tomato paste

Directions:

1. Place a large skillet pan over medium-high heat, add the beef, half of both the garlic and the onion, and a pinch of salt and ground black pepper.
2. Cook for 5 to 7 minutes, stirring regularly until the meat is nicely golden brown.
3. Drain off the fat, and add to the slow-cooker.
4. Stir in remaining ingredients, and place the lid on the slow-cooker.
5. Set the cooking timer for 6 to 8 hours and cook at a low heat setting.
6. To serve, allow people to help themselves to cilantro, grated cheese, and sour cream.

Nutrition:

Energy: 306 Kcal

Carbohydrates: 13 g

Net Carbs: 10 g

Fats: 18 g

Protein: 23 g

## Thit Bo Xao Dua

Preparation time: 15 minutes

Cooking Time: 20 minutes

Serving: 2

Ingredients:

- One bowl beef chunks
- One minced garlic clove
- Pepper
- 1 tsp. cornstarch
- 3 tbsp. oil
- 1/2 thinly sliced onion
- 2 cups trimmed green beans
- 1/4 cup chicken stock
- 1 tsp. soy sauce

Directions:

1. Mix garlic paste, pepper, cornstarch, and oil in a bowl and add the beef chunks.
2. Heat oil and cook the marinated beef till it turns brown.
3. Cook onions in some oil till soft. Transfer beans and broth to it.

4. Boil till beans turn tender and add the soy sauce and beef. Serve.

Nutrition:

Net carbs: 6.3grams

Proteins: 23.1grams

Fats: 28.6grams

Calories: 376kcal

## The Best Meatloaf

Preparation time: 10 minutes

Cooking Time: 1hr

Serving: 2

Baked minced mutton with plenty of low-carb ingredients can be a perfect lunch or dinner.

Ingredients:

- 1/8 cup milk
- 1/3 cup bread crumbs
- 1-1/2 cup minced mutton
- Salt
- Pepper
- 1 whisked egg
- 1 tbsp. low-carb steak sauce
- 1/3 chopped onion
- 1/8 cup diced bell pepper

Directions:

1. Preheat oven to 350F.
2. Dip the bread crumbs in milk till they become mushy.
3. Assemble the mutton, salt, pepper, egg, steak sauce, onion, and bell pepper in a bowl and pour the breadcrumb mixture over it.
4. Combine well and pour on a loaf pan.
5. Bake for an hour. Slice and serve.

Nutrition:

Net carbs: 10.1grams

Proteins: 20.9grams

Fats: 17.9grams

Calories: 288kcal

## Super Delicious Meatballs

Preparation time: 15 minutes

Cooking Time: 45 minutes

Serving: 2

Nothing tastes better than meatballs with herbs and cheese. Try it for lunch or dinner.

Ingredients:

- 1/4 pound minced lamb meat
- 1/8 pound ground veal and pork
- 1/2 minced garlic cloves
- 1/2 egg
- 1/4 cup shredded cheese
- 1-1/2 cup parsley
- Salt
- Pepper
- 1/4 cup of warm water
- 1/4 cup olive oil

Directions:

1. Mix meat, pork, and veal in a bowl. Add garlic, cheese, parsley,

salt, and pepper to it and combine well.
2. Add the little warm water to the mixture and roll it into meatballs.
3. Fry the balls in oil till brown and serve.

Nutrition:

Net carbs: 6.6grams

Proteins: 26.6grams

Fats: 53.2grams

Calories: 613kcal

## Rolled Flank Steak

Preparation time: 10 minutes

Cooking Time: 50 minutes

Serving: 2

Ingredients:

- 2 pounds beef flank steak
- 1/4 cup soy sauce
- 1/2 cup olive oil
- 2 tsp. steak seasoning
- 8 ounces sliced cheese
- Four slices cut bacon
- 1/2 cup spinach and mushrooms
- 1/2 diced bell pepper

Directions:

1. Cut the flank steaks into strips.
2. Combine soy sauce, oil, and steak seasoning in a Ziploc bag and marinate the beef overnight.
3. Preheat the oven to 350F.
4. Layer the beef strips with cheese, bacon, spinach, bell pepper, and mushrooms and roll the strips into a wheel.
5. Bake the beef wheels for 15 minutes at 145F. Serve.

## Foolproof Rib Roast

Preparation time: 15 minutes

Cooking Time: 3hrs and 30 minutes

Serving: 2

Ingredients:

- 1/3 pound lamb or beef ribs
- Salt
- Pepper
- 1/3 tsp. garlic powder

Directions:

1. Preheat the oven to 375F.
2. Mix salt, pepper, and garlic powder in a small bowl.
3. Adjust the ribs on a grill with the fatty side up.
4. Thoroughly season it with the spice mix.
5. Roast for an hour and let it rest in the oven for 3 hours.
6. Before serving, roast it again for 30 minutes.

Nutrition:

Net carbs: 0.6grams

Proteins: 37grams

Fats: 46.2grams

Calories: 576kcal

## London Broil

Preparation time: 12hrs

Cooking Time: 7 minutes

Serving: 2

Marinated and grilled steak is a fantastic lunch or dinner option.

Ingredients:

- 1/4 minced garlic clove
- Salt
- 3/4 tbsp. soy sauce
- 1/4 tbsp. tomato puree
- 1/4 tbsp. olive oil
- Pepper
- 1/8 tsp. oregano
- 1 pounds flank steak

Directions:

1. Combine all the ingredients in a bowl to make a subtle marinade.
2. Make deep cuts into the meat and rub the marinade all over it.
3. Marinate overnight.
4. Grease the grill with some oil and preheat it.
5. Grill the meat for 7 minutes per side till it is done. Serve.

Nutrition:

Net carbs: 1.2grams

Proteins: 48.6grams

Fats: 20.6grams

Calories: 396kcal

## German Rouladen

Preparation time: 15 minutes

Cooking Time: 1hr

Serving: 2

Bacon and a few other ingredients rolled into a filet is a perfect low-carb recipe.

Ingredients:

- 1-1/2 cup lamb steak
- Ground mustard
- 1/8 pound sliced bacon
- 1 sliced onion
- 1/3 jar of dill pickles
- 2tbsp. butter
- 2-1/2 cups water
- 1/3 cup bone broth

Directions:

1. Chop the flanks into filets.
2. Rub mustard on each filet on one side.
3. Adjust bacon, onions, and pickles on the fillets and make a roll of each.
4. Melt butter and sauté the rolls to brown.

5. Boil water and bone broth and add the rolls. Cook for an hour. Serve.

Nutrition:

Net carbs: 7.7grams

Proteins: 19.1grams

Fats: 17.4grams

Calories: 264kcal

## Jalapeno Steak

Preparation time: 10 minutes

Cooking Time: 5 minutes

Serving: 2

Grilled steak with a lot of jalapenos is a low-carb dish relished by all.

Ingredients:

- 1 1/3 sliced jalapeno
- 1 1/3 peeled garlic cloves
- Pepper
- Salt
- 1/8 cup lime juice
- 1/3 tbsp. dried oregano
- 1-1/2 pound sirloin steak

Directions:

1. Grind all the ingredients in a mixer into a fine blend.
2. Place the steak in a Ziploc bag and pour over the marinade.
3. Marinate overnight.
4. Preheat an oil-coated grill and adjust the marinated steak on it.
5. Grill for 5 minutes on each side till it is tender. Serve.

Nutrition:

Net carbs: 3.1grams

Proteins: 19.1grams

Fats: 10.5grams

Calories: 186kcal

Serving size: 6

## Mexican Beef Supreme

Preparation time: 10 minutes

Cooking Time: 10 minutes

Serving: 2

Beef cooked in plenty of veggies and herbs makes a hunger-killer dinner.

Ingredients:

- 1 tbsp. olive oil
- One diced onion
- 1 pound beef stew meat
- 1 tsp. minced garlic
- 2 tsp. lime juice
- One chopped jalapeno
- Three chopped green onions
- 1/4 cup chopped cilantro
- 1 tsp. dried oregano
- One can green salsa

Directions:

1. Heat oil and sauté the onions till soft.
2. Add beef and garlic and cook till meat turns brown.
3. Combine the rest of the ingredients in a bowl and stir into the pot.
4. Cook for 10 minutes till meat is done. Serve.

Nutrition:

Net carbs: 8.6grams

Proteins: 30.2grams

Fats: 27.9grams

Calories: 414kcal

# CHAPTER 14:

# Vegetables

## Supreme Air-Fried Tofu

Preparation time: 20 minutes

Cooking Time: 55 minutes

Serving: 2

Ingredients:

- One block of pressed and sliced into 1-inch cubes of extra-firm tofu
- Two tablespoons of soy sauce
- One teaspoon of seasoned rice vinegar
- Two teaspoons of toasted sesame oil
- One tablespoon of cornstarch

Directions:

1. Using a bowl, add and toss the tofu, soy sauce, seasoned rice vinegar, sesame oil until it is adequately covered.
2. Place it inside your refrigerator and allow it to marinate for 30 minutes.
3. Preheat your air fryer to 370 degrees Fahrenheit.
4. Add the cornstarch to the tofu mixture and toss it until it is adequately covered.
5. Grease your air fryer basket with a nonstick cooking spray and add the tofu inside your basket.
6. Cook it for 20 minutes at 370 degrees Fahrenheit, and shake it after 10 minutes.
7. Serve and enjoy!

Nutrition:

Calories: 80, Fat: 5.8g, Protein: 5g, Carbohydrates: 3g, Dietary Fiber: 1.2g

## Not Your Average Zucchini Parmesan Chips

Preparation time: 10 minutes

Cooking Time: 15 minutes

Serving: 2

Ingredients:

- Two thinly sliced zucchinis
- One beaten egg
- ½ cup of panko breadcrumbs
- ½ cup of grated Parmesan cheese
- One teaspoon of salt
- One teaspoon of black pepper

Directions:

1. Prepare your zucchini by using a mandolin or a knife to slice the zucchinis thinly.
2. Use a cloth to pat dry the zucchini chips.
3. Then using a bowl, add the eggs and beat it properly. After that, pick another bowl, and add the breadcrumbs, Parmesan cheese, salt, and black pepper.
4. Dredge the zucchini chips into the egg mixture and then cover it with the Parmesan-breadcrumb mixture.
5. Grease the battered zucchini chips with a nonstick cooking spray and place it inside your air fryer.
6. Cook it for 8 minutes at 350 degrees Fahrenheit.
7. Once done, carefully remove it from your air fryer and sprinkle another teaspoon of salt to give it some taste.
8. Serve and enjoy!

Nutrition:

Calories: 100, Fat: 16g, Protein: 4g, Carbohydrates 9g, Dietary Fiber: 1.8g

## Outstanding Batter-Fried Scallions

Preparation time: 10 minutes

Cooking Time: 10 minutes

Serving: 2

Ingredients:

- Four bunches of trimmed scallions
- 1 cup of flour
- 1 cup of white wine
- One teaspoon of salt
- One teaspoon of black pepper

Directions:

1. Preheat your air fryer to 390 degrees Fahrenheit.
2. Using a bowl, add and mix the white wine, the flour and stir until it gets smooth.
3. Add the salt, the black pepper, and mix again.
4. Dip each scallion into the flour mixture until it is adequately covered and remove any excess batter.
5. Grease your air fryer basket with a nonstick cooking spray and add the scallions. At this point, you may need to work in batches.
6. Cook the scallions for 3 to 5 minutes or until it has a golden brown color and crispy texture, while still shaking it after every 2 minutes.

7. Carefully remove it from your air fryer and check if it's correctly done. Then allow it to cool before serving.

8. Serve and enjoy!

Nutrition:

Calories: 190, Fat: 22g, Protein: 4g, Carbohydrates: 9g, Dietary Fiber: 0.8g

## Delectable French Green Beans With Shallots And Almonds

Preparation time: 15 minutes

Cooking Time: 25 minutes

Serving: 2

Ingredients:

- 1 ½ pound of steamed French green beans
- ½ pound of peeled, stemmed quartered shallots
- ¼ cup of lightly toasted slivered almonds
- Two tablespoons of olive oil
- One tablespoon of salt
- One teaspoon of garlic salt
- One teaspoon of white pepper

Directions:

1. Using a large pot, fill it with water and boil it under an average pressure of heat.

2. Add the green beans, a tablespoon of salt, stir for a while, and cook it for 2 minutes.

3. Once done, drain it using a colander and allow it to cool off.

4. Using a large bowl, add the green beans, shallots, garlic salt, white pepper, olive oil, and toss it until it is adequately covered.

5. Place the green beans and shallots inside your air fryer basket and cook it for 25 minutes at a 400 degrees Fahrenheit, shaking it halfway through.

6. Then pick a large bowl, add the cooked green beans, shallots, almonds and toss it until it is adequately covered.

7. Serve and enjoy!

Nutrition:

Calories: 110, Fat: 9g, Protein: 3g, Carbohydrates: 7g, Dietary Fiber: 4g

## Super-Healthy Air-Fried Green Tomatoes

Preparation time: 10 minutes

Cooking Time: 25 minutes

Serving: 2

Ingredients:

- Four sliced into ¼-inch pieces green tomatoes
- Two beaten eggs

- Two tablespoons of milk
- 1 cup of flour
- ½ cup of cornmeal
- ½ cup of panko breadcrumbs
- One teaspoon of garlic powder
- One teaspoon of paprika
- One teaspoon of salt
- One teaspoon of black pepper

Directions:

1. Using a bowl, add 1 cup of flour.
2. Pick a second bowl, add the eggs, milk, and mix properly.
3. Using a third bowl, add the cornmeal, panko breadcrumbs, and seasonings and mix properly.
4. For each tomato slice, dredge it in the flour, dip it into the egg mixture, and then cover it with the cornmeal-breadcrumb mixture.
5. Grease your air fryer basket with a nonstick cooking spray.
6. Working in batches, add the green tomatoes, cook it for 20 minutes at 360 degrees Fahrenheit of heat, and flip it after 10 minutes.
7. Repeat the above step with any leftover. Serve and enjoy!

Nutrition:

Calories: 190, Fat: 12g, Protein: 4g, Dietary Fiber: 6g, Protein: 4.25g

## Luscious Air-Fried Broccoli Crisps

Preparation time: 10 minutes

Cooking Time: 35 minutes

Serving: 2

Ingredients:

- One large chopped into florets broccoli head
- Two tablespoons of olive oil
- One teaspoon of salt
- One teaspoon of black pepper

Directions:

1. Preheat your air fryer to 360 degrees Fahrenheit.
2. Using a bowl, add and toss the broccoli florets with the olive oil, salt, and black pepper.
3. Add the broccoli florets and cook it for 12 minutes, then shake after 6 minutes.
4. Carefully remove it from your air fryer and allow it to cool off.
5. Serve and enjoy!

Nutrition:

Calories: 120, Fat: 19g, Protein: 4.5g, Carbohydrates: 8.3g, Dietary Fiber: 4.5g

## Veggie Tuna Salad

Preparation time: 10 minutes

Cooking Time: 5 minutes

Serving: 2

Ingredients:

- Tomatoes (6, plum, chopped)
- Celery (8 stalks, leafy, chopped)
- Onion (1, medium, chopped)
- Chickpeas (1 can be drained)
- Black olives (½ cup, black, pitted, coarsely chopped).
- Parsley leaves (½ cup, fresh, chopped)
- Lemons (2)
- Tuna (2 cans, drained, flaked)
- Olive oil (1/3 cup)

Directions:

1. In a bowl, combine the tomatoes, chickpeas, celery, parsley, olives, and onion.
2. When finished, add the tuna flakes and mix them thoroughly until combined.
3. Add the olive oil and lemon juice to the salad and mix well.
4. Season salad with pepper and salt before serving. Enjoy!

Nutrition:

Total carbs per serving: 5.2g

## Creamy Green Beans

Preparation time: 10 minutes

Cooking Time: 13 minutes

Serving: 1

This Creamy green bean recipe is a nutritious and tasty meal, perfect for you and your family.

Ingredients:

- Double cream (4 tbsp.)
- Sour cream (5 tbsp.)
- Green beans (300 g)
- Dijon mustard (2 tbsp.)
- Capers (1 tbsp., chopped)
- Zest of half of lemon

Directions:

1. In boiling water, cook green beans for 5 minutes.
2. Afterward, combine sour cream, capers, double cream, lemon zest, and mustard altogether.
3. When beans are finished cooking, season with salt and pepper, serve immediately for best taste.

Nutrition:

Total carbs per serving: 2.1g

## Stir-Fried Steak With Asparagus

Preparation time: 10 minutes

Cooking Time: 15 minutes

Serving: 1

An easy way to make a delicious recipe. Sure to leave you craving.

Ingredients:

- Sirloin steak (12 oz., boneless, ¼ inch strips)
- Canola oil (5 tsp., divided)
- Cornstarch (1 tsp.)
- Garlic (2 tsp., minced)
- Ginger (2 tsp., fresh, peeled, grated)
- Soy sauce (1 ½ tbsp., low sodium)
- Oyster sauce (1 ½ tbsp.)
- Chicken stock (¼ cup, unsalted)
- Bell pepper (1, red, medium, cut into strips)
- Asparagus (1 ¼ cup, medium, cut into 2' pieces)
- Onions (3, green, chopped)
- Red pepper (½ tsp., crushed)

Directions:

1. In a bowl, combine oyster sauce, chicken stock, fresh ginger, soy sauce. Ensure to use a whisk to stir.
2. When finished, heat skillet over medium-high heat and add a tsp. of oil, add beef and stir-fry until it becomes brown.
3. Transfer beef to another plate and discard liquid.
4. Add two additional tbsp. of oil into the skillet, add the asparagus and bell pepper, and stir-fry for an additional 2 minutes, then reduce the heat to medium-high.
5. Pour the stock mixture into skillet and cook until the sauce becomes thick, about 3 minutes.
6. Return juices to the skillet and continue cooking for an additional minute. Serve.

Nutrition:

Total carbs per serving: 9g

## The Great Gazpacho

Preparation time: 10 minutes

Cooking Time: 2-4 hrs.

Serving: 2

A healthy, warm gazpacho was sure to leave you speechless.

Ingredients:

- Lime juice (1 tbsp., fresh)
- Garlic (1 clove)
- Onion (¼ cup, sweet, chopped)
- Cucumber (1, English, peeled, chopped)
- Bell pepper (1, red, seeded, chopped)
- Tomatoes (500 g, cored, chopped)
- Wine vinegar (3 tbsp., red)

- Olive oil (1 tsp.)
- Parsley (2 tbsp., fresh, chopped)
- Kosher salt (¾ - 1 tsp.)
- Tomato juice (2 cups)
- Red pepper flakes
- Ground black pepper

Directions:
1. Place tomatoes, cucumber, pepper, onion, garlic clove, tomato juice, lime juice, olive oil, and herbs in a blender and process mixture until smooth.
2. Add your kosher salt, red pepper flakes, and wine vinegar and process until you achieve the desired taste.
3. Refrigerate for 2-4 hours if desired or overnight.
4. Drizzle the 1 tsp. olive oil on top and use green onion, black pepper, and chopped peppers. Enjoy.

Nutrition: Total carbs per serving: 2.3g

## Mexican Surprise

Preparation time: 20 minutes

Cooking Time: 55 minutes

Serving: 2

That is certainly a surprise because one bite cannot be forgotten. A delicious authentic dish.

Ingredients:
- Salsa (1/3 cup)
- Cheddar cheese (1 cup, shredded)
- Sour cream (½ cup, fat, reduced)
- Skim milk (1 cup)
- Egg (1, whole)
- Egg whites (3)
- Turkey sausage (6 oz., ground)
- Bread (5 slices, brown, cubed)

Directions:
1. The first step is to use some cooking spray to spray a pie dish.
2. When finished, evenly place bread cubes on the pie dish you have prepared and set aside.
3. In a medium-high skillet, cook sausage until well browned and ensure that you break up the pieces, as required.
4. Place the sausage on top of the bread cubes, beat egg whites, sour cream, milk, and whole egg in a bowl.
5. Add the cheddar cheese and mix until combined thoroughly.
6. When finished, pour cheese and egg mixture over sausage and let freeze for approximately 2 hours or overnight.
7. After removing from the fridge, bake for a minimum of 35 minutes in an oven at 325

degrees Celsius and let mixture stand for about 10 minutes.

8. After 10 minutes has elapsed, begin to cut the bread. For tastiest results, top each slice of Mexican surprise with salsa.

Nutrition:

Total carbs per serving: 8g

## Cheesy Kale and Tomato Chips

Preparation time: 12.5hrs

Cooking Time: 12hrs 30 minutes

Serving: 1

This exotic Cheesy kale Tomato Chip is a healthy and nutritious alternative for regular chips.

Ingredients:

- Tomatoes (30 g, organic)
- Tomatoes (2, sun-dried, soaked for about an hour in water)
- Kale (1 bunch, stems removed, leaves ripped)
- Garlic (2 cloves, large)
- Cashews (1 cup, raw)
- Basil (2-4 tbsp., fresh)
- Tomato soaking water (¾ cup + 2 tbsp.)
- Sea salt (¾ tbsp.)
- Nutritional yeast (2 tbsp.)
- Lemon juice (2 tbsp., fresh)

Directions:

1. The first step is to soak cashews and tomatoes together for about an hour in the water until they are softened.
2. Set aside soaking water after removing cashews and tomatoes.
3. In a food processor, pulse until thoroughly minced.
4. When finished, add the remaining ingredients except for sea salt and process until smooth.
5. Add salt when finished for additional taste.
6. After kale leaves have been washed, tear them into small pieces, and ensure to discard stems.
7. Afterward, pour the cheesy sauce that you have made over the kale and stir until well coated.
8. Place the kale into a dehydrator and process at 110 Fahrenheit for approximately 12 hours. Once chips become crispy, it means that they're ready to be served. Enjoy!

Nutrition:

Total carbs per serving: 5.5g

## Super Stacked Eggplants

Preparation time: 10 minutes

Cooking Time: 1hr

Serving: 2

A mouthwatering recipe that is fit for you and your family.

Ingredients:

- Red wine vinegar (3 tbsp.)
- Olive Oil (6 ½ tbsp.)
- Oregano (1 tbsp., dried)
- Garlic (1 clove, large, pressed)
- Salt (1 tsp.)
- Pumpkin seeds (¼ cup, toasted)
- Parmesan Cheese (¼ cup, grated)
- Basil leaves (1 cup)
- Eggplant (1, 1-1 ½' thick pieces)
- Black pepper (1/8 tsp., ground)
- Mozzarella (4 oz., fresh, sliced thinly)
- Tomato (1, medium, sliced thinly)
- Balsamic vinegar (1 tsp.)

Directions:

1. Combine red wine vinegar, oregano, olive oil, garlic, salt, and pepper altogether in a large bowl.
2. Add the eggplant and begin to toss until thoroughly combined.
3. Let mixture stand for approximately an hour and ensure to turn the eggplant occasionally.
4. Pulse basil, parmesan, pine nuts, and the olive oil in a food processor until a paste is formed and transfer to a bowl. Use plastic wrap to cover and secure.
5. Combine balsamic vinegar, ½ tsp. of salt and ¼ oil with tomato (sliced) and black pepper (pinch) on a pie plate. Gradually mix until tomatoes are well coated.
6. Evenly arrange the pieces by placing each eggplant slice on a platter and evenly spreading ½ tsp. of pesto on top of each.
7. Use a slice of tomato and a slice of mozzarella to top. Add eggplant pesto, cheese, and tomato. Drizzle the eggplant stacks with remaining juice from cooking (optional). Serve.

Nutrition: Total carbs per serving: 3.25g

## Turnips And Caviar Afternoon Snack

Preparation time: 10 minutes

Cooking Time: 20 minutes

Serving: 1

Ingredients:

- Turnips (4, small, peeled, sliced)
- Caviar
- Olive oil

Directions:

1. The first step is to preheat the oven to 400 degrees F. In a small bowl, place some olive oil and start to dip the turnips in the bowl.
2. Place the olive oil-coated turnips on a baking sheet coated with wax paper.
3. Use pepper and salt to season. Bake the turnips for approximately 15 minutes or until it becomes golden brown. Ensure to flip the turnips to bake evenly on each side.
4. When baked, top with a little sour cream and a small amount of caviar.

Nutrition: Total carbs per serving: 8g

## Roasted Vegetables In Herbs

Preparation time: 5 minutes

Cooking Time: 40 minutes

Serving: 1

A meal fit for a family; this recipe will have your family members begging for the recipe.

Ingredients:

- Onion (1, small, red, sliced)
- Parsnip (1, medium, peeled, 1" pieces)
- Carrots (2, peeled, 1" pieces)
- Potatoes (2, medium, sweet, 1" cubes)
- Black pepper (½ tsp., ground)
- Salt (½ tsp.)
- Basil (2 tsp.)
- Thyme (2 tsp.)
- Oregano (2 tsp.)
- Garlic (3 cloves, minced)

Directions:

1. Heat the oven to 425 degrees Fahrenheit. Place the potatoes, carrots, onion, and parsnip in a baking dish.
2. Mix the garlic, herbs, oil, salt, and pepper in a medium-sized bowl and pour mixture over the vegetables. Mix until well coated.
3. Bake dish for approximately 30 minutes, ensuring that it is adequately covered.
4. Stir vegetables and bake for an extra 10 minutes, then serve.

Nutrition: Total carbs per serving: 4.5g

## Salmon Croquettes

Preparation time: 10 minutes

Cooking Time: 20 minutes

Serving: 2

These Salmon Croquettes are a fantastic meal that is sure to leave you craving for more.

Ingredients:

- Salmon (1, 15 oz. Can drain)

- Soy flour (2 tbsp.)
- Egg (1)
- Onion (¼ cup, green, minced)
- Salt and pepper (for seasoning)
- Olive oil

Directions:

1. Place salmon in a medium-sized bowl, then remove any skin and bones.
2. When finished, use a fork and mash the salmon before adding in the following: egg, flour, and onions. Add pepper and salt to taste.
3. Form small patties, using the mixture.
4. Each patty should not exceed 2 inches in diameter. When finished, heat 2-2 ½ tablespoon of olive oil in a medium-sized skillet and fry patties until cakes become golden brown. Ensure not to burn them.
5. When cooked, place croquettes on a paper towel to drain the excess oil. Serve with sour cream and hot sauce.

Nutrition:

Carbs per serving: Less than 1g per patty

# Red Grapefruit Salad

Preparation time: 15 minutes

Cooking Time: 25 minutes

Serving: 2

This Red Grapefruit Salad is a naturally sweet, healthy, and delicious recipe that combines sweet and juicy fruits with vegetables.

Ingredients:

- Grapefruit (2 pcs, white, sectioned)
- Grapefruit (2 pcs, red or pink, sectioned)
- Tarragon leaf (1 tsp.)
- Mustard seeds (¼ tsp., yellow)
- Olive oil (3 tbsps.)
- Salad leaves (5 cups, mixed, fresh)
- Onion (½, small, red, chopped)

Directions:

1. The first step is to cut each grapefruit by removing the membranes and outer covering.
2. When finished, squeeze out all remaining juice and set aside in a small bowl for further use.
3. For the dressing:
4. Take 1 tbsp. of grapefruit juice and mix with the mustard seeds in a small mixing bowl.
5. Whisk together with the olive oil until thoroughly blended. Add in the salt, tarragon, and pepper (freshly grounded) for seasoning.

6. Taste occasionally and adjust accordingly to preference.
7. Place the salad leaves, grapefruits, and red onion in another salad bowl. Pour in the dressing and lightly toss.

Nutrition:

Total carbs per serving: 11g

## Stuffed Cherry Tomatoes

Preparation time: 10 minutes

Cooking Time: 20 minutes

Serving: 2

Ingredients:

- 3 large cherry Tomatoes
- 1/4 stalk, finely chopped Celery
- 1 1/3 tbsp. Mayonnaise
- 1/4 cup Tuna
- 1/2, small, finely chopped Onion

Directions:

1. The first step is to slice a small portion from each tomato's top and begin to core them out.
2. Discard the cores and set tomatoes aside. Place the tuna, celery, mayonnaise, and onion together in a medium-sized bowl.
3. Mix ingredients thoroughly using a spatula. Afterward, fill the tomatoes with the mix.
4. Place into a small decorative dish and serve.

Nutrition: Total carbs per serving: 9g

## Scrambled Egg Burritos Served With Black Bean Salsa

Preparation time: 20 minutes

Cooking Time: 20 minutes

Serving: 2

Ingredients:

For the burritos

- ¼ cup reduced-fat sour cream
- 1/2 cup pepper Jack cheese or Cheddar cheese (grated)
- One 4-ounce can of chopped green chilies
- One teaspoon extra-virgin oil
- Freshly ground pepper (to taste)
- 1/8 teaspoon salt
- Four pieces large eggs
- Four parts 8-inch whole-wheat flour tortillas

For the Salsa

- 1/8 teaspoon salt
- ½ teaspoon minced chipotle chili in adobo sauce
- 1 ½ teaspoon extra-virgin oil
- One tablespoon lime juice
- One tablespoon fresh parsley or cilantro (chopped)
- Two tablespoons scallion (chopped)
- 1 cup canned black beans (rinsed)

- 1 cup diced seeded plum tomatoes (about four pieces)

Directions:

1. To make the salsa, simply mix all the ingredients in a large bowl. Make sure to stir thoroughly to blend and then store in the refrigerator until it is ready to serve.

2. To prepare the burritos: In a medium bowl, blend 1/8 teaspoon salt and pepper and the eggs using a fork until everything is combined well. Heat a teaspoon of oil in a small nonstick skillet over low heat. Place in the green chilies and then allow cooking with constant stirring for about a minute.

3. Pour in the egg mixture and cook with constant stirring (slowly) using a heatproof rubber spatula or wooden spoon until fluffy, soft curd starts to form. That should take about 3 minutes.

4. Divide the egg mixture evenly among the flour tortillas, and then sprinkle about two tablespoons of grated cheese. Roll up the filled tortillas, then top, and then serve with the salsa and sour cream.

Additional Tips:

1. You can prepare the salsa ahead, then cover and store for up to 2 days in the refrigerator.

2. Chipotle chili peppers prepared in adobo sauce are smoked jalapenos in a spicy and flavorful sauce. You can purchase these at supermarkets in the Mexican food. Once the bottle is opened, they can last for about two weeks in the ref or six months in the freezer.

Nutrition:

381 calories; protein 17.7g carbohydrates 39.2g

## Lemon Cranberry Muffins

Preparation time: 10 minutes

Cooking Time: 25 minutes

Serving: 2

Ingredients:

- 1 ½ cups cranberries, frozen or fresh (chopped coarsely)
- ¼ teaspoon salt
- One teaspoon baking soda
- Two teaspoons baking powder
- ½ cup cornmeal, ideally fine or medium stone-ground
- 1 ½ cups of white whole-wheat flour
- One teaspoon vanilla extract
- Two tablespoons lemon juice
- Three teaspoons lemon zest (freshly grated)
- One-piece large egg

- 1/3 cup canola oil
- ¾ cup nonfat plain yogurt
- ½ cup plus two tablespoon sugar

Directions:

1. Preheat the oven to 400 degrees Fahrenheit. Line 12 muffin cups with paper liners or coat with cooking spray.
2. In a medium bowl, whisk vanilla, lemon juice, two teaspoons lemon zest, egg, oil, yogurt, and ½ cup sugar.
3. In a separate large bowl, whisk salt, baking soda, baking powder, cornmeal, and flour. Pour in the yogurt mixture and fold until entirely blended. Slowly add in the cranberries.
4. Pour in the resulting batter among the muffin cups.
5. In a small bowl, mix the remaining teaspoon of lemon zest and two tablespoons sugar and sprinkle evenly over the muffin tops.
6. Bake the muffin for 20 to 25 minutes or until golden brown, and they spring back slowly to the touch. Allow to cool in the pan for about 10 minutes and then transfer to a wire rack. Allow cooling for about 5 minutes before serving.
7. Additional Tips:
8. You can individually wrap the muffins in plastic and place in the freezer for about a month. When serving, reheat the frozen muffin by removing the plastic, then wrapping it in a paper towel and heat in the microwave on high for about 60 seconds.
9. White whole-wheat flour is prepared from a special kind of white wheat. It is light in flavor and color but has similar nutritional contents as the standard whole-wheat flour. White whole-wheat flour is available in big supermarkets and can be stored in the freezer.
10. To make fast work of chopping the cranberries, but the whole berries in a food processor and pulse for a couple of times until your desired texture are achieved.

Nutrition:

390Cal., 56gCarbs, 16gFat, 7gProtein

## Florentine Hash Skillet

Preparation time: 10 minutes

Cooking Time: 7 minutes

Serving: 2

Ingredients:

- Two tablespoons sharp Cheddar cheese (shredded)
- Pinch of freshly ground pepper
- Pinch of salt
- One large piece of egg

- ½ cup frozen spinach (chopped)
- ½ cup precooked shredded potatoes or frozen hash browns
- One teaspoon extra-virgin olive oil

Directions:

1. Heat oil over medium heat in a small non-stick pan.
2. Spread the spinach and hash browns into the pan. Crack the egg on top and sprinkle with cheese, pepper, and salt.
3. Cover and lower the heat to medium and allow cooking until the potatoes or hash browns are beginning to brown at the bottom. Cook for about 7 minutes until the cheese is melted and the egg is set.

Additional Tip:

Shredded cooked potatoes are commercially available at the refrigerated dairy or produce a team of the majority of supermarkets.

Nutrition:

226 calories; protein 13.6g DV; carbohydrates 11g

## Whole-Grain Waffles In Cherry Sauce

Preparation time: 10 minutes

Cooking Time: 5 minutes

Serving: 2

Cornmeal places a tasty texture to this waffle recipe. The delicious hot cherry sauce is a nutrient-packed substitute for maple syrup. Any type of fine cornmeal will work for this yummy breakfast recipe. If you wish to use whole-grain cornmeal, search for finely ground cornmeal labeled "stone-ground" or "whole-grain" in the grocery's natural foods.

Ingredients:

For the waffles:

- Two teaspoons vanilla extract
- One tablespoon canola oil or extra-virgin olive oil
- 2 cups of nonfat or reduced-fat buttermilk
- Two pieces large eggs
- ¼ teaspoon salt
- ½ teaspoon baking soda
- 1 ½ teaspoon baking powder
- 1/2 cup fine cornmeal

For the Cherry Sauce

- One teaspoon vanilla extract
- One teaspoon lemon juice
- Two teaspoons cornstarch
- ¼ cup honey
- ¼ cup of water
- 2 cups frozen or fresh pitted cherries

Directions:

1. To prepare the waffles: Preheat the oven to 200 degrees Fahrenheit. Put a big baking sheet on the rack's center.

2. In a large bowl, whisk the salt, baking soda, baking powder, cornmeal, and whole-wheat flour. In a separate bowl, gently beat the brown sugar and eggs. Pour in the vanilla, oil, and buttermilk. Continue to whisk until well mixed. Add all the wet ingredients to the dry ingredients while continually stirring until well blended.

3. Preheat the waffle iron and lightly coat it with a cooking spray. Pour in just enough batter to cover about 2/3 of the surface. Use a spatula to distribute the batter evenly. Close and allow cooking for 5 minutes or until golden brown.

4. Place the waffles into the baking sheet to keep warm until it is ready to serve.

5. Re-do the entire process with the remaining batter using more cooking spray as required.

6. To prepare the cherry sauce: In a small saucepan, mix the vanilla extract, lemon juice, cornstarch, honey, water, and cherries. Bring to a boil over medium heat and cook with occasional stirring until the mixture thickens for about 1 minute. Pour on top of the waffles when ready to serve.

Additional Tips:

To measure flours, use the "spoon and level" method. That can be done by using a spoon to scoop flour from its container into a measuring cup gently. To level the flour with the measuring cup's top, level with a knife or other straight edge.

Prepare the cherry sauce, cover, and store in the refrigerator for up to 3 days. Gently reheat when ready to serve. Wrap the waffles tightly and store in the ref for up to 3 days or freeze up to 3 months. When ready to serve, reheat in the toaster.

## Smoked Tofu And Quinoa Salad

Preparation time: 10 minutes

Cooking Time: 20 minutes

Serving: 2

This dish featured the fresh and tangy flavors of tabbouleh. It paired them with quinoa and smoky tofu to make a perfect main-dish salad that is deliciously served on a bed of green vegetables. This salad recipe is loaded with heart-healthy food items such as legumes (soy-based tofu), whole grains (quinoa), and plenty of vegetables.

Ingredients:

- ½ cup fresh mint (chopped)
- ½ cup fresh parsley (chopped)
- 1 cup diced cucumber
- 1 cup grape tomatoes (cut in halves)
- One small yellow bell pepper (diced)

- One-piece 8-ounce package baked smoked tofu
- ¼ teaspoon freshly ground pepper
- Two little cloves garlic (minced)
- Three tablespoons extra-virgin olive oil
- ¼ cup lemon juice
- 1 cup quinoa (well rinsed)
- 2 cups of water

Directions:

1. In a medium saucepan, bring water and half a teaspoon of salt to boil.
2. Place in the quinoa and then return to a boil.
3. Lessen to a simmer, cover, and allow cooking until the water has been fully absorbed. That should take about 20 minutes.
4. Spread the quinoa on a baking sheet and allow cooling for about 10 minutes.
5. In the meantime, whisk pepper, salt, garlic, oil, and lemon juice in a big bowl.
6. Pour in the cooled quinoa, mint, parsley, cucumber, tomatoes, bell pepper, and tofu. Toss thoroughly to combine.
7. Additional Tips
8. Quinoa is a protein-rich, delicately flavored grain. It contains saponin, which is its natural, bitter protective covering. When rinsed, quinoa loses its saponin. Quinoa is commercially available in raw food stores as well in many supermarkets.
9. This recipe can be stored in an airtight container inside the refrigerator and can last for up to 1 day.
10. Pre-cooked "baked tofu" is a lot firmer than water-packed tofu and is available in different flavors. You may also like to use flavored baked tofu in a stir-fry or on a sandwich.

Nutrition:

228Cal. 26gCarbs. 10gFat. 9gProtein.

## Egg Salad Bento Box

Preparation time: 10 minutes

Cooking Time: 20 minutes

Serving: 2

This recipe makes a hearty lunch and snack all in one. Place the egg salad into a lettuce bed to make it look pretty and enjoy a cocktail of vegetables and bread. Toss blueberries and banana with yogurt to prevent the latter from turning brown. Save the pistachios and chocolate chips for an afternoon quick snack.

Ingredients:

- One tablespoon bittersweet chocolate chips

- One tablespoon shelled unsalted pistachios
- Three slices of cocktail-size pumpernickel bread
- Six pieces cherry tomatoes
- 2/3 cup broccoli florets, raw or cooked
- Two tablespoons low-fat it non-fat vanilla yogurt
- ½ cup banana slices
- ½ cup blueberries
- Two leaves Bibb or Boston lettuce
- Freshly ground pepper (to taste)
- One teaspoon scallion greens (minced)
- Two teaspoons Dijon mustard
- One tablespoon low-fat mayonnaise
- Two tablespoons finely diced celery
- Two pieces of eggs (hard-boiled, peeled, and chopped)

Directions:

1. In a small bowl, mash the eggs with the use of a fork.
2. Add in the pepper, scallion greens, mustard, mayonnaise, and celery until well combined.
3. Line one container with the lettuce leaves and place egg salad on top.
4. In a separate container, combine yogurt, banana, and blueberries.
5. In the third container, place the bread.
6. Arrange the tomatoes and broccoli in the fourth container.
7. Place the bread in a dip-size box, then fill with chocolate chips and pistachios.

Nutrition:

Calories 337

Total Fat 25.56g

Saturated Fat 5.424g

Sugars 3.66g

Protein 15.2g

# CHAPTER 15:

# Soups And Stews

## Amazing Jalapeno Lime Chicken Soup

Preparation time: 10 minutes

Cooking Time: 15 minutes

Serving: 2

Ingredients:

- 2 pounds boneless chicken breasts, chopped
- Two tablespoons olive oil
- Six jalapenos, chopped
- One red onion, chopped
- Two garlic cloves, minced
- 2 (16-ounce) jars salsa verde
- 4 cups chicken broth
- Four limes, juiced
- One teaspoon salt

Directions:

1. Press the Sauté button. Add the olive oil, red onion, garlic, and jalapeno and cook until softened.
2. Add the chicken broth and chicken.
3. Close and seal the lid; cook at high pressure for 15 minutes, or press the Poultry button.
4. Once the cooking is done, quick-release the pressure and carefully remove the lid.
5. Carefully remove the chicken and shred using two forks. Once shredded, return to the Instant Pot.
6. Stir in the salsa verde, lime juice, and salt until well combined and warmed through.
7. Serve and enjoy!

Nutrition:

Energy (calories): 250 kcal

## Terrific Cream Of Red Bell Pepper Soup

Preparation time: 10 minutes

Cooking Time: 30 minutes

Serving: 2

Ingredients:

- 2 ½ pounds red bell peppers
- One tablespoon olive oil

- Four tablespoons coconut, melted
- 1 cup shallots, chopped
- Two garlic cloves, minced
- 1 cup of water
- 3 cups vegetable broth
- ½ cup heavy cream
- Two teaspoons red wine vinegar
- ½ teaspoon cayenne pepper
- One teaspoon salt
- One teaspoon black pepper

Direction:

1. Place 1 cup of water and a trivet inside the Instant Pot.
2. Place the red bell peppers on top of the trivet.
3. Close and seal the lid; cook at high pressure for 5 minutes.
4. When the cooking is done, naturally release the pressure.
5. Remove the bell peppers and discard the water.
6. Once the bell peppers have cooled, peel, deseed and slice them
7. Press the Sauté button and add the olive oil.
8. Once the oil is hot, add the shallots and garlic cloves. Cook until translucent, stirring frequently.
9. Add the bell peppers and remaining ingredients, except for the heavy cream, to the Instant Pot.
10. Close and seal the lid and cook at high pressure for 3 minutes.
11. Quick-release the pressure when the cooking is done.
12. Use an immersion blender to puree the soup until smooth.
13. Stir in the heavy cream and adjust the seasoning as needed.
14. Serve and enjoy!

Nutrition:

Energy (calories):

Per one serving: 250 kcal

## Brilliant Italian Sausage And Pepper Soup

Preparation time: 15 minutes

Cooking Time: 10 minutes

Serving: 2

Ingredients:

- 2 pounds hot Italian sausage, cut into bite-sized pieces
- Two tablespoons olive oil
- Four garlic cloves, minced
- One onion, chopped
- Three red or green bell peppers, chopped

- Two tablespoons red wine vinegar
- 4 cups chicken broth
- 1 (28-ounce) can diced tomatoes, undrained
- ¼ cup parsley, freshly chopped
- ¼ cup basil, freshly chopped
- 1 cup spinach, chopped
- ½ cup Parmesan cheese, grated

Directions:
1. Press the Sauté button and add the olive oil.
2. Once the oil is hot, add the sausage and cook until brown. Remove and set aside.
3. Add the onions, peppers, and garlic and cook until softened.
4. Add the sausage and remaining ingredients.
5. Close and seal the lid and cook at high pressure for 10 minutes.
6. When the cooking is done, quick-release the pressure, serve, and enjoy!

Nutrition:

Per one serving: 521 kcal

Protein: 30.7g

## Remarkable Jalapeno Bacon Cheddar Soup

Preparation time: 10 minutes

Cooking Time: 15 minutes

Serving: 2

Ingredients:
- Eight slices bacon
- Four jalapeno peppers, chopped
- Four tablespoons butter
- One onion, chopped
- 3 cups chicken broth
- 1 cup heavy cream
- 6-ounces cream cheese softened
- 8-ounces cheddar cheese, shredded
- One teaspoon dried thyme
- One teaspoon garlic powder
- One teaspoon onion powder
- ½ teaspoon celery seed
- ½ teaspoon cumin
- One teaspoon salt
- One teaspoon black pepper

Directions:
1. Press the Sauté button. Add the bacon and cook until brown and crispy. Remove and set aside. Reserve the bacon grease.
2. Add the jalapenos and onions and sauté until lightly browned. Add butter as needed.

3. Add the chicken broth and cream cheese.
4. Close and seal the lid; cook at high pressure for 5 minutes.
5. Quick-release the pressure when the cooking is done.
6. Press the Sauté button again and stir in the bacon, cheddar cheese, thyme, garlic powder, onion powder, celery seed, cumin, salt, and black pepper.
7. Sprinkle the xanthan gum and cook until the soup has thickened.
8. Serve and enjoy!

Nutrition:

Per one serving: 555 kcal

Protein: 24.

## Surprising Avocado Chicken Soup

Preparation time: 10 minutes

Cooking Time: 20 minutes

Serving: 2

Ingredients:

- 1 cup chicken stock
- 1/2 tablespoon olive oil
- 1/2 pound boneless, skinless chicken thighs
- 1/4 green onion, chopped
- 1/4 jalapeno, seeded and chopped
- 1 1/2 garlic cloves, minced
- 1/2 teaspoon ground cumin
- 1/8 cup cilantro, freshly chopped
- 1/2 lime, juice
- 1/2 large avocado, cubed

Directions:

1. Press the Sauté button and add the olive oil.
2. Once the oil is hot, add the chicken thighs and brown on each side.
3. Add the chicken stock, onions, jalapeno, garlic, and seasonings.
4. Close and seal the lid; cook at high pressure for 8 minutes.
5. , Quick-release the pressure when the cooking is done.
6. Remove the chicken and shred with two forks. Allow cooling as needed.
7. In the Instant Pot, stir in the cilantro and avocado.
8. Use an immersion blender to blend until smooth and creamy.
9. Stir in the shredded chicken and adjust the seasoning as needed. Serve!

Nutrition:

Per one serving: 486 kcal

Protein: 46.1g

## Outstanding Taco Soup

Preparation time: 10 minutes

Cooking Time: 25 minutes

Serving: 2

Ingredients:

- 2/3 pound ground beef
- 1 tablespoon olive oil
- 1/3 onion, chopped
- 1/3 red bell pepper, chopped
- 1/3 poblano pepper, chopped
- 1 garlic cloves, minced
- 1 2/3 cups beef broth
- 1 1/3 cups diced tomatoes
- 2/3 tablespoon green Tabasco sauce
- 1/3 lime, juiced
- 2/3 teaspoon ground cumin
- 1tsp. of ground ancho chili pepper
- 1/3 teaspoon chili powder
- 1/3 teaspoon salt
- 1/3 teaspoon black pepper
- Mexican blend cheese, shredded (optional topping)
- Lime wedges (optional topping)
- Sour cream (optional topping)
- Tabasco sauce (optional topping)

Directions:

1. Press the Sauté button and add the ground beef. Cook until browned, stirring occasionally.
2. Add the garlic, onion, red pepper, and poblano pepper and cook for 2 to 3 minutes, stirring frequently.
3. Add the remaining ingredients (except for the topping ingredients).
4. Close and seal the lid; cook at high pressure for 10 minutes.
5. When the cooking is done, naturally release the pressure and remove the lid.
6. Press the Sauté button and cook until most of the liquid has reduced, or the soup reaches your desired texture.
7. Portion into bowls, add toppings, and serve.

Nutrition:

Per one serving: 621 kcal

Protein: 77.4g

## Very Good Broccoli Cheese Soup With Chicken

Preparation time: 15 minutes

Cooking Time: 25 minutes

Serving: 2

Ingredients:

- 2 pounds boneless, skinless chicken breasts, chopped into 1" pieces
- Two large heads of broccoli, chopped into florets
- Two tablespoons olive oil
- One onion, chopped
- Two garlic cloves, minced
- ½ cup butter
- 8 cups chicken broth

- ½ cup almond flour
- 4 cups almond milk
- 8-ounces cream cheese, room temperature
- 4 cups cheddar cheese, shredded
- ½ cup Parmesan cheese, shredded
- One teaspoon salt
- One teaspoon garlic powder
- One teaspoon black pepper
- ½ teaspoon cayenne pepper

Directions:

1. Press the Sauté button. Add the olive oil and chicken chunks and cook until browned. Remove and set aside.
2. Add the butter. Once the butter is melted, add the onions and garlic cloves. Cook until the onions become translucent.
3. Add the flour and stir for 1 minute.
4. Add the chicken broth and continue to stir and cook until any flour lumps are gone.
5. Stir in the broccoli and chicken.
6. Close and seal the lid; cook at high pressure for 8 minutes
7. Quick-release the pressure once the cooking is done,
8. Stir in the almond milk, cream cheese, cheddar cheese, Parmesan cheese, salt, garlic powder, black pepper, and cayenne pepper.
9. Continue to cook until the cheese has melted and the soup is warm. Adjust the thickness as needed. Serve and enjoy!

Nutrition:

Per one serving: 946 kcal

Protein: 57.

## Hungarian Mushroom Soup With Fresh Dill

Preparation time: 5 minutes

Cooking Time: 20 minutes

Serving: 2

Ingredients:

- 1 pound mushrooms, sliced
- Four tablespoons butter
- Three tablespoons flour
- One tablespoon paprika
- Three tablespoons soy sauce
- One tablespoon lemon juice
- One tablespoon fresh dill, chopped
- ¼ cup parsley, chopped
- 1 cup milk
- ½ cup sour cream
- 3 cups chicken stock
- One large onion, chopped

- One teaspoon salt
- One teaspoon black pepper

Directions:
1. Press the Sauté button. Add the butter.
2. Once the butter has melted, add the onions and cook until translucent.
3. Add the mushrooms and cook for 10 minutes, stirring occasionally, or until brown. Remove and set aside.
4. Add the onions and cook for 3 minutes, stirring occasionally.
5. Stir in the flour and mushrooms.
6. Add the chicken stock and soy sauce.
7. Close and seal the lid; cook at high pressure for 5 minutes.
8. Quick-release the pressure once the cooking is done,
9. Stir in the remaining ingredients and adjust the seasoning as needed.
10. Serve and enjoy!

Nutrition:

Energy (calories):

Total: 1107 kcal

Per one serving: 277 kcal

## Creamy Garlic Mushroom Soup

Preparation time: 10 minutes

Cooking Time: 20 minutes

Serving: 2

Ingredients:
- 1 pound cremini mushrooms, thinly sliced
- Four garlic cloves, minced
- One tablespoon olive oil
- ¼ cup arrowroot flour
- Two tablespoons ghee
- One teaspoon salt
- One teaspoon black pepper
- 2 cups chicken broth
- 2 cups of water
- 1/8 teaspoon dried thyme
- ½ cup of coconut milk

Directions:
1. Press the Sauté button and add the olive oil.
2. Once hot, add the mushrooms, garlic, salt, and black pepper.
3. Cook for 10 minutes or until mushrooms is brown, stirring occasionally.
4. Stir in the ghee and arrowroot powder and cook for 2 minutes. Stir to cover the mushrooms with the combination.

5. Stir in the chicken broth and water.
6. Close and seal the lid; cook at high pressure for 5 minutes.
7. Once the cooking is done, quick-release the pressure and carefully remove the lid.
8. Stir in the coconut milk until well combined.
9. Garnished with dried thyme.
10. Serve and enjoy!

Nutrition:

Energy (calories): Total: 857 kcal

Per one serving: 214 kcal

## Superb French Onion Soup

Preparation time: 15 minutes

Cooking Time: 30 minutes

Serving: 2

Ingredients:

- 1 1/2 tablespoons butter
- 1/2 tablespoon olive oil
- 3/4 pound onions, sliced
- 1 garlic cloves, minced
- 1/4 pound Gruyere cheese, grated
- 1/8 cup dry sherry
- 2 cups chicken stock
- 1/2 sprigs thyme
- 1/4 bay leaf
- 1/4 teaspoon fish sauce
- 1/4 teaspoon apple cider vinegar
- 1/4 teaspoon salt
- 1/4 teaspoon black pepper

Directions:

1. Press the Sauté button and add the butter and olive oil.
2. Once the olive oil and butter are hot, add the onions and cook until softened, stirring frequently.
3. Add the remaining ingredients.
4. Close and seal the lid; cook at high pressure for 20 minutes.
5. When the cooking is done, naturally release the pressure and remove the lid.
6. Press Sauté again and cook until the soup thickens or reaches your desired consistency. Serve and enjoy!

Nutrition: Energy (calories):

Per one serving: 455 kcal

## Soup With Pork And Fennel (In A Slow Cooker)

Preparation time: 10 minutes

Cooking Time: 6hrs

Serving: 2

Ingredients:

- 450 g pork neck
- 450 g of cauliflower chopped into flowers
- 280 g sliced fresh fennel
- Two cloves of garlic, chopped into quarters

- tsp. salt
- ½ tsp. ground white pepper
- cups of water
- cup chicken stock
- 1 cup of fat cream

Directions:
1. Put all the ingredients except the cream in a slow cooker.
2. Cook at high temperature for 6 hours.
3. Remove the pork from the soup and chop. Set aside.
4. Beat the soup with a blender until smooth.
5. Add cream and minced pork. Try it and, if necessary, add extra salt and pepper.

## Low Carb Chicken Noodle Soup

Preparation time: 15 minutes

Cooking Time: 10 minutes

Serving: 2

INGREDIENTS

- 3 tbsp. coconut oil
- Three minced cloves of garlic
- chopped onion
- 0.5 tsp. ground turmeric
- One medium turnip, diced
- Eight stalks of celery, chopped
- l chicken bone broth
- 450 g pre-cooked and chopped chicken
- 4 tsp. fresh chopped basil
- 4 tsp. fresh chopped parsley
- 0.5 tsp. sea salt
- bay leaves
- 455 g zucchini chopped with spirals

Directions:
1. Heat 1 tablespoon of coconut oil in a saucepan over medium heat. Add garlic and fry until fragrant.
2. Add onions and turmeric. Cook until onion is transparent.
3. Add turnips and celery with the remaining two tablespoons of coconut oil. Cook for about 10 minutes.
4. Add the broth, chicken, basil, parsley, salt, and bay leaf. Bring to a boil, and then reduce heat.
5. Cover and simmer for about 40 minutes. Remove from heat.
6. Remove the bay leaf. Add the spiralized zucchini and cover the pan. Leave to brew for 10 minutes to soften the zucchini noodles.

Nutrition:

Calories. 108. Fat. 3.5 g. Carbs. 16.03 g. Protein. 5.95 g

# Creamy Salmon Soup With Coconut Milk

Preparation time: 20 minutes

Cooking Time: 1hr minutes

Serving: 2

INGREDIENTS

- 908 g chicken bone broth
- 2 tbsp. lard or coconut oil
- One small chopped onion
- Four minced cloves of garlic
- Two medium turnips, peeled and diced
- Two medium carrots, chopped
- Three stalks of celery, chopped
- 1 tbsp. cider vinegar
- Five sprigs of fresh thyme, chopped
- 0.5 tsp. sea salt (or more to taste)
- 455 g sliced salmon fillet
- 400 g canned coconut milk
- 2 tbsp. lime juice or lemon juice
- Two green chopped onions (optional)

Directions

1. Melt lard or coconut oil in a large saucepan. Sauté the onion until transparent (about 5 minutes).
2. Add the garlic and continue to simmer until fragrant. Then add turnips, carrots, and celery. Cook for another 5-10 minutes until the vegetables are lightly browned.
3. Add the broth, vinegar, thyme, and salt. Reduce heat, cover, and simmer for 30 minutes to soften vegetables.
4. Put 2 cups of soup in a blender (remove the carrots so that the liquid does not turn orange) and beat everything until smooth. Add mashed potatoes to the remaining soup.
5. Add salmon and coconut milk, and continue cooking until the fish is cooked.
6. Season with lime (or lemon) juice and garnish with green onions.

Nutrition:

Calories: 402kcal | Carbohydrates: 35g | Protein: 36g | Fat: 13g | Saturated Fat: 2g |

# Creamy Cheese Soup with Broccoli

Preparation time: 10 minutes

Cooking Time: 20 minutes

Serving: 2

INGREDIENTS

- 1 tbsp. butter
- One chopped small onion
- Two medium chopped garlic cloves
- Salt and pepper to taste
- ½ tsp. xanthan gum

- ½ cup chicken stock
- 1 cup chopped broccoli
- 1 cup of fat cream
- 1 ½ cup grated cheddar cheese

Directions:

1. Preheat the pan on the stove. Put onion, chopped garlic, salt, pepper, and oil and cook over medium heat until soft.
2. Add xanthan gum and chicken stock. Mix well.
3. Put the broccoli in the pan and make sure it is covered with the stock.
4. Quickly add cream. Bring the soup to a boil, stirring often.
5. Slowly start adding cheese, stirring again.
6. Serve with plenty of broccoli and cheese.

Nutrition:

173Cal. 15gCarbs. 9gFat. 7gProtein.

## Ginger Pumpkin Soup

Preparation time: 20 minutes

Cooking Time: 40 minutes

Serving: 2

INGREDIENTS

- One small pumpkin
- 44.36 g of olive oil
- One clove of garlic
- One small onion
- 0.5 l vegetable stock
- 7 g fresh ginger
- 1 g of salt
- 1 g black pepper

Directions:

1. Cut the pumpkin in half and pull out the core.
2. Trim the tail and pull out the seeds, and cut the pumpkin into cubes.
3. In a large saucepan, heat 2 tbsp. Olive oil.
4. Add onions and garlic, and cook until tender, stirring frequently.
5. Add pumpkin and ginger, and cook for 2-3 minutes.
6. Add vegetable stock and bring to a boil.
7. Season with salt and pepper.
8. Cook over low heat for 35–40 minutes until the pumpkin is soft.
9. Using a hand blender beat the soup until smooth.
10. Serve with whipped cream.

Nutrition:

Calories 80

Total Carbohydrate 18 g

Dietary fiber 2 g

Sugar 1.7 g

Protein 1.8 g

## Creamy Cheese Soup With Vegetables

Preparation time: 15 minutes

Cooking Time: 10 minutes

Serving: 2

INGREDIENTS

- 2 cups broccoli (coarsely chopped)
- One medium carrot (chopped)
- One small onion (chopped)
- 2 tbsp. olive oil
- 1 tsp. garlic powder
- 3/4 tsp. salt
- 1/2 tsp. pepper
- 1/8 tsp. nutmeg
- 2 cups chicken or beef broth
- One small spinach
- 1/2 cup fat cream
- 113 g Cheddar Cheese
- 113 g gouda cheese

Directions

1. Add olive oil to a large saucepan and put on medium heat. Add chopped carrots and onions mix well and cook for 1-2 minutes. Add garlic, broccoli, seasoning, and spices. Mix and cook for another 1 minute.
2. Add bone broth, mix and cook for 8-10 minutes until the vegetables are soft. Turn off the heat and mix with heavy cream.
3. Pour 1/2 of the soup mixture into the blender, add the spinach and beat until smooth. You can mix the whole soup if you prefer an utterly thick consistency.
4. Return the blender's contents to a large pan and mix with two kinds of cheese until they are completely melted. Season to taste and sprinkle with broccoli and cheese if desired.

Nutrition:

Calories128.1 Saturated Fat2.3 g

Total Carbohydrate14.0 g

Protein11.5 g

## Spicy Sausage And Pepper Soup

Preparation time: 20 minutes

Cooking Time: 5hrs

Serving: 2

INGREDIENTS

- 211 g spicy Italian sausages
- 2 cups raw spinach
- 1/3 medium green bell pepper
- 1/3 medium red bell pepper
- 1/8 medium onion
- 1/3 cup jalapeno tomatoes
- 2/3 cup beef
- 2/3 teaspoon chili powder
- 2/3 teaspoon of caraway seeds
- 2/3 teaspoon minced garlic
- 1/3 teaspoon Italian seasoning
- 1/8 teaspoon kosher salt

Directions:

1. Cut the sausage and sauté it.
2. Add chopped peppers, tomatoes, beef, and spices to the pan. Add the sausage on top and mix well.
3. Sauté your onions and garlic to a translucent state and add to the pan.
4. Top with spinach and cook for 3 hours.
5. After 3 hours, mix, reduce heat, and simmer another 2 hours.

Nutrition:

658.25 Calories, 54g Fats, 9.65g Net Carbs, and 29.57g Protein.

## Soup With Red Pepper And Cauliflower

Preparation time: 30 minutes

Cooking Time: 1hr minutes

Serving: 2

INGREDIENTS

- Two red bell peppers
- 1/2 head of cauliflower
- 6 tbsp. duck fat
- Three medium green onions, diced
- 3 cups chicken stock
- 1/2 cup fat cream
- 1 tsp. garlic powder
- 1 tsp. dried thyme
- 1 tsp. smoked paprika
- 1/4 tsp. red pepper
- 113 g goat cheese
- Salt and pepper to taste

Directions:

1. Cut the bell pepper in half and peel the seeds. Bake for 10-15 minutes or until the skin is charred and blackened.
2. Once the pepper is ready, remove it from the oven and place it in a container with a lid or bag for storing food. Let the pepper steam to make it softer.
3. Cut the cauliflower into inflorescences and season with 2 tbsp. molten duck fat, salt, and pepper. Bake cabbage for 30-35 minutes at 200 degrees.
4. Remove the peel from the pepper by thoroughly cleaning it.
5. Pour 4 tbsp. into the pan. Duck fat. When it heats, add the cubes of green onions, seasoning, chicken stock, red pepper, and cabbage. Cook for 10-20 minutes.
6. Mix everything well with a blender, then add cream and mix again.

7. Serve with crispy bacon and goat cheese. Garnish with thyme and green onions.

Nutrition:

Calories: 68.1

Total Carbohydrate: 8.5 g

Dietary Fiber: 2.3 g

Protein: 1.4 g

## Spicy Low-Carb Spinach Soup

Preparation time: 15 minutes

Cooking Time: 5 minutes

Serving: 2

INGREDIENTS

- One teaspoon fresh ginger
- One clove of garlic
- 100 ml of coconut milk
- One hot water
- One large bag of washed spinach
- Soy sauce

Directions:

1. Cook 1 teaspoon of raw 1 in oil in a soup pot for 1 minute. Stir in a piece of garlic for 2 minutes.
2. Pour and crush 100 ml coconut milk and 360 ml water
3. Take a broth tablet with you
4. Cook with a pan lid.
5. Put the spinach in a spoon (hold a little behind)
6. Cook for 2-3 minutes. Cut the spinach leaves into slices.
7. Grate the soup with a hand mixer or food processor,
8. Season to taste with soy sauce.
9. Decorate the soup with spinach bars and red thread

Nutrition:

357kcal | Carb: 4.35g | Prot: 44.06g | Fat: 16.94g

## 358. Creamy Zucchini Soup With Salmon Chips

Preparation time: 10 minutes

Cooking Time: 15 minutes

Serving: 2

INGREDIENTS

- One clove of garlic
- Two courgettes
- Two vegetable stock cubes
- 1-liter water
- 125 ml fresh whipped cream
- Salt and pepper
- 150 grams of smoked salmon chips

Directions:

1. Cut the onion, garlic, and dice the zucchini. Heat olive oil a little in a soup pan and fry onions and garlic until it becomes glassy.

2. Add zucchini cubes and cook for another 3 minutes on high heat.

3. Add 1 liter of water to the stock cube and bring it to a boil. Boil at low temperature for 8 minutes.

4. Puree the soup with a hand blender and stir in the whipped cream. Season with salt and pepper.

5. Divide the soup into plates and add the appropriate amount of salmon chips. You can also heat the salmon for another minute.

Nutrition:

307 calories; fat 28g;

## Pumpkin Soup With Coconut And Curry

Preparation time: 15 minutes

Cooking Time: 25 minutes

Serving: 2

INGREDIENTS

- 800 grams sliced pumpkin cubes
- 1-2 cloves of garlic
- 2 tsp. curry powder
- salt and pepper
- 400 ml chicken broth
- 400 ml of water
- 200 ml of coconut milk

Directions:

1. Melt a piece of butter in a large soup pot.

2. Heat the chicken broth in another pan at the same time.

3. Cut the onion into small pieces and fry gently in the pan for 5 minutes.

4. Add the diced pumpkin and fry it until softer.

5. Add the garlic, curry powder, salt, and pepper to the onion and cook together for 1 minute.

6. Simultaneously heat the coconut milk in a separate pan and stir in occasionally.

7. Add the chicken stock and water to the whole and mix well.

8. Lower your gas burner to a lower position.

9. Boil slowly for 20 minutes and stir occasionally.

10. Put the soup in the blender together with the coconut milk and mix until smooth.

11. Then add it to the soup pan again and heat it until it is warm enough to be served.

Nutrition:

335Cal. 27gCarbs. 18gFat. 23gProtein

## Quick Seafood Chowder

Preparation time: 20 minutes

Cooking Time: 15 minutes

Serving: 2

Ingredients

- One teaspoon garlic
- Six tablespoons shallots, chopped
- Four tablespoons light olive oil
- Two stalks of celery, chopped
- 12 cherry tomatoes
- Six tablespoons clam juice, all-natural
- 2 cups chicken broth, organic and homemade
- 1/6 teaspoon Italian seasoning
- 1/8 teaspoon black pepper
- 1 lb. shrimp
- 4 oz. blue crab
- 8 oz. clams

Directions

1. Heat the oil in a large sauté pan or skillet.
2. Using medium heat, sauté the garlic and shallots for approximately 2 minutes (the onions should be translucent and the garlic fragrant).
3. Add in the celery, tomatoes, clam juice, and broth, continually stirring; season with pepper and Italian seasoning.
4. Simmer for 3 minutes, stirring occasionally.
5. Stir in the shrimp, crab, and clams.
6. Bring the mixture to a simmer and cook 5 minutes (the shrimp should be pink and firm); stir occasionally.
7. Remove to a serving bowl.
8. Serve warm.

Nutrition:

Calories 484 Total Carbs 28.2g Net Carbs 23.3g Fat 19g Protein 38g

## Atkins Diet Soup

Preparation time: 25 minutes

Cooking Time: 35 minutes

Serving: 2

Ingredients

- Three slices bacon, chopped
- Two teaspoons olive oil
- 1/3 cup onion, chopped
- One tablespoon fresh garlic, minced
- 1/2 cup sundried tomatoes, chopped
- 1/2 cup sliced white mushrooms
- 10 cups chicken stock
- 2 cups of water
- 3 cups celery root, peeled and chopped

- 5 cups cooked chicken breast, chopped
- 1 cup yellow squash, sliced
- ½ cup green beans cut into 1 inch
- 5 cups Swiss chard, chopped
- Three tablespoons of red wine vinegar
- ¼ cup fresh basil, chopped
- Salt and freshly ground black pepper to taste

Directions

1. Using a large soup pot, cook the bacon and olive oil for 2 minutes on medium heat.
2. Stir in the onions, sundried tomatoes, garlic, and mushrooms.
3. Cook for 6 minutes, stirring occasionally.
4. Add the water and stock, stir to mix.
5. Stir in the celery root and chicken.
6. Simmer for 15 minutes, stirring occasionally.
7. Add the squash, green beans, and Swiss chard.
8. Simmer for 10 minutes, stirring occasionally.
9. Stir in the red wine vinegar; add salt and pepper to taste.
10. Stir in the fresh basil before serving.
11. Serve.

Nutrition:

Calories 360 Total Carbs 22.2g Net Carbs 17.4g Fat 13g Protein 38g

## Blue Cheese And Bacon Soup

Preparation time: 10 minutes

Cooking Time: 35 minutes

Serving: 2

Ingredients

- Four medium slices of bacon
- Three tablespoons butter
- One leek, chopped
- 2 cups mushroom pieces and stems
- 1 cup cauliflower
- 25 oz. can chicken broth
- 1/2 cup tap water
- 3 oz. blue cheese

Directions

1. Cook the bacon over medium heat in a skillet or griddle.
2. Cook until the bacon is crispy on one side; flip the bacon over and cook until it is crisp all the way through.
3. Remove the bacon to a paper towel; pat it to remove any excess fat.
4. When the bacon is cold, crumble it and set it aside.
5. In the meantime, melt the butter in a large soup pot.

6. Add the leeks, mushrooms, and cauliflower.
7. Stir the ingredients together.
8. Cover the pot, and cook the vegetables for 5 minutes, stirring occasionally.
9. Pour in the chicken broth and water; bring the pot to a boil.
10. Reduce the heat; cover and simmer for 10 minutes (the vegetables should be very tender).
11. Remove the soup from the stove and puree it in a blender or food processor; when pureeing the last batch of soup, add the blue cheese.
12. Return the soup to the soup pot on the stove.
13. Heat until warmed through on low heat, if necessary.
14. Pour into bowls and top with crumbled bacon. Serve.

Nutrition:

Calories 331 Total Carbs 10.4g Net Carbs 7.7 g Fat 24 g Protein 20g

## Versatile Vegetable Soup

Preparation time: 15 minutes

Cooking Time: 25-30 minutes

Serving: 2

Ingredients

- Four tablespoons olive oil
- One stalk celery
- 1/2 teaspoon of ground thyme, dried
- One teaspoon garlic, minced
- Two small zucchini
- 1/4 cup green snap beans
- 1/4 teaspoon salt
- 1/4 teaspoon black pepper
- 4 cups vegetable broth
- One small onion, sliced
- One red tomato, chopped
- 1/4 cup parsley

Directions

1. Heat the oil in a large saucepan or soup pot.
2. Stir in the celery, onion, and thyme.
3. Sauté approximately for 5 minutes, occasionally stirring, until the vegetables are soft.
4. Add the garlic and sauté for approximately 30 seconds, until it is fragrant.
5. Stir in the zucchini, green beans, salt, and pepper.
6. Sauté for approximately 2 minutes, until these vegetables are slightly soft.
7. Add the broth and tomato.
8. Increase the temperature to high, and bring the mixture to a boil.

9. Reduce the heat to low; cover the pan with the lid, and simmer for 10 minutes.
10. Chop the parsley and stir it in.
11. Remove from the heat.
12. Serve hot.

Nutrition:

Calories 371 Total Carbs 13.6g Net Carbs 9.9g Fat 31g Protein 13 g

## Roasted Red Pepper Soup

Preparation time: 15 minutes

Cooking Time: 20 minutes

Serving: 2

Ingredients

- Two tablespoons olive oil
- Two stalks of celery
- Two small onions, chopped
- Two cloves garlic
- 1 cup bell peppers, roasted
- 12 fluid oz. tap water
- 24 oz. chicken broth
- 2/3 cup heavy cream
- 1/4 cup parmesan cheese (grated)
- Salt and black pepper, to taste

Directions

1. Using medium heat, heat oil in a large saucepan.
2. Dice the celery and onion; mince the garlic.
3. Add the celery, onion, and garlic to the pan.
4. Cook for approximately 8 minutes, occasionally stirring (vegetables should be soft).
5. Dice the roasted red peppers.
6. Stir in the red peppers, water, and broth.
7. Bring the mixture to a boil; reduce the heat and simmer for approximately 5 minutes.
8. Remove the soup from the heat.
9. Puree it in a blender or food processor.
10. Return the soup to the saucepan.
11. Stir in the cream.
12. Slowly reheat the soup.
13. Add salt and pepper to taste.
14. Pour soup into bowls.
15. Sprinkle with Parmesan cheese.
16. Serve.

Nutrition:

Calories 215 Total Carbs 8.6g Net Carbs 7.7 g Fat 18g Protein 9.2g

## Low Carb Beef Stew

Preparation time: 30 minutes

Cooking Time: 2hrs and 45 minutes

Serving: 2

Ingredients

- 48 oz. beef chuck
- 4 oz. of raw bacon
- Four tablespoons olive oil
- 2 cups onions, chopped
- ½ cup carrots, chopped
- Two stalks of celery
- Four cloves garlic
- 16 fluid oz. red table wine
- 16 oz. beef broth, homemade
- One teaspoon bay leaf
- 8 oz. mushroom, chopped
- Three teaspoons thyme
- One tablespoon parsley
- ¼ cup of almond flour
- Salt and black pepper, to taste

Directions

1. Cut the beef into cubes and season with salt and pepper to taste.
2. Put ¼ cup of the almond flour in a bowl; lightly coat the beef cubes.
3. In a large stockpot or Dutch oven, cook the bacon until crisp over medium heat.
4. Remove the bacon, crumble it, and set it aside.
5. Dice the onion and carrots, chop the celery, and dice the garlic; mix the vegetables and set them aside.
6. Add oil to the bacon fat in the pot.
7. Brown the beef cubes in batches over medium-high heat.
8. Remove the beef from the pot to a mixing bowl.
9. Add the onion, carrot, and celery to the pot; sauté for approximately 8 minutes on medium heat (the vegetables should be soft).
10. Add the garlic and cook for approximately 30 seconds (until it is fragrant).
11. Pour in the wine; increase the heat to high.
12. Boil the wine for approximately 5 minutes, until it is reduced to 1 cup.
13. Return the beef and its juices to the pot.
14. Add the beef broth, and stir in the bay leaf.
15. Reduce the heat to low.
16. Partially cover the pot and simmer for 2 hours.
17. Stir in the mushrooms, thyme, and parsley.
18. Cook for an additional 30 minutes (the beef should be tender and the sauce thickened).

19. Remove the bay leaf.
20. Serve with the crumbled bacon.

Nutrition:

Calories 1585Total Carbs 30.2g Net Carbs 27g Fat 48g Protein 119g

## Hearty Beef Stew

Preparation time: 25 minutes

Cooking Time: 50 minutes

Serving: 2

Ingredients

- Four cloves of garlic
- 1.5 cups Cauliflower
- 1.5 cups broccoli
- 1/3 cup of zucchini
- Four tablespoons of butter
- 4 cups of beef broth
- 3 cups of tomatoes
- Two onions cut into large pieces
- 1.5 lb. of beef roast

Directions

1. Cut the onions into large pieces.
2. Pour the beef broth into a large roasting or Dutch oven; heat it to boiling.
3. Reduce the heat, and add the beef roast and onion.
4. Cook the beef on medium heat until it is tender.
5. When the beef is tender, remove it from the broth and dice it.
6. Return the beef to the pan.
7. Add the remaining ingredients.
8. Simmer until the vegetables are soft, stirring occasionally.
9. Serve hot.

Nutrition:

Calories 530Total Carbs 16.9g Net Carbs12.1 g Fat 24g Protein 60g

## Beef Chuck and Vegetable Stew

Preparation time: 60 minutes

Cooking Time: 3 hours

Serving: 2

Ingredients

- 1 1/3 tablespoons olive oil
- 1 lb. beef chuck, cubed and trimmed
- 1/3 teaspoon thyme leaves
- 1/3 teaspoon oregano
- 2/3 teaspoon rosemary (dried)
- 1/8 teaspoon paprika
- Salt and black pepper, to taste
- 1 1/3 tablespoon butter
- 1/3 cup white onions, chopped
- 1 1/3 cloves garlic
- 6 fluid oz. water
- 1/3 lb. green snap beans
- 1/3 medium carrot, chopped

Directions

1. Preheat the oven to 325 degrees F.
2. In a Dutch oven, heat half the oil over medium-high heat.
3. Combine the thyme, oregano, rosemary, paprika, salt, and pepper. Toss half of the beef in it.
4. Remove the beef and put it in the Dutch oven to brown.
5. Remove the beef to a bowl.
6. Repeat steps 2-5 for the remaining beef, using the spices leftover from the first batch of meat.
7. Set aside the beef.
8. Chop the garlic.
9. Melt the butter in the Dutch oven.
10. Add the diced onions and cook them for 7-8 minutes (they should begin to brown); add the garlic for the last 2 minutes.
11. Stir in the beef and its juices, the wine, and 2 cups of water.
12. Bring the mixture to a boil.
13. Cover the Dutch oven and place it in the preheated oven.
14. Cook for 2 hours (the beef should be tender).
15. Stir in the green beans and carrot; cook for an additional 15 minutes (the vegetables should be tender).
16. Remove the Dutch oven from the oven and place it on a burner with medium-high heat.
17. Stir and serve immediately.

Nutrition:

Calories 353 Total Carbs 11.3g Net Carbs 8.1g Fat 24g Protein 36 g

# CHAPTER 16:

# Snacks

## Apricot-Apple Cloud

Preparation time: 65 minutes

Cooking Time: 10 minutes

Serving: 2

Ingredients:

- 1/2 cup heavy cream
- 2/3 cup unsweetened applesauce baby food
- 2/3 Tbsp. sucralose based sweetened

Directions:

1. In a large bowl, using an electric mixer, whip the heavy cream. Add the sugar substitute. Beat until firm peaks form.
2. Gently fold in applesauce. Stir until combined.
3. Pour into six individual serving bowls.
4. Chill for 1 hour. Serve.

Nutrition:

Calories: 9.9

Fat: 22.4

Carbs: 25g

Protein: 1.5g

## Artichoke With Three Kinds Of Cheese

Preparation time: 20 minutes

Cooking Time: 40 minutes

Serving: 2

Ingredients:

- 2 cups artichoke hearts
- ½ cup vegetable broth
- 3 Tbsp. extra virgin olive oil
- 1 tsp. lemon juice
- Two garlic cloves, minced
- Fresh parsley, chopped
- Fresh basil, chopped
- ½ cup shredded Fontina cheese
- ½ cup of shredded Swiss cheese
- ½ cup shredded Parmesan cheese

Directions:

1. Preheat oven to 400F
2. Arrange artichokes in a single layer of a deep baking dish.
3. Drizzle oil, lemon juice, garlic, vegetable broth over the artichokes.

4. Start with fontina cheese, then Swiss cheese, parmesan cheese last.
5. Cover baking dish with aluminum foil. Bake 15 minutes.
6. Remove foil. Bake an additional 15 minutes until cheese is golden and bubbly.
7. Remove from the oven. Let it cool to room temperature. Serve.

Nutrition:

Calories: 57

Fat: 14g

Carbs: 3g

Protein: 4g

Dietary Fiber: 2.6g

## Peanut Butter Granola Bar With Strawberries And Yogurt Parfait

Preparation time: 5 minutes

Cooking Time: 0 minutes

Serving: 1

Granola bars are an excellent energy source, and combined with yogurt and strawberries, they can turn into a great Atkins suitable snack.

Ingredients:

- 1 cup plain Greek yogurt
- 1 Atkins Peanut Butter Granola Bar
- Five strawberries, sliced

Directions:

1. Place the granola bar in a baggie. Break up into small pieces.
2. Spoon a layer of yogurt at the bottom of a dish.
3. Add a layer of the smashed granola bar.
4. Spoon in a layer of yogurt.
5. Top with strawberries.
6. Serve immediately or chill in the refrigerator.

Nutrition:

Calories: 314

Fat: 9.5g

Carbs: 12.6g

Protein: 24.1g

Dietary Fiber: 6.8g

## Blackberry Peach Compote

Preparation time: 10 minutes

Cooking Time: 20 minutes

Serving: 2

Ingredients:

- 1/8 cup Sauvignon Blanc wine
- 1/3 Tbsp. Xylitol
- 1/8 tsp. ground ginger
- 1/8 tsp. Cinnamon
- 1/2 medium peaches
- 1/8 cup blackberries
- 1/8 tsp. thick it up

Directions:

1. In a large saucepan, combine the wine, Xylitol, ginger, peaches, and cinnamon.
2. Simmer for 15 minutes.
3. Add the blackberries. Simmer another 5 minutes until berries are tender.
4. Stir in the thick it up. Simmer approximately 5 minutes.
5. Remove from heat. Cool to room temperature. Serve.

Nutrition:

Calories: 35

Fat: 0.2g

Carbs: 4.2g

Protein: 0.5g

Dietary Fiber: 3.4g

## Baked Brie

Preparation time: 5 minutes

Cooking Time: 10 minutes

Serving: 2

Ingredients:

- 2 2/3 oz. Brie wheel cheese
- 1/8 cup pine nuts

Directions:

1. Heat oven to 450F
2. Trip top of white rind off the cheese.
3. Cover top with pine nuts.
4. Place cheese on aluminum foil pan or pie dish.
5. Bake 10 minutes. Serve.

Nutrition:

Calories: 144

Fat: 12.1g

Carbs: 2.g

Protein: 8.2g

Dietary Fiber: 0.1g

## Indian Chicken Curry

Preparation time: 8 minutes

Cooking Time: 20 minutes

Serving: 2

Ingredients:

- 1 Tbsp. unsalted butter
- 2/3 garlic cloves, minced
- 1 1/3 chicken breasts, boneless, skinless
- 1/3 tsp. cumin
- 1/8 tsp. coriander
- 1/8 tsp. ground ginger
- 1/8 tsp. crushed red pepper flakes
- 1/8 cup chicken broth
- 1/8 cup heavy cream
- Fresh cilantro

Directions:

1. In a large skillet, melt the butter. Sauté the garlic for 2 minutes.

2. Add the chicken breasts. Cook thoroughly.
3. Once cooked, remove the chicken and cut it into chunks. Return to the pan.
4. Pour in the chicken broth, cumin, coriander, ginger, red pepper flakes.
5. Turn down the heat to medium-low. Simmer 5 minutes.
6. Stir in the cream. Simmer another 3 minutes.
7. Serve in bowls over rice. Garnish with fresh cilantro.

Nutrition:

Calories: 413

Fat: 22.1g

Carbs: 1g

Protein: 49.1g

Dietary Fiber: 0.3g

## Avocado Salsa

Preparation time: 10 minutes

Cooking Time: 0 minutes

Serving: 2

Avocados are great; turning it into a salsa, even more remarkable.

Ingredients:

- One red tomato
- ⅛ cup fresh cilantro, rough chopped
- One red onion, diced
- ½ jalapeno pepper, diced
- Two avocadoes, diced
- 2-3 Tbsp. fresh lime juice
- Pinch of salt and new ground black pepper

Directions:

1. Chop all the vegetables.
2. Add them to a bowl.
3. Squeeze in the lime juice. Season with salt and pepper. Stir.
4. Refrigerate for 30 minutes. Serve.

Nutrition:

Calories: 71

Fat: 5.3g

Carbs: 3.3g

Protein: 1.1g

Dietary Fiber: 3g

## Chicken Wings

Preparation time: 10 minutes

Cooking Time: 35 minutes

Serving: 2

Ingredients:

- 1/8 serving all-purpose low carb baking mix
- 1/2 Tbsp. chili powder
- 1/4 tsp. cayenne pepper
- 1/2 tsp. yellow mustard seed
- 1/2 tsp. salt
- 12-16 chicken wings

Directions:

1. Preheat oven to 450F
2. Rinse the chicken wings.
3. Line a baking sheet with aluminum foil. Spray with non-stick cooking spray.
4. Take a Ziploc bag; add the baking mix, chili powder, cayenne pepper, and mustard seed, salt. Place the wings in the bag. Massage the chicken wings through the pack to coat them with seasoning.
5. Transfer to the baking sheet. Cook 30-35 minutes, until golden brown.
6. Serve immediately.

Nutrition:

Calories: 276

Fat: 18.5g

Carbs: 3.4g

Protein: 22.4g

Dietary Fiber: 0.3g

## Cauliflower Mushroom Risotto

Preparation time: 10 minutes

Cooking Time: 10 minutes

Serving: 2

Ingredients:

- 1 Tbsp. olive oil
- Two garlic cloves, minced
- Four baby Bella mushrooms, diced
- 1 cup chicken broth
- 2 cups riced cauliflower
- ¼ cup parmesan cheese
- ¼ cup heavy cream
- 1 tsp. tarragon
- Pinch of salt and pepper

Directions:

1. In a blender, process the cauliflower until rice-like consistency.
2. In a skillet, heat the olive oil. Sauté the garlic mushrooms for 3 minutes.
3. Pour in the chicken broth and cauliflower. Stir well. Simmer 5 minutes.
4. Once the liquid has cooked away, add the parmesan cheese and tarragon, salt, and pepper. Stir well. Stir in the cream. Keep stirring until the cheese has melted.
5. Serve hot.

Nutrition:

Calories: 245.5

Fat: 20g

Carbs: 8.5g

Protein: 7g

Fiber: 2.5g

Net Carbs: 6g

## Coconut Orange Creamsicle Fat Bombs

Preparation time: 2-3 minutes

Cooking Time: 10 minutes

Serving: 2

Enjoy a savory combination of coconut and orange in this fat bomb recipe.

Ingredients:

- ½ cup of coconut oil
- ½ cup heavy whipping cream
- ¼ cup cream cheese
- 1 tsp. orange-vanilla Mio
- 10 drops liquid Stevia

Directions:

1. Add the coconut oil to a blender. Pulse until smooth.
2. Add the whipped cream. Pulse until combined.
3. Add the cream cheese. Pulse until smooth.
4. Add the orange Milo and Stevia. Pulse until smooth.
5. Spoon the mixture into a silicone tray mold or ice cube tray. Freeze 3 hours.
6. Pop-out to eat. Store uneaten bombs in a bag in the freezer.

Nutrition:

Calories: 176

Fat: 20g

Carbs: 0.7g

Protein: 0.8g

Fiber: 0g

Net Carbs: 0.7g

## Corndog Muffins

Preparation time: 10 minutes

Cooking Time: 15 minutes

Serving: 4 Muffins

Turn your ordinary muffin into a delightful meaty combination with these cute muffins.

Ingredients:

- ½ cup blanched almond flour
- ½ cup flaxseed meal
- 1 Tbsp. psyllium husk powder
- 3 Tbsp. swerve sweetener
- ¼ tsp. salt
- ¼ tsp. baking powder
- ¼ cup melted butter
- One egg
- ¼ cup of coconut milk
- ⅓ cup sour cream
- Three all-beef hot dogs

Directions:

1. Preheat oven to 375F
2. In a bowl, add the almond flour, flaxseed, husk powder, granulated

sweetener, salt, and baking powder. Whisk together.

3. In a separate bowl, combine the egg, coconut milk. Whisk together. Add the butter. Stir until combined. Add the sour cream. Stir until combined.
4. Add the dry ingredients to the wet ingredients. Stir until a smooth batter forms.
5. Grease a 12 mini muffin tin.
6. Slice the hot dogs into four.
7. Fill the muffin cup halfway. Add the sliced hot dog to the batter.
8. Bake 12 minutes.
9. Then broil 1-2 minutes until golden brown. Serve.

Nutrition:

Calories: 78.5

Fat: 6.8g

Carbs: 2.1g

Protein: 2.4g

Fiber: 1.5g

Net Carbs: 0.7g

## Layered Fried Queso Blanco

Preparation time: 10 minutes

Cooking Time: 10 minutes

Serving: 2

Think frying up your cheese might be a bad idea? Think again.

Ingredients:

- ½ cup Queso Blanco
- 1½ Tbsp. olive oil
- Pinch red pepper flakes or salt and pepper

Directions:

1. Cut the cheese into cubes. Chill in the freezer as you heat the oil.
2. In a skillet, heat the olive oil. Once the pan is hot, add the cubes of cheese.
3. As it cooks, it will melt. Once it is golden brown on one side, flip it over. Press down against the cheese to flatten it slightly and push out the oil. Once it is golden brown on both sides, tilt the edges against the pan and cook until golden brown. It will seal the cheese into a square.
4. Remove from pan. Place on paper towel. Pat lightly. Slice into cubes again.
5. Sprinkle red pepper flakes or salt and pepper over the cubes. Serve immediately.

Nutrition:

Calories: 525

Fat: 43g

Carbs: 4g

Protein: 30g

Fiber: 2g

Net Carbs: 2g

## Raspberry Lemon Popsicles

Preparation time: 10-15 minutes

Cooking Time: 2hrs

Serving: 2

Ingredients:

- 1/3 cup of raspberries
- Juice from 1/2 a lemon
- 1/8 cup of coconut oil
- 1/3 cup of coconut milk
- 1/8 cup sour cream
- 1/8 cup heavy cream
- 1/8 tsp. Guar Gum
- 6 2/3 drops liquid Stevia

Directions:

1. Combine all the ingredients in a blender. Pulse until smooth. Strain the liquid.
2. Pour mixture into Popsicle molds. Freeze 2 hours.
3. If stuck, run the mold under hot water briefly.

Nutrition:

Calories: 150.5

Fat: 16.0g

Carbs: 3.3g

Protein: 0.5

Fiber: 1.3g

Net Carbs: 2.0g

## Neapolitan Fat Bombs

Preparation time: 15-30 minutes

Cooking Time: 1hr

Serving: 2

Ingredients:

- ½ cup butter
- ½ cup coconut oil
- ½ cup sour cream
- ½ cup cream cheese
- 2 Tbsp. liquid stevia
- 2 Tbsp. cocoa powder
- 1 tsp. pure vanilla extract
- 2 strawberries

Directions:

1. In a blender, add the butter, coconut oil, sour cream, cream cheese. Pulse until smooth.
2. Set out three bowls. Add cocoa powder to a bowl. Add vanilla extract to another bowl. Add strawberries to a bowl. Mash them.
3. Pour the mixture evenly between the three bowls. Stir each mixture until smooth.
4. Pour vanilla mixture into the bottom of the silicone mold or ice cube tray. Freeze for 30 minutes. Place other bowls in the fridge. Pour the chocolate layer into the silicone mold or ice cube tray.

Freeze 30 minutes. Pour the strawberry layer into the silicone mold or ice cube tray. Freeze 2 hours. Ready to serve.

Nutrition:

Calories: 102.2

Fat: 10.9g

Carbs: 0.6g

Protein: 0.6g

Fiber: 0.2g

Net Carbs: 0.4g

## Atkins Special Burger

Preparation time: 30 minutes

Cooking Time: 30 minutes

Serving: 2

Ingredients :

- 2/3 lb. ground beef
- 1/3 tablespoon chives, chopped
- 1/8 cup scallion, minced
- 2 ounces cheddar cheese, coarsely grated
- 1/4 teaspoon tarragon, crumbled
- 2/3 teaspoon seasoning salt
- 1/8 cup fresh parsley, chopped
- 1 tablespoon butter, melted (optional)
- 1 small tomato, diced
- 1 egg, beaten

Directions:

1. You will have to mix the beef, tarragon, salt parsley, chives, scallions, eggs, and tomato and then shape the mixture into 12 equal sized balls. These balls are to be flattened to make pan cakes.
2. Divide the cheese in six piles, place each share of cheese on a pan cake and cover it with another pan cake. Press the edges to lock the cheese inside the meat pan cakes.
3. You will cook these pan cakes on an outdoor grill. You can also broil them in the oven or sauté with butter in a non-stick pan.

## Atkins Special Grilled Chicken

Preparation time: 30 minutes

Cooking Time: 1hr 25 minutes

Serving: 2

Ingredients :

- 1/4 cup mayonnaise
- 1 tablespoon minced fresh tarragon
- 1 small garlic clove, minced
- 1 teaspoon salt
- 4 bell peppers, whole, any color
- 1/4 cup olive oil
- 1 teaspoon granular sugar substitute
- 1/2 teaspoon pepper
- 2 tablespoons extra virgin olive oil
- 3 tablespoons fresh lemon juice
- 2 tablespoons minced fresh parsley

- 1 large scallion, thinly sliced
- 1 1/2 lbs boneless skinless chicken breast halves, each split in half horizontally

Directions:

1. You will mix the mayonnaise, lemon juice, parsley, oil, scallion, garlic, tarragon, sugar substitute and salt in a plastic bag (the bag must be a re-sealable one gallon size). Now, add the chicken and seal the bag and shake it properly to make the coating even. You will have to keep the bag inside the fridge for an hour.
2. Now, heat the charcoal or gas grill (medium heat) and then grill the chicken by occasionally turning the pieces. Proper cooking of the chicken will take about 7 minutes.
3. Instructions for the peppers:
4. You will have to roast the peppers over the open flame or under a broiler till the skins are charred from all sides.
5. Now, keep the pepper in the plastic bag and seal it. You will have to let the peppers steam for 10 minutes and as they are cool enough to handle, you will peel them, seed them and cut into strips (1/3 inch wide).
6. Transfer them into glass plates and drizzle with olive oil. You can preserve the peppers up to a week.

## Blueberry Bliss

Preparation time: 30 minutes

Cooking Time: 1hr

Serving: 2

Ingredients :

- 1 1/3 tablespoons butter
- 1/8 teaspoon almond extract
- 1/3 cup fresh blueberries or 1 cup frozen blueberries, patted dry
- 1 1/3 tablespoons Atkins baking mix, divide
- 1/8 cup water
- 1 large egg
- 1 (1/8 ounce) packets sugar substitute (I use Splenda)
- 1/3 pinch salt
- 1/4 cup heavy cream

Directions:

1. Preparation part will include preheating the oven at 350 degrees Fahrenheit.
2. You will now melt the butter (in a tart pan or 9 inch pie plate).
3. Mix 2 tablespoons of bake mix along with the sugar substitute and salt in a medium sized bowl.
4. Take a separate smaller bowl and whisk the cream along with the eggs, water and almond extract. Here you will pour the excess amount of melted butter from the pan.
5. You will have to add the liquid ingredients to the dry ones and mix them till they are properly smooth.

6. You will now toss the blueberries with the remaining bake mix (1 tablespoon) and gently fold them into a batter. You will have to pour this batter into the pan which has already been prepared.

7. You will bake them for 45 minutes and make sure that they are golden and puffy and serve immediately after baking.

8.

## Ham Salad – Simple Version

Preparation time: 10 minutes

Cooking Time: 0 minutes

Serving: 2

Ingredients :

- 1 pound ham, finely chopped
- 2 tablespoons Dijon mustard
- 1 shallot, finely chopped
- 1 tablespoon dill pickle, finely chopped
- 3 tablespoons mayonnaise
- 1/4 teaspoon cayenne pepper (optional)

Directions:

1. Just take a mixing bowl and mix the ham, mayonnaise, cayenne and mustard properly.

2. Stir the mixture in a shallot and add pickle before serving.

## Banana Muffin Delight

Preparation time: 30 minutes

Cooking Time: 30 minutes

Serving: 2

Ingredients :

- 3 large eggs
- 3/4 cup butter, melted
- 1 1/2 teaspoons baking powder
- 1 cup walnuts (optional)
- 4 tablespoons mayonnaise
- 2 teaspoons vanilla
- 1/2 cup water
- 1 cup flax seed meal
- 1/2 cup davinci sugar-free banana syrup
- 3/4 cup Atkins baking mix

Directions:

1. You will have to preheat the oven at 350 degrees temperature and prepare the muffin pan by inserting the coil cupcakes and spraying them with oil. You must not use paper cup cakes or liners as they will get attached to the muffins and you cannot separate them later.

2. Now, it is time to make the batter. Beat the eggs and mix the melted butter slowly into it. After this you will add the Davinci syrup along with water and continue to mix.

3. Take a separate bowl and mix the Atkins bake mixture and the flax

meal, salt, baking powder and make sure that the baking powder is evenly distributed.

4. It is now that you will add the wet ingredients and mix well.
5. Distribute this batter in 12 muffin cups and bake for 30 minutes. Check with the toothpicks and make sure that the center is properly cooked.
6. You can also use a loaf pan to make the muffins.

## Crispy Apple

Preparation time: 30 minutes

Cooking Time: 40 minutes

Serving: 2

Ingredients:

- 1 1/3 cups sliced apples
- 1/3 cup Splenda Sugar Blend for Baking
- 1/3 teaspoon cinnamon
- 1/8 cup soft butter
- 1/3 teaspoon salt
- 1/3 tablespoon butter
- 1/4 cup Atkins baking mix

Directions:

1. You will have to butter the baking dish and then place the 4 cups of sliced apples on them.
2. Mix the remaining ingredients properly and sprinkle the mixture over the sliced apples.
3. Bake them for 40 minutes at 350 degrees temperature.

## Atkins Chicken Wrap Special

Preparation time: 10 minutes

Cooking Time: 12 minutes

Serving: 2

Ingredients :

- 1 tablespoon butter
- Onion powder
- Salt
- Pepper
- 4 teaspoons blue cheese dressing
- 2 boneless skinless chicken breasts
- garlic powder
- Frank's red hot sauce
- 4 iceberg lettuce or 4 romaine leaves

Directions:

1. You will have to slice the breasts of chicken in 4 or 5 strips.
2. Now, melt the butter over medium heat.
3. Both sides of the chicken strips are to be sprinkled with garlic powder, salt, onion powder and pepper (this is to be done according to your taste).
4. You will now cook the chicken in the butter till they are tender and brown in color.
5. Serve by wrapping the chicken in lettuce leaves. You can add hot sauce before wrapping if you want the hot taste.

## Salad Wrappings With Chicken

Preparation time: 15 minutes

Cooking Time: 10 minutes

Serving: 2

Ingredients :

- 1 pound poached chicken breast
- 1 tablespoon chopped fresh parsley
- 3 large lettuce leaves
- 1/2 teaspoon finely chopped chipotle chili in adobo (optional, for a spicier version)
- 1 celery rib, chopped
- 3 tablespoons mayonnaise
- 1 teaspoon Dijon mustard

Directions:

1. Start by cutting the chicken in cubes (1/2 inch).
2. Now, mix the celery, parsley and mustard in the bowl and then add the chicken to it and toss to combine properly.
3. Wrap the whole thing in large lettuce leaves before serving.

## Atkins Special Soup

Preparation time: 20 minutes

Cooking Time: 25 minutes

Serving: 2

Ingredients :

- 2 tablespoons olive oil
- 1/2 teaspoon salt
- 1/4 teaspoon pepper
- 4 cups lower sodium vegetable broth
- 1 celery rib, chopped
- 1/2 small onion, chopped
- 1/2 teaspoon dried thyme
- 2 garlic cloves, sliced
- 1 large tomatoes, chopped
- 1 small zucchini, cut into 1/4-inch dice
- 1/2 cup chopped green beans
- 1/4 cup chopped fresh parsley

Directions:

1. You will have to use a heavy bottomed sauce pan to heat the oil and then add the celery, onion and thyme and then sauté the vegetables till they are tender (this will take about 5 minutes).
2. Now, you will add the zucchini along with the green beans, pepper, salt and again sauté them till they are soft (this will take about 2 minutes).
3. It is time to add the stock along with the tomato and you will also have to increase the heat and bring it to boil.
4. Once it starts to boil, you will reduce the heat and cover the pan and then allow simmering for 10 more minutes. Serve hot by sprinkling the chopped parsley.

## Atkins Mahi-Mahi

Preparation time: 30 minutes

Cooking Time: 30 minutes

Serving: 2

Ingredients :

- Salt & freshly ground black pepper
- 1/2 small green bell pepper, thinly sliced (1/2 cup)
- 1/2 cup chopped canned tomato, with juice
- 1 tablespoon unsalted butter
- 1/2 small onion, thinly sliced (1/2 cup)
- 1/2 small red bell pepper, thinly sliced (1/2 cup)
- 4 (6 ounce) mahi mahi fillets
- 1 tablespoon fresh lemon juice (1/2 lemon)
- 1 tablespoon fresh cilantro, chopped
- hot pepper sauce
- 1 tablespoon olive oil

Directions:

1. You will have to sprinkle the mixture of lemon juice, salt and pepper on the fish and set them aside.
2. Take a sauce pan and melt the butter in it over medium heat. You will sauté the peppers and onion in this butter till they are slightly soft (this will take about 2 minutes).
3. Now, add the tomatoes and reduce the heat and simmer till the sauce becomes thick (this will take about 8 minutes). You will now stir in the cilantro along with the hot pepper sauce according to your taste.
4. Take a large non-stick skillet and heat the oil in it. Sauté the fish till they are just cooked through (this will take about 3 minutes per side). Spoon the sauce over the fish just before serving.

## Pork Delight With Poblano Pepper

Preparation time: 15 minutes

Cooking Time: 25 minutes

Serving: 2

Ingredients :

- 1 tablespoon olive oil
- 1/4 cup water
- 1 cup poblano pepper, seeded and chopped
- 1 cup yellow onion, chopped
- 1 cup heavy cream
- 4 center-cut pork chops (about 10 oz. each)
- Salt and pepper

Directions:

1. You will heat the olive oil in a big skillet till it is hot enough (but not smoking).

2. You will season the pork with pepper and salt and cook them in olive oil, till they are tender and golden brown in color (this will take about 4 to 5 minutes for each side). Take the port to another plate and keep it warm.

3. You will now take the skillet and add the poblano chilis, salt, pepper and onions and cook by stirring them occasionally (this may take about 6 or 7 minutes).

4. You will now stir in the cream and water and bring the mixture to simmer.

5. Now, you will just have to add the pork chops and cook for another 2 minutes on each side.

6. Pour the cream sauce before serving.

## Almonds And Strawberries

Preparation time: 2 minutes

Cooking Time: 0 minutes

Serving: 1

Ingredients:

- 15 almonds
- Four fresh strawberries

Directions:
1. Serve the almonds with the strawberries.

Nutrition:

Net Carbohydrate: 5.4 grams

Proteins: 4.2 grams

## Apple And Cheese Snack

Preparation time: 5 minutes

Cooking Time: 0 minutes

Serving: 1

Ingredients:

- 0.4 part of apple
- 30 gr. cheddar cheese

Directions:
1. Dice the cheese and enjoy with slices of apple.

Nutrition:

Net Carbohydrates: 8 3 grams

Proteins: 5.2 grams

## Avocado with Strawberries

Preparation time: 2 minutes

Cooking Time: 0 minutes

Serving: 1

Ingredients:

- 0.5 avocado
- Six fresh strawberries

Directions:
1. Chop the strawberries, peel the avocado
2. Squeeze the seed and enjoy them together!

Nutrition: Carbohydrates: 7. grams

Proteins: 2 grams Fat: 11.1grams

## Apples and Almond Butter

Preparation time: 2 minutes

Cooking Time: 0 minutes

Serving: 1

Ingredients:

- One tbs. almond butter
- 0.5 apple

Direction:

Cut one apple into slices and dip in the almond butter.

Nutrition:

Net Carbohydrates: 13.1 grams

Proteins: 7 grams

## Asparagus and Ham

Preparation time: 15 minutes

Cooking Time: 5 minutes

Serving: 2

Ingredients

- 2 asparagus
- 1 slice ham
- 1/4 tbsp. olive oil

Directions:

1. Cover a piece of ham just about every asparagus ends.
2. Heat the grillwork or grill to maximal heat. Spurge the asparagus softly with olive oil.
3. Roast for 3 - 4 minutes until the ham gets the golden brown texture, and the asparagus is bright green, crisp, and soft. Put them in a serving dish.

Nutrition:

Net Carbohydrate: 0.3 grams

Protein: 4.4 grams

## Atkins Rye Biscuits with Ham

Preparation time: 2 minutes

Cooking Time: 0 minutes

Serving: 1

Ingredients:

- One rye crackers
- Atkins, 30 gr. Ham

Direction:

Serve with ham on a cookie and enjoy it!

Nutrition:

Net Carbohydrates 2.9 grams

Proteins 11.1 grams

## Balls Of Cheese With Bacon

Preparation time: 10 minutes

Cooking Time: 10 minutes

Servings: 2

Ingredients:

- 1 2/3 smoked bacon
- 1 2/3 Tbsp. cream cheese

- 20 gr. cheddar cheese
- 1/4 Tsp. onion powder
- 1/4 Tsp. garlic powder
- 1/4 Tbsp. Worcestershire sauce
- 2 pecans in halves

Directions:

1. Cook the bacon, drain it and crumble it.
2. Combine with the rest of the ingredients (except nuts) and form a ball. Pass the walnuts well chopped.

Nutrition:

Carbohydrates: 1.2 grams

Proteins: 8.3 grams

Fat: 12.2 grams

## Celery And Hummus

Preparation time: 5 minutes

Cooking Time: 0 minutes

Serving: 1

Ingredients:

- One stalk of celery
- Two tbs. hummus

Directions:

Cut the celery into sticks and put them in hummus.

Nutrition:

Carbohydrates: 3.2 grams

Proteins: 2.7 grams

Fat: 2.9 grams

## Celery Stalk With Peanut Butter

Preparation time: 5 minutes

Cooking Time: 0 minutes

Serving: 1

Ingredients:

- 2 of celery
- Two tbs. peanut butter with thick chunks

Directions:

Wash the celery stalks and then fill them with peanut butter and enjoy!

Nutrition:

Carbohydrates: 6 grams

Proteins: 8.2 grams Fat: 16.2 grams

## Cheese With Avocado

Preparation time: 1 minute

Cooking Time: 0 minutes

Serving: 1

Ingredients

- 0.5 avocado
- 30 gr. cheddar cheese

Directions:

Enjoy the cheese with ripe avocado sliced.

Nutrition:

Carbohydrates: 1.3 grams

Proteins: 6.4 grams  Fat: 16.5 grams

## Taco Salad

Preparation time: 10 minutes

Cooking Time: 55 minutes

Serving: 2

Ingredients:

- One tablespoon chili powder
- One teaspoon ground cumin
- One teaspoon gluten-free Thicken Up (low carb food thickener)
- ½ teaspoon onion powder
- ½ teaspoon garlic powder
- 1 pound lean ground beef
- ¾ cup of water
- 6 cups shredded Romaine lettuce
- Four tablespoons taco sauce
- 4 ounces medium jicama (Mexican turnip), cut into thin strips
- 1 cup shredded fat-free Monterey Jack cheese
- ½ cup shredded fat-free cheddar cheese
- Four tablespoons fat-free sour cream

Directions

1. Make the seasoning mix: In a small bowl, combine the chili powder, cumin, Thicken Up, onion powder, and garlic powder. Set aside.
2. In a large skillet, cook the ground beef over medium heat until browned, about 15 minutes.
3. Drain off fat, if any. Add the water and seasoning mix; stir to combine. Reduce heat to medium-low, and cook until liquid is almost completely absorbed 10 to 12 minutes.
4. In a large bowl, toss lettuce with taco sauce. Divide among four large serving bowls, about 1 ½ cups each. Top each with ¼ cup chopped jicama.
5. In a medium bowl, toss the Monterey jack and cheddar cheeses together; divide and sprinkle over the jicama.
6. Spoon the beef mixture (about ½ cup per serving) over the cheese.
7. Top each with one tablespoon sour cream.

Nutrition:

Calories: 293, Calories from Fat: 90, Saturated Fat: 4.2g, Cholesterol: 109mg, Total Carbs: 11.1g, Dietary Fiber: 2.8g, Protein: 37.9g

## Shrimp Gumbo

Preparation time: 20 minutes

Cooking Time: 50 minutes

Serving: 2

Ingredients:

- 1 tablespoon extra-virgin olive oil, divided
- 2/3 tablespoon gluten-free All-Purpose Low-Carb Baking Mix
- 1 celery stalk, chopped

- 1 small green bell pepper, seeded and chopped
- 1/3 small onion, chopped
- 1 3/4 cups chicken broth
- 1/3 cup diced stewed tomatoes
- 2/3 teaspoons Creole seasoning blend
- 2/3 tablespoons garlic cloves, chopped
- 1/3 pound collard greens, washed, cut in strips, or two packages (10-ounces each) frozen
- 1/3 (10-ounce) package frozen cut okra
- 2/3 pounds large shrimp, shelled and deveined

Directions

1. In a large saucepan, heat oil over medium heat, whisk in baking mix, and cook, whisking, until deep golden brown, about five minutes.
2. Add celery, bell pepper, and onion and cook 5 minutes, occasionally stirring, five minutes. Add garlic and creole seasoning and cook for one minute longer.
3. Add chicken broth and tomatoes to vegetable mixture and bring to a boil. Add collards and okra, cover, and cook until collards are tender, about five minutes.
4. Add shrimp to gumbo, mix well, cover, and cook four minutes, until shrimp are pink and cooked through.
5. Season to taste with hot pepper sauce, salt, and pepper.

Nutrition:

Calories: 279, Calories from Fat: 81, Cholesterol: 216mg, Sodium: 952mg, Total Carbs: 17g, Sugars: 3.1g, Protein: 36.1g

## Roast Beef And Mixed Greens With Pickled Okra And Radishes

Preparation time: 15 minutes

Cooking Time: 30 minutes

Serving: 2

Ingredients:

- 12 ounces lean roast beef
- 2 cups mixed greens
- 4 ounces pickled okra
- 10 radishes, sliced
- 2 servings fat-free Creamy Italian Dressing

Directions:

1. Season roast beef with salt and freshly ground pepper.
2. Slice or cut the beef into cubes, and serve cold or slightly warmed in the microwave.
3. Toss greens, okra, and radishes with dressing. Serve salad with roast beef.

Nutrition:

Calories: 385, Fat: 44, Saturated Fat: 1.6g, Cholesterol: 122mg, Total Carbs: 36.7g, Sugars: 6.1g, Protein: 44.8g

## Pork Tenderloin With Tomatoes And Green Olives

Preparation time: 20 minutes

Cooking Time: 1 hr.

Serving: 2

Ingredients:

- 2/3 plum tomato, seeded and chopped
- 2/3 ounces chopped green olives
- 1/8 cup dry white wine
- 1/3 teaspoon chopped fresh rosemary
- 2/3 garlic cloves pushed through a press
- 1/3 tablespoon extra-virgin olive oil
- 1/2 pound whole pork tenderloins
- 1/8 teaspoon salt
- 1/8 teaspoon ground pepper
- 1/3 cup of low sodium chicken broth
- 2/3 teaspoon chicken Up (food thickener)

Directions:

1. Preheat oven to 400°F.
2. Combine tomatoes, olives, white wine, rosemary, and garlic in a bowl.
3. Heat oil in a heavy ovenproof skillet over medium-high heat until hot. Season pork with salt and pepper. Sauté pork on both sides, about five minutes. Add tomato mixture.
4. Insert ovenproof meat thermometer into the thickest part of pork. Place skillet in oven and bake 30 minutes or until thermometer registers 160°F. Remove pork from skillet; cover and keep warm.
5. Place skillet over medium heat; add broth and Thicken Up. Bring to a boil; reduce heat and simmer until slightly thickened, five minutes. Drizzle sauce over pork and serve hot!

Nutrition:

Calories: 159, Saturated Fat: 1.8g, Cholesterol: 43mg, Total Carbs: 8g, Sugars: 3.1g, Protein: 15.1g

## Pumpkin-Spice Brownies

Preparation time: 20 minutes

Cooking Time: 40 minutes

Serving: 4 Brownies

Ingredients:

- 1/4 ounces unsweetened baking chocolate
- 1/8 cup unsalted butter
- One tablespoon unsweetened cocoa powder
- 1/2 ounces powdered erythritol (sugar alcohol food additive)
- 1 large eggs
- Two teaspoons vanilla extract
- 1/8 cup coconut flour
- 1/8 teaspoon baking soda
- 1/8 teaspoon salt
- 1/8 teaspoon ground cinnamon
- 1-ounce fat-free cream cheese
- 1/8 cup unsweetened pumpkin puree
- 1/8 cup granular sugar substitute (sucralose)
- 1/4 teaspoons pumpkin pie spice

Directions:

1. Preheat oven to 350°F.
2. Grease an 8x8-inch pan.
3. Melt butter and chocolate in a small bowl at 30-second intervals in the microwave until melted. Thoroughly mix the chocolate and butter, add in the cocoa powder and powdered erythritol, and continue to blend until smooth. Add one teaspoon vanilla and three eggs; whisk until incorporated. Whisk the coconut flour, baking soda, salt, and cinnamon in a small bowl. Add to the chocolate mixture and stir until thickened. Set the brownie mixture aside.
4. Using a hand blender, mix the cream cheese with the sucralose in a small bowl. Add one egg, pumpkin purée, pumpkin spice blend, and one teaspoon vanilla; beat until smooth.
5. Spread 2/3 of the brownie mixture into the prepared pan. Pour cream cheese mixture over the top. Drop the remaining 1/3 of the brownie batter by spoonful's over the cream cheese mixture and then take a knife and gently swirl the layers together. Bake for 30 minutes. Allow cooling before cutting. Best served at room temperature but keep refrigerated in an airtight container for up to one week.

Nutrition:

Calories: 142, Saturated Fat: 8.3g, Cholesterol: 77mg, Total Carbs: 9.8g, Dietary Fiber: 1.2g, Sugars: 7.7g, Protein: 3.4g

## Spicy Turnip Fries

Preparation time: 15 minutes

Cooking Time: 40 minutes

Serving: 2

Ingredients:

- 1 1/3 turnips, trimmed and peeled (about one 1/4 pound)
- 2/3 tablespoon extra virgin olive oil
- 1/3 teaspoon Kosher salt
- 1/8 teaspoon chili powder

Directions:

1. Heat oven to 425°F. Cut turnips into 2½-inch sticks. Place on a foil-lined pan. Drizzle with oil and sprinkle with salt and chili powder. Toss with your hands to coat. Spread out in a single layer.
2. Bake fries 25 minutes, turning halfway through cooking time for even browning. Bake five more minutes under the broiler for extra crispy. Serve immediately.

Nutrition: Calories: 64, Saturated Fat: 0.7g, Total Carbs: 5.5g, Dietary Fiber: 1.4g, Sugars: 3.4g, Protein: 0.7g

## Kale Chips

Preparation time: 10 minutes

Cooking Time: 35 minutes

Serving: 2

Ingredients:

- 2 1/3 ounces curly kale (trimmed from about 13 ounces, discard stems)

- 1/3 tablespoon extra-virgin olive oil
- 1/8 teaspoon sea salt

Directions:

1. Preheat oven to 250°F and prepare a sheet pan with parchment paper.
2. Remove the leaves from the stems of the kale stalk. Tear leaves into bite-sized pieces.
3. Toss kale with olive oil by hand in a bowl, then arrange equally spaced on the baking sheet and season with sea salt.
4. Place pan in the oven and set a timer for 30 minutes. After 20 minutes, check to see if pieces are dried and crispy. If not, continue to study at five-minute intervals. Store in an airtight container for up to one week.

Nutrition:

Calories: 36, Saturated Fat: 0g, Trans Fat: 0g, Total Carbs: 3.5g, Protein: 1g

## Ham N' Cheese Frittata

Preparation time: 10 minutes

Cooking Time: 40 minutes

Serving: 2

Ingredients:

- 1/3 tablespoon chopped yellow onion ( 1/2 small onion)
- 1/8 medium green bell pepper, chopped
- 2 2/3 ounces chopped cooked lean ham
- 1 tablespoon chopped Italian (flat-leaf) parsley leaves, divided
- 3 large eggs, beaten
- 1/8 cup half and half
- 1/8 cup of water
- 1/8 teaspoon salt
- 1/2 teaspoon Italian seasoning
- 1/3 cup grated fat-free Swiss cheese, divided

Directions:

1. Preheat broiler.
2. Melt butter in a large non-stick skillet over medium-high heat; add onion, pepper, ham, and half the parsley. Cook five minutes, until onion is soft and translucent.
3. Combine eggs, half and half, water, salt, Italian seasoning, and half the grated cheese.
4. Add egg mixture to pan. Cook, constantly stirring, until the eggs form soft, creamy curds, about five minutes. Remove from heat; sprinkle remaining cheese over top of eggs.
5. Place skillet under broiler; cook until cheese is bubbly and golden, about three minutes. Cool slightly.
6. Slide frittata onto a serving platter; top with remaining parsley.
7. Cut into wedges.

Nutrition:

Calories: 166, Saturated Fat: 3.3g, Cholesterol: 300mg, Total Carbs: 2.2g, Dietary Fiber: 0g, Protein: 17g

## Roast Chicken And Vegetable Stew

Preparation time: 20 minutes

Cooking Time: 45 minutes

Serving: 2

Ingredients

- 3/4 pounds roasted whole chicken
- 1 1/8 cups of low sodium chicken broth
- 1/3 bay leaf
- 1/4 cup half and half
- 1 tablespoon butter
- 1/4 cup chopped red bell pepper
- 1/8 cup chopped white onion
- 1/8 pound fresh sliced mushrooms
- 5 2/3 ounces fresh asparagus spears, cut into 1-inch pieces
- 1/3 cup fresh green beans, cut into 1-inch pieces
- 1/3 tablespoon chopped fresh thyme
- 1/8 teaspoon salt
- 1/8 teaspoon ground black pepper

Directions

1. Remove chicken meat from the bones and skin. Cut into bite-sized pieces and place into a bowl, and set aside.
2. Place half and half in a small saucepan and cook over medium heat until thick, five to seven minutes. While "cream" reduces, melt butter in a medium saucepan over high heat. Sauté bell pepper and onion until softened, about 3 minutes. Add broth and bay leaf and bring to a boil, about 10 minutes.
3. Add mushrooms, asparagus, and green beans to the broth and cook until tender, about seven minutes. Add chicken and simmer on low until heated through about three minutes.
4. Turn off heat and stir in reduced cream and thyme. Season to taste with salt and pepper.

Nutrition:

Calories: 423, Saturated Fat: 11.9g, Cholesterol: 160mg, Total Carbs: 11.4g, Protein: 34.4g

## Baked Spaghetti

Preparation time: 10 minutes

Cooking Time: 50 minutes

Serving: 2

Ingredients:

- 2 cups of cooked spaghetti squash -- (2 to 3)
- 1 pound of lean ground beef – (cooked and drained)
- 2 cups of fresh mushrooms
- One small onion -- diced
- 2 cups of your favorite low carbohydrates spaghetti sauce -- or canned tomatoes
- 2 cups of grated cheese

Directions:

1. Sauté; mushrooms and onion in 1 tbsp. butter.
2. Combine all ingredients and top with the cheese.
3. Bake at 350 degrees for 30 minutes.

Nutrition: 409Cal. 53gCarbs. 13gFat. 24gProtein

## Beef And Been Entrée

Preparation time: 10 minutes

Cooking Time: 15 minutes

Serving: 2

Ingredients:

- 1 pound of lean ground beef
- 1 cup of diced onion
- One can of tomatoes with green chilies
- One can of trappers black eye peas
- 1/2 cup of shredded cheddar cheese
- Salt and pepper – to taste

Directions:

1. Brown the ground beef and onions until they are cooked lightly.
2. Drain well and add everything except the cheese.
3. Reduce heat to low, cover, and allow simmering for 15 minutes.
4. Serve with cheese sprinkled over the top.

Nutrition: Calories. 13g. Sat Fat. 970mg. Sodium. 4g. Sugars

## Blondies

Preparation time: 20 minutes

Cooking Time: 30 minutes

Serving: 2

Ingredients:

- 8 tbsp. of butter
- 1 cup of sweetener
- 2 tsp. of vanilla
- Two eggs
- 1 tsp. of Almond extract
- 1 tbsp. of lemon juice
- 1/2 cup of Atkins bakes mix

Directions:

1. Mix the softened butter, sweetener, and vanilla.
2. Add in the eggs one at a time.
3. Add almond extract as well as the lemon juice.
4. Stir in the bake mix.
5. Pour in greased pan and bake at 350 degrees for about 30 minutes.

(This recipe also makes a dozen mini muffins. bake 20 minutes for mini muffins)

Nutrition: 256Cal. 36gCarbs. 9gFat. Three %2gProtein.

## Brandy Mochaccino

Preparation time: 20 minutes

Cooking Time: 0 minutes

Serving: 2

Ingredients:

- Two scoops of chocolate Kato shake mix
- 1 cup of cold-brewed decaf coffee
- 1 cup of chopped ice
- Two tablespoons of heavy cream
- One tablespoon of ground flaxseed -- optional
- One capful of Brandy Extract
- One package of artificial sweetener – optional

Directions:

1. Blend all the listed ingredients in a blender. Serve.

Nutrition:

290Cal. 42gCarbs. 12gFat. 12gProtein

## Bruschetta Style Tomato Turkey Salad

Preparation time: 20 minutes

Cooking Time: 0 minutes

Serving: 2

Ingredients:

- 1 cup of ground turkey
- 1 cup of mixed lettuce
- One tomato
- 4 or 5 kalamata olives
- Salt
- Pepper
- 1 or 2 tablespoons of olive oil
- 1 tsp. of crushed garlic
- 1 tsp. basil paste (or a few leaves of finely chopped fresh basil)

Directions:

1. Using a small bowl, dice the tomato.
2. Add the chopped olives, olive oil, garlic, basil, and salt and pepper to taste.
3. Brown the turkey mince in a suitable saucepan. Add the tomato mix to the turkey and mix them.
4. Serve over a bed of mixed lettuce.

Nutrition:

Calories 70 Total Fat 5g Saturated fat 1g

Protein 1g

## Butterscotch Fudge

Preparation time: 15 minutes

Cooking Time: 0 minutes

Serving: 2

Ingredients:

- 1 cup of heavy cream

- 8 oz. of cream cheese
- 2 tbsp. of Splenda
- 1/2 cup of peanut butter
- One small box of butterscotch pudding

Directions:
1. Blend the heavy cream, cream cheese & sweetener together until very smooth.
2. Add the peanut butter to the mixture until smooth.
3. Add pudding mix until smooth.
4. Pour into sprayed 7 x 11 pans.
5. Place in the refrigerator and allow chilling for 2-3 hours.

Nutrition:

Energy 389.2kcal

Fat 7.2g

Protein 2.0g

## Ceviche

Preparation time: 10 minutes

Cooking Time: 15 minutes

Serving: 2

Ingredients:
- Shrimp (raw)
- Cilantro
- Onion
- Tomatoes
- Lime juice (fresh)
- Salt
- Pepper
- Garlic
- Jalapenos (optional)

Directions:
1. First, peel and wash all the shrimp.
2. Dice all the veggies and drop them in the same bowl along with the shrimp.
3. Add lime juice and add seasoning- salt, pepper, garlic powder to taste.
4. Let it sit for 10 to 15 minutes, and when shrimp is pink, it's ready to be served.

Nutrition:

130Cal. 8gCarbs. Seven %1gFat. 22gProtein

## Chicken Bacon Club Salad

Preparation time: 10 minutes

Cooking Time: 50 minutes

Serving: 2

Ingredients:
- Four boneless skinless chicken breasts
- 1 cup of Mayo
- Six slices of bacon
- 2 cups of shredded cheddar cheese

Directions:

1. First, cook the bacon until they become crisp, and then crumble.
2. Cube the chicken breast and cook thoroughly.
3. Mix all the ingredients.
4. Spread into an 8-inch cake pan.
5. Bake for about 15 minutes.
6. Serve on top of a bed of lettuce. Top with black olives if you like.

Nutrition:

416 •Carbs: 34g •Fat: 23g •Protein: 21g

## Chicken, Peas, Pecans & Grapes Salad

Preparation time: 10 minutes

Cooking Time: 50 minutes

Serving: 2

Ingredients:

- 3 cups of cooked chicken, diced
- 1/2 cup of red grapes, halved
- 1 cup of frozen peas
- 1/2 cup of pecan pieces
- 1/4 cup of red onion, chopped
- One hard-boiled egg
- 1/4 cup of mayo
- Salt and pepper to taste
- Romaine leaves

Directions:

1. Mix ingredients
2. Serve on romaine leaves.

Nutrition:

Calories: 327.3

Protein: 37.5 g

Dietary Fiber: 1.2 g

Total Fat: 15.8 g

## Chili Relleno With Or Without Chicken

Preparation time: 10 minutes

Cooking Time: 45 minutes

Serving: 2

Ingredients:

- 1 lb. of cheddar cheese (grated)
- 1 lb. of Monterey cheese (grated)
- 3 (7 oz.) cans of diced green chilies
- Five beaten eggs
- 2 to 3 chicken breasts (cooked and chopped, optional)

Directions:

1. First, mix the cheese cooked chicken and green chilies together in a suitable baking dish.
2. Pour the eggs all over the mixture.

3. Transfer to the oven and bake at 350 degrees for 45 minutes.

Nutrition:

300Cal. 14gCarbs. 20gFat. 15gProtein

## Chocolate Chip Muffins

Preparation time: 25 minutes

Cooking Time: 25-30 minutes

Serving: 2

Ingredients:

- 12 oz. box of Atkins Brownie mix
- 3/4 cup of oil
- Three eggs
- 1 1/2 cups of water
- 1 cup of Atkins Pancake Mix
- 1/2 cup of sugar-free chocolate chips

Directions:

1. Using a suitable bowl, beat together the eggs, oil, and water.
2. Add brownie mix; beat on low speed for about 1 minute.
3. Add the pancake mix; beat on medium speed for about 2 minutes.
4. Add the chocolate chips and mix thoroughly.
5. Divide into 24 paper-lined muffin cups.

6. Transfer to the oven and bake at 400 degrees for 25-30 minutes.

Nutrition:

130 grams. 419. Cal. . 73g. Carbs.

## Chocolate French Silk Pie

Preparation time: 20 minutes

Cooking Time: 0 minutes

Serving: 2

Ingredients:

- 1 cup of heavy cream (whipped)
- Three tablespoons of unsweetened cocoa
- 3/4 cup of artificial sweetener
- One teaspoon of vanilla
- 8 ounces of cream cheese

Directions:

1. Mix thoroughly until velvety smooth.
2. Transfer to the refrigerator and leave to refrigerate.

Nutrition:

Fat 261, Calories 420, Total Fat 29g

## Zucchini Crisp

Preparation time: 20 minutes

Cooking Time: 10 minutes

Serving: 2

Ingredients

- Two medium zucchini
- Salt and pepper
- 2 tbsp. olive oil
- 2 tbsp. grated parmesan cheese

Direction

1. Slice the zucchini into ¼ inch slices.
2. Brush both sides with extra-virgin olive oil.
3. Season it with salt and pepper. Add parmesan.
4. Set a baking sheet in a single layer and bake in a preheated 400 degree Fahrenheit oven for 10 minutes. Serve and enjoy!

Nutrition:

Calories: 15.2

Total Fat: 0.1 g

Dietary Fiber: 1.3 g

## Cinnamon Churros

Preparation time: 15 minutes

Cooking Time: 50 minutes

Serving: 2

Ingredients:

- 2/3 tbsp. coconut flour
- 1/8 cup almond flour
- 1/8 tsp. baking powder
- 1 large egg
- 1 tbsp. sugar substitute
- 2/3 tsp. ground cinnamon
- 1/8 cup unsweetened coconut milk
- 1/3 tbsp. unsalted butter
- Salt, to taste

Direction:

1. Prepare a fryer or deep skillet with 2-3 inches of oil.
2. Heat at 350 degrees Fahrenheit.
3. In a mixing bowl, combine the almond flour, baking powder, coconut flour, cinnamon, and salt.
4. In a saucepan, boil the coconut milk, butter, and sugar substitute.
5. Remove from the heat and add the flour mixture.
6. Stir until very thick. Cool for a few minutes. Once cool, add one egg and mix.
7. Drop balls of the mixture into the fryer.
8. Fry until golden brown and crisp, about 3 minutes long. That should make about 16 balls.
9. In a blender, pulse the remaining sugar substitute with one teaspoon of cinnamon.
10. Roll the balls into the cinnamon and sugar mixture until coated.

11. Place on a serving platter. Serve and enjoy!

Nutrition:

Calories 247 Saturated fat 0.3 g

Total Carbohydrate 81 g

Dietary fiber 53 g Protein 4 g

## Guacamole Bacon Stuffed Pepper Poppers

Preparation time: 20 minutes

Cooking Time: 10 minutes

Serving: 2

Ingredients:

- Eight bacon, chopped and crisped up
- 1 pound sweet baby peppers
- Two ripe Haas avocados
- Juice from 1 lime
- 1/2 chopped cilantro
- 1 tsp. chili garlic or hot sauce
- Salt, to taste

Direction

1. Preheat oven to 350 degrees Fahrenheit.
2. Prepare the peppers by cutting them lengthwise.
3. Place the peppers on a baking sheet and bake until tender, about 10 minutes.
4. Assemble the guacamole by mashing together the avocados, lime juice, hot sauce, cilantro, and salt.
5. Fill the peppers with the guacamole mix.
6. Top with bacon crumbles. Serve and enjoy!

Nutrition:

Calories: 65.6 Dietary Fiber: 0.4 g

## Tomato-Mozzarella Melt

Preparation time: 5 minutes

Cooking Time: 1 minute

Serving: 2

Ingredients:

- 1/4 cup shredded mozzarella cheese
- One medium tomato

Direction:

1. Cut tomato in half.
2. Place 1/2 of cheese on each tomato half.
3. Place in microwave for 30 to 60 seconds until cheese melts or under the broiler for 1 minute until cheese melts. Enjoy!

Nutrition:

Calories: 424 •Carbs: 12g •Fat: 34g •Protein: 36g

## Roast Beef, Red Bell Pepper And Provolone Lettuce Wraps

Preparation time: 10 minutes

Cooking Time: 0 minutes

Serving: 2

Ingredients:

- 4 oz. sliced roast beef
- Large lettuce leaves
- 1/2 tsp. prepared horseradish
- 2 oz. sliced provolone cheese
- 1/4 sliced red bell pepper
- 1 tbsp. mayonnaise
- Salt and pepper

Direction:

1. Lay lettuce leaves flat on a clean surface.
2. Top each with a slice of cheese.
3. Combine the horseradish, mayonnaise, and garlic powder.
4. Season with salt and pepper.
5. Spread onto cheese slices. Then place a layer of roast beef.
6. Cut the red bell pepper into ¼-inch thick strips.
7. Lay on one end of the cheese, lettuce, and roast beef.
8. Roll and secure with a toothpick. Serve and enjoy!

Nutrition:

44.5g Protein, 44.9g Fat, 1g Fiber, 603.5kcal Calories

## Chocolate Coconut Haystacks

Preparation time: 10 minutes

Cooking Time: 12 minutes

Serving: 2

Ingredients:

- 2 tbsp. unsweetened cocoa powder
- Two large egg whites
- 1 cup sugar substitute
- 2 cups grated unsweetened dried coconut
- 2 tbsp. sugar-free chocolate syrup

Direction

1. Heat oven to 325 degrees Fahrenheit.
2. Line baking sheets with aluminum foil.
3. Whip egg whites. Gradually beat in sugar substitute and cocoa powder.
4. Fold in coconut and syrup.
5. Drop mixture by rounded teaspoonful onto baking sheets.
6. Shape into pyramids.
7. Bake for 12 minutes.

8. Cool for 1 minute before transferring to wire racks to cool completely. Serve and enjoy!

Nutrition:

150Cal. 32g Carbs. 4g Fat. 1gProtein

## Cereal Treat

Preparation time: 10 minutes

Cooking Time: 2.5 minutes

Serving: 2

Ingredients:

- 5 cups crispy rice cereal
- 1/4 cup butter
- One package miniature marshmallows

Direction:

1. Grease a pan with butter or cooking spray.
2. In a microwave-safe bowl, combine butter and marshmallows.
3. Microwave on high for 2 minutes, stirring every 30 seconds, until smooth.
4. Remove from the oven and stir in the cereal.
5. Press into the pan with the back of a buttered spoon. Let the treats cool.
6. Cut into squares and serve. Enjoy!

Nutrition:

120Cal. , 26gCarbs , 1g Fat 1gProtein

## Spiced Coconut Bark

Preparation time: 10 minutes

Cooking Time: 10 minutes

Serving: 2

Ingredients

- 7 oz. sugar-free chocolate
- 1 tsp. ground cinnamon
- 1/8 tsp. ground chipotle or cayenne pepper
- 5 tbsp. unsweetened shredded coconut
- Kosher salt, to taste

Direction

1. Melt chocolate.
2. Stir in cinnamon and chipotle or cayenne pepper.
3. Stir in shredded coconut. Pour the mixture into the parchment paper, spread out evenly in rectangles.
4. Sprinkle shredded coconut on top.
5. Sprinkle a little bit of kosher salt.
6. Place in the refrigerator for 10 minutes, and then divide into 12 equal portions. Serve and enjoy!

Nutrition:

Calories: 120 •Carbs: 0g •Fat: 0g •Protein: 33g

## Double Chocolate Express Smoothie

Preparation time: 10 minutes

Cooking Time: 0 minutes

Serving: 2

Ingredients:

- 3/4 tsp. decaffeinated espresso powder
- 1/2 cup water
- 1 1/2 scoops chocolate powder
- 1 tbsp. unsweetened cocoa powder
- 3 tbsp. half and half

Direction

1. Combine the water, half-and-half, cocoa and espresso powders, protein powders in a blender. Add ice cubes one at a time.
2. Blend until smooth.
3. Pour into a tall glass and garnish with cocoa powder or drizzle with sugar-free chocolate syrup. Serve and enjoy!

Nutrition:

33.6 oz. 651Cal. , 129gCarbs. , 17gFat. 15gProtein

## Zesty Oven Baked Fries

Preparation time: 10 minutes

Cooking Time: 10 minutes

Serving: 2

Ingredients:

- Two large baking potatoes, peeled and cut into thin strips
- One tablespoon grated parmesan cheese
- One tablespoon oil
- 1/4 teaspoon salt
- 1/4 teaspoon garlic powder
- 1/4 teaspoon paprika
- 1/4 teaspoon black pepper

Directions:

1. Heat oven to 450°.
2. Spray a baking sheet with cooking spray.
3. Combine all dry ingredients and combine with potatoes, tossing to coat.
4. Drizzle with oil, tossing again to coat.
5. Arrange potatoes in a single layer on a baking sheet and bake for 35 minutes or until golden brown.

Nutrition:

Calories 312 Total Fat 15 g

Saturated fat 2.3 g Polyunsaturated fat 5 g

Protein 3.4 g

## Oven-Baked Carrot Fries

Preparation time: 15 minutes

Cooking Time: 20 minutes

Serving: 2

Ingredients

- 1 1/2 lbs. carrots
- One teaspoon sugar
- Two tablespoons olive oil
- 1/2 teaspoon salt
- Two tablespoons fresh rosemary, finely chopped
- One pinch pepper

Directions:

1. Heat oven to 425 degrees F. Line a shallow pan with foil.
2. Using a sharp knife, slice away the tip and end of each carrot; peel each completely.
3. Cut carrots in half crosswise, then cut lengthwise, then cut lengthwise again.
4. In a mixing bowl, combine the carrot sticks, olive oil, rosemary, sugar, salt, and pepper. Stir until all are evenly coated.
5. Place carrots in the pan, spreading sticks out as much as possible. Bake for 20 minutes or until carrots is tender.
6. Serve hot or at room temperature

Nutrition:

Calories: 136.3

Sugars: 8.9 g

Dietary Fiber: 4.9 g

Protein: 1.6 g

## Zesty Baked Fries

Preparation time: 10 minutes

Cooking Time: 50 minutes

Serving: 2

Ingredients

- 1/4 cup grated parmesan cheese
- One tablespoon olive oil
- Two teaspoons basil
- One teaspoon oregano
- One teaspoon garlic powder
- Four medium red potatoes

Directions

1. Mix the first five ingredients.
2. Cut potatoes in the sticks.
3. Toss potatoes with cheese mixture.
4. Place on a baking sheet coated with cooking spray.
5. Spray potatoes lightly with cooking spray.

6. Bake at 425* for 15 minutes, turn potatoes over, and bake 15 more minutes, until crisp.

Nutrition:

Calories 312

Total Fat 15 g

Saturated fat 2.3 g

Protein 3.4 g

## Baked Fresh Chili Fries

Preparation time: 20 minutes

Cooking Time: 18 minutes

Serving: 2

Ingredients

- 2 jalapeno peppers
- 1 1/3 poblano peppers
- 1/3 cup all-purpose flour, plus 2 tbsp.
- 1 egg, beaten
- 1/8 cup milk
- 2/3 tablespoons spicy mustard
- 1/3 cup breadcrumbs
- 1/8 cup parmesan cheese, grated
- 1/3 teaspoon garlic powder
- 1/3 tablespoon cajun seasoning
- salt and pepper

Directions

1. Preheat oven to 400. Remove seeds from peppers and cut into 1/2 inch lengthwise strips.
2. Set up a breading station: 1 pan of 1 cup of flour; 1 pan of beaten eggs with milk, 2 tbsp. flour, and mustard; and one pan of breadcrumbs seasoned with cheese, garlic powder, Cajun seasoning, and salt and pepper.
3. Coat the peppers in the flour, then in the egg mixture, and then in breadcrumbs. Arrange the chili fries on a nonstick baking sheet and roast for 18 minutes, turning once.
4. Remove from oven and serve.

Nutrition:

194calories, 4g fat, 37g carbs, 4g protein

## Spicy Baked Sweet Potato "Fries"

Preparation time: 25 minutes

Cooking Time: 20 minutes

Serving: 2

Ingredients

- Two medium sweet potatoes washed and cut lengthwise into strips 1/3 inch on each side
- 1 1/2 tablespoons olive oil
- One teaspoon ground cumin
- 1/2 teaspoon chili powder
- 1/4 teaspoon salt
- 1/2 teaspoon onion powder

Directions

1. Preheat oven to 450°F. With aluminum foil or parchment paper, line a cookie sheet.

2. In a medium bowl, combine sweet potatoes with olive oil and seasonings. Mix well to evenly coat potatoes. Place potato strips on the foil or parchment-lined cookie sheet and leave space between strips for even baking.

3. Bake for approximately 15 minutes or until potatoes become crispy. Turn strips every 5 to 7 minutes as needed. Serve immediately.

Nutrition:

Calories 86

Total Fat 0.1 g

Sugar 4.2 g

Protein 1.6 g

## Garlic Oven Fries

Preparation time: 25 minutes

Cooking Time: 50 minutes

Serving: 2

Ingredients

- 2 lbs. small russet potatoes, peeled and cut into 1/2 inch wedges
- Two tablespoons olive oil
- Two tablespoons butter
- 3 -4 garlic cloves, minced
- salt
- fresh ground white pepper

Directions

1. Preheat oven to 400 degrees.
2. Toss the potatoes with the olive oil.
3. Spread in a roasting pan and roast for 45 to 50 minutes, occasionally tossing until cooked through and golden brown.
4. Just before the potatoes have finished roasting, melt the butter in a small sauté pan.
5. Add the garlic and sauté over medium-low heat for 2-3 minutes, until garlic begins to soften.
6. Set aside.
7. Transfer the potatoes to a large serving bowl and drizzle the garlic and butter over them.
8. Season generously with salt and pepper and toss to combine.
9. Keep warm until ready to serve.

Nutrition:

Calories 312 Total Fat 15 g Protein 3.4 g

## Peppery Turnip "Fries"

Preparation time: 15 minutes

Cooking Time: 35 minutes

Serving: 2

Ingredients

- Four medium turnips (about 1 1/2 lbs.)
- 1/2 teaspoon grated nutmeg

- One teaspoon fresh ground pepper
- 3-4 tablespoons freshly ground parmesan cheese
- olive oil
- One tablespoon lime juice (optional)

Directions

1. Preheat the oven to 425 degrees F.
2. Lightly grease a large cookie sheet with olive oil.
3. Pare the turnips and cut them into 2 1/2 x 1/2 inch sticks.
4. Combine the spices, Parmesan, and turnips in a large plastic bag.
5. Seal and shake to coat.
6. Spread the posts in a single layer on the prepared pan and brush with a little olive oil.
7. Bake for 30-35 minutes, turning once until spears are tender and golden.
8. Serve with or without a sprinkling of lime.

## Oven-Baked Fries

Preparation time: 10 minutes

Cooking Time: 30 minutes

Serving: 2

Ingredients

- Eight russet potatoes, unpeeled, scrubbed well

- 1/2 cup extra virgin olive oil
- Two teaspoons sweet paprika
- coarse salt, to taste
- fresh ground black pepper, to taste

Directions

1. Preheat oven to 400. Cut the potatoes into lengthwise quarters, and then cut each piece in half crosswise. Place them in a bowl and toss with the olive oil, paprika, and salt and pepper.
2. Arrange the potatoes in a single layer on a baking sheet and bake until tender in the center and brown and crisp outside, about 30 minutes, shaking them once while cooking.
3. Carefully remove the fries with a metal spatula and pile them on a platter. Sprinkle with a little more coarse salt and enjoy with your favorite dipping sauce.

Nutrition:

Calories 312 Total Fat 15 g Protein 3.4 g

## Spicy 'Fries'

Preparation time: 10 minutes

Cooking Time: 35 minutes

Serving: 2

Ingredients

- 1 1/2 lbs. baking potatoes, scrubbed left unpeeled and julienned

- 1 ½ tablespoons olive oil
- Two teaspoons chili powder
- ½ teaspoon oregano, crumbled
- ½ teaspoon salt
- ¼ teaspoon pepper
- ¼ teaspoon cumin

Directions

1. Preheat oven to 450F.
2. Combine all ingredients in a bowl; toss well.
3. Arrange potatoes in a single layer on a foil-lined baking sheet.
4. Bake for 35 minutes or until golden and crisp.
5. Enjoy!

Nutrition:

Calories 312

Total Fat 15 g

Protein 3.4 g

## Baked Spicy French Fries (Ww Core)

Preparation time: 15 minutes

Cooking Time: 25 minutes

Serving: 2

Ingredients

- Two egg whites

- ½ teaspoon chili powder
- ¾ teaspoon ground cumin
- ¼ teaspoon black pepper
- ½ teaspoon table salt
- Two large potatoes

Directions

1. Preheat oven to 425 degrees F. Sprays a nonstick baking sheet with nonstick cooking spray.
2. In a large bowl, combine all ingredients; toss to coat. Transfer to the baking sheet.
3. Bake until potatoes are barely tender, about 15 minutes.
4. Increase the oven temperature to broil; broil until crispy, about 10 minutes. Serve at once.

Nutrition:

Calories 312

Total Fat 15 g

Protein 3.4 g

## Twice Baked French Fries

Preparation time: 10 minutes

Cooking Time: 15 minutes

Serving: 2

Ingredients

- Four russet potatoes peeled and cut into French fry strips.
- ¼ cup butter, melted

- salt and pepper
- garlic powder
- onion powder
- One dash cayenne pepper

Directions

1. Spread potatoes on lightly greased jelly roll pan and bake at 375° for 15 minutes.
2. Drizzle melted butter over (use more if needed to coat all of the potatoes).
3. Sprinkle liberally with salt and pepper, and then add other seasonings as desired.
4. Toss together to be sure all of the potatoes are coated with butter and herbs.
5. Return to oven until potatoes are crisp and tender.

Nutrition:

Calories 312

Total Fat 15 g

Protein 3.4 g

## Baked Sweet Potato Fries

Preparation time: 10 minutes

Cooking Time: 20 minutes

Serving: 2

Ingredients

- nonstick spray coating
- Four small sweet potatoes (about 1 lb.)
- One tablespoon margarine or one tablespoon butter, melted
- 1/4 teaspoon seasoning salt
- One dash nutmeg

Directions

1. Spray a 15x10x1-inch baking pan with nonstick coating.
2. Scrub potatoes; cut lengthwise into quarters, then cut each quarter into two wedges.
3. Arrange potatoes in a single layer in a pan.
4. Combine margarine or butter, salt, and nutmeg.
5. Brush onto potatoes.
6. Bake in a 450° oven for 20 minutes or until brown and tender

Nutrition:

Calories 312 Total Fat 15 g

Protein 3.4 g

## Sweet Potato Fries

Preparation time: 10 minutes

Cooking Time: 25 minutes

Serving: 2

Ingredients

- 1 lb. sweet potato

- One egg white
- Two teaspoons chili powder
- 1/4 teaspoon garlic powder
- 1/4 teaspoon onion powder
- 1/8 teaspoon salt

Directions

1. Peel and cut potatoes into 1/4 inch x 1/2 inch strips.
2. In a bowl, combine egg white and seasonings; beat well.
3. Add potatoes; toss to coat.
4. Spray two baking sheets with nonstick cooking spray.
5. Place potatoes in a single layer on the two baking sheets.
6. Bake, uncovered at 450 degrees for 20-25 minutes or until golden brown.

Nutrition:

Calories 312

Total Fat 15 g

Protein 3.4 g

## Oven-Baked French Fries

Preparation time: 15 minutes

Cooking Time: 40 minutes

Serving: 2

Ingredients

- One egg white, beaten until foamy
- One tablespoon chili powder
- 1/2 teaspoon crushed red pepper flakes
- Two large baking potatoes, skins left on, thinly sliced
- One large sweet potato, peeled, thinly sliced
- salt

Directions

1. In a large bowl or zipper storage bag, mix the egg white, chili powder, and red pepper. Add potatoes and toss together.
2. Coat a large cookie sheet with non-stick spray (or use non-stick aluminum foil). Spread potatoes in a single layer.
3. Bake 450' for 30-35 minutes or until potatoes are crisp and browned. Season with salt.

Nutrition:

Calories 312 Total Fat 15 g Protein 3.4 g

## Garlicky French Fries

Preparation time: 15 minutes

Cooking Time: 30 minutes

Serving: 2

Ingredients

- 1 (32 ounces) bag frozen French fries
- Three teaspoons vegetable oil

- ¾ teaspoon salt
- cooking spray
- Two tablespoons butter
- Eight garlic cloves, minced
- Two tablespoons fresh parsley, finely chopped
- Two tablespoons parmesan cheese

Directions

1. Preheat oven to 400°.
2. Combine first three ingredients in a large zip-top plastic bag, tossing to coat.
3. Arrange potatoes in a single layer on a baking sheet coated with cooking spray. Bake at 400° for 20 minutes or until potatoes are tender and golden brown, turning after 10 minutes.
4. Place butter and garlic in a large nonstick skillet; cook over low heat for 2 minutes, stirring constantly. Add potatoes, parsley, and cheese to pan; toss to coat. Serve immediately.

Nutrition:

Calories 312

Total Fat 15 g

Protein 3.4 g

# CHAPTER 17:

# Desserts

## Panna Cotta

Preparation time: 3hours 13 minutes

Cooking Time: 5 minutes

Serving: 2

Ingredients:

- 1/3 oz. gelatin powder, unsweetened
- 2 2/3 packets sweetener, sucralose-based
- 2/3 cups heavy cream
- 1/3 teaspoon vanilla extract
- Water

Directions

1. Grease 6 6-oz. cups lightly.
2. Place gelatin in 3 tablespoons of water and let it rest for 5 minutes.
3. Pour ½ cup water in a saucepan together with heavy cream, vanilla extract, and sweetener. Cook gently over medium heat and mix well.
4. Remove saucepan from heat before adding the gelatin mixture. Mix well, it melts.
5. Transfer the mixture into the prepared cups and cover the surface with a plastic wrap.
6. Store them in the refrigerator for at least 3 hours.

Nutrition:

Each serving contains 2.6 grams of protein, 29.6 grams of fat, 287 calories, and 3.7 grams of net carbohydrates.

## Raspberry Parfait

Preparation time: 5 minutes

Cooking Time: 0 minutes

Serving: 2

Ingredients:

- ½ cup heavy cream
- Two packets sweetener, sucralose-based
- 4 oz. mascarpone
- ½ cup raspberries

Directions

1. Whisk heavy cream.
2. Once soft peaks form, add sweetener and mascarpone. Continue whisking until smooth.

3. Divide the mixture equally into two parfait glasses. Place raspberries on top of each.

Nutrition:

Each serving contains 5.6 grams of protein, 2 grams of fiber, and 48.7 grams of fat, 470 calories, and 4.3 grams of net carbohydrates.

## Brownie Drops

Preparation time: 15 minutes

Cooking Time: 10 minutes

Serving: 2

Ingredients:

- 1/8 cup whole wheat pastry flour
- Two eggs
- Two tablespoons whole grain soy flour
- ¾ cup sweetener, sucralose-based
- Six tablespoons heavy cream
- ¼ teaspoon double-acting baking powder, straight phosphate
- Two tablespoons butter, unsalted
- 3 oz. baking chocolate squares, unsweetened

Directions

1. Set the oven to 375 degrees. Prepare a baking sheet lined with parchment paper.
2. Combine pastry flour, baking powder, and soy flour in a bowl. Mix well.
3. Place chocolate, butter, and cream in a bowl. Heat it in the microwave for about 2 minutes. Remove from heat and let it rest for another 2 minutes. Whisk until smooth.
4. Using an electric mixer, whisk sweetener and eggs together on medium speed for about 3 minutes.
5. Slowly add the chocolate mixture into the egg mixture and continue whisking until blended well.
6. Reduce the mixer speed to low and add flour mixture until well combined.
7. Using a teaspoon, place slightly rounded pieces of dough into the baking sheet. Cook in the oven for about 5-6 minutes.
8. Once done, transfer to a wire rack and let it cool.

Nutrition:

Each serving contains 2.5 grams of protein, 1.4 grams of fiber, and 9.4 grams of fat, 104 calories, and 3.9 grams of net carbohydrates.

## Chocolate Walnut Cookies

Preparation time: 20 minutes

Cooking Time: 6 minutes

Serving: 10 cookies for 2 persons

Ingredients:

- 1/8 cup whole wheat pastry flour
- 1/8 cup English walnuts, lightly toasted and chopped
- 2/3 tablespoons whole-grain soy flour
- 1/3 teaspoon vanilla extract
- 1/8 teaspoon baking soda
- 2/3 tablespoons butter, unsalted
- 1 1/2 tablespoons heavy cream
- 1/4 cup sweetener, sucralose-based
- 1 egg
- 1/2 oz. baking chocolate squares, unsweetened

Directions

1. Preheat the oven to 375 degrees. Prepare two baking sheets lined with parchment paper.
2. Place soy flour, pastry flour, and baking soda in a bowl and mix well.
3. Whisk sweetener and eggs using an electric mixer on medium speed until slightly thick.
4. Put the cream, chocolate, and butter together in a bowl. Heat it in the microwave for about 2 minutes. Let it rest for 5 minutes, then whisk mixture until smooth.
5. Slowly add the vanilla extract and chocolate mixture into the egg mixture while whisking.
6. Reduce the mixer speed to low and add flour mixture until well combined. Cover and refrigerate for 30 minutes.
7. Using a teaspoon, place slightly rounded pieces of dough on the baking sheet. Lightly press on the dough balls and place walnut pieces on top of each.
8. Cook for about 6 minutes and let it rest for a minute. Transfer into wire racks to cool.

Nutrition:

Each serving contains 0.9 grams of protein, 0.4 grams of fiber, and 3.2 grams of fat, 37 calories, and 1.3 grams of net carbohydrates.

## Caprese Salad

Preparation time: 10 minutes

Cooking Time: 0 minutes

Serving: 1

Ingredients:

- Five cherry tomatoes, sliced
- One tablespoon olive oil, extra virgin
- 2 oz. mozzarella, sliced
- One tablespoon basil, chopped

Directions

1. Combine mozzarella and tomatoes in a bowl.
2. Spread olive oil on top.

3. Garnish with basil.

Nutrition:

Each serving contains 10.1 grams of protein, 1.1 grams of fiber, and 27.4 grams of fat, 294 calories, and 2.3 grams of net carbohydrates.

## Baked Brie With Tomatoes And Nuts

Preparation time: 5 minutes

Cooking Time: 10 minutes

Serving: 2

Ingredients:

- 2 2/3 oz. brie pieces of cheese
- 1/3 tablespoon parsley, chopped
- 1/3 tablespoon sundried tomatoes, chopped
- 1/8 oz. pine nuts, dried

Directions

1. Preheat the oven to 450 degrees.
2. Remove the white rind from the top of the cheese.
3. Put the cheese in a pie plate
4. Combine parsley and tomatoes in a bowl. Mix well.
5. Distribute the tomato mixture evenly over the cheese. Sprinkle pine nuts on top.
6. Cook in the oven for about 10 minutes.

Nutrition:

Each serving contains 8.1 grams of protein, 0.1 grams of fiber, and 11.6 grams of fat, 138 calories, and 0.5 grams of net carbohydrates.

## Carrot Nut Muffins

Preparation time: 10 minutes

Cooking Time: 25 minutes

Serving: 6 muffins for 2 persons

Ingredients:

- 1/2 cup whole grain soy flour
- 1 teaspoons vanilla extract
- 3/4 cups sweetener, sucralose-based
- 1/2 cup almond flour, blanched
- 1 teaspoons cinnamon
- 1/2 cup carrots, grated
- 1/4 teaspoon salt
- 1/2 cup of vegetable oil
- 2 eggs
- 1/4 teaspoon double-acting baking powder, straight phosphate

Directions

1. Preheat your oven to 350 degrees. Grease a 12-cup muffin tin using a non-stick cooking spray and set aside.
2. Combine soy flour, baking powder, almond flour, salt, sweetener, and cinnamon in a bowl.
3. Place the remaining ingredients in a separate bowl and mix thoroughly.
4. Combine the two mixtures until blended well. Pour equal amounts of

the batter into the muffin tins. Cook in the oven for about 20-25 minutes.
5. Once done, place muffins in a wire rack to cool.

Nutrition:

Each serving contains 6.2 grams of protein, 2.1 grams of fiber, and 25.6 grams of fat, 282 calories, and 6.2 grams of net carbohydrates.

## French Quesadillas

Preparation time: 10 minutes

Cooking Time: 5 minutes

Serving: 2

Ingredients:

- 3 oz. boneless ham, cooked and sliced
- ¼ cup almonds, sliced
- One pear, sliced
- 4 oz. brie cheese, sliced
- Four tortillas, low-carb

Directions

1. Preheat your oven to 350 degrees.
2. Arrange the tortillas on a sheet pan. Place pear slices on top of the tortillas, followed by ham, cheese, and almonds.
3. Fold the tortillas and cook for about 5 minutes.

Nutrition:

Each serving contains 16.3 grams of protein, 6.1 grams of fiber, and 15.4 grams of fat, 245 calories, and 9.2 grams of net carbohydrates.

## Chocolate Coconut Smoothie

Preparation time: 10 minutes

Cooking Time: 25 minutes

Serving: 1-2

Ingredients:

- ½ of sizeable ripe avocado
- One ¼ cup of almond milk
- ¼ cup of coconut cream
- One tablespoon flax seeds
- tablespoons cacao powder
- One teaspoon MCT oil
- One generous tablespoon almond butter
- Sweetener to taste if necessary

Directions

Place all elements in a blender and pulse until creamy smooth. Serve.

Nutrition:

Calories 510

Fat 42.8 g

Protein 12.4 g

Carbohydrates 23.3 g

Fiber 16.5 g

## Mint Chocolate Smoothie

Preparation time: 15 minutes

Cooking Time: 30 minutes

Serving: 2

Ingredients:

- ½ cup of coconut milk
- Two tablespoons of chocolate collagen protein
- ½ ripe avocado
- 1 cup of water
- ½ cup of ice
- Four leaves of fresh mint
- Two tablespoons of shredded coconut
- One tablespoon of cacao butter

Directions

1. Place all of the elements in a food processor except for the collagen protein and shredded coconut.
2. Blend on high for one minute.
3. Now add in the collagen protein and pulse on low for five to ten seconds.
4. Top your smoothie with the coconut flakes. Serve and enjoy.

Nutrition:

Calories 552  Fat 44 g

Protein 26 g  Carbohydrates 10 g

Fiber 9 g

Sugar 2 g

## Coffee Cake Muffins

Preparation time: 10 minutes

Cooking Time: 45 minutes

Serving: 6 muffins for 2 persons

Ingredients for Batter:

- One tablespoon of butter
- Two eggs
- 1 ounce of cream cheese
- sweetener (approximately 1/5 cup)
- One teaspoon of vanilla extract
- ½ cup of almond flour
- ¼ cup of almond milk, unsweetened
- ¼ cup of coconut flour
- ½ teaspoon of baking powder
- 1/6 teaspoon of salt

Ingredients for the Topping:

- ½ cup of almond flour
- 1/6 cup of softened butter
- One tablespoon coconut flour
- 1/6 cup of sweetener
- ½ teaspoon of ground cinnamon

Directions

1. Preheat your oven to 350° F.
2. Put paper liners in a single muffin tin and spray with a little cooking spray.

3. In a blender or food processor, combine the batter ingredients well.
4. Place the batter equally in the muffin tin.
5. Now combine the topping ingredients in your blender or food processor and pulse until you achieve a crumb texture.
6. Sprinkle each muffin liner with batter with the crumb topping.
7. Place in the oven and bake for twenty minutes until the muffins are golden brown. Enjoy.

Nutrition:

Calories 222

Fat 18 g

Protein 7 g

Carbohydrates 3 g

Fiber 4 g

Sugar 1 g

## Atkins Almond Flour Pancakes

Preparation time: 10 minutes

Cooking Time: 45 minutes

Serving: 2

Ingredients:
- Four large eggs
- 4 ounces of almond flour (1 cup)
- 4 ounces of heavy whipping cream
- Four teaspoons of granulated sweetener
- ½ teaspoon of baking powder
- Two teaspoons of unsalted butter
- Pinch of salt

Directions

1. Separate the eggs.
2. In a bowl, mix the egg yolks, cream, sweetener, and salt until creamy smooth.
3. Combine the flour with the baking powder.
4. Add in the egg yolk mixture and whisk until amalgamated.
5. Beat the egg whites in a discrete bowl with an electric mixer until peaks are formed.
6. Now fold the egg whites into the pancake batter.
7. In a large non-stick skillet, melt the butter evenly.
8. Spoon in two tablespoons of the batter to form your pancakes.
9. Cook until the cakes are lightly browned on both sides.
10. Serve with butter, berries, maple syrup, or the topping of your choice.

Nutrition:

Calories 339 Fat 30 g

Protein 12 g Carbohydrates 7 g

Fiber 3 g

## Cinnamon Pancakes

Preparation time: 15 minutes

Cooking Time: 25 minutes

Serving: 2

Ingredients:

- Three eggs
- ½ cup of almond flour
- One teaspoon of cinnamon
- Two tablespoons of coconut flour
- ½ teaspoon of baking powder
- 1 or 2 tablespoons of granulated sweetener
- ¼ cup of milk
- Two tablespoons of coconut butter for the glaze
- One teaspoon of cinnamon for the glaze

Directions

1. Put all batter elements into a blender or food processor and blend until thoroughly mixed into a thick batter.
2. Rest the batter for ten minutes.
3. Preheat a greased skillet on low to medium heat.
4. Pour portions of batter of about ¼ cup. Shield the pan and cook for two minutes, then flip to cook the other side. Use all of the batters.
5. When you have finished cooking the pancakes, melt the coconut butter in the pan and add the cinnamon.
6. Add the milk, stir and drizzle on top of the pancakes.

Nutrition:

Calories 125

Fat 7 g

Protein 7 g

Carbohydrates 3.5 g

Fiber 3 g

## Bacon & Egg Muffins

Preparation time: 5 minutes

Cooking Time: 25 minutes

Serving: 2

Ingredients:

- 4 eggs
- 2/3 finely chopped scallions
- 1 2/3 ounces of cooked bacon
- 2 ounces of shredded cheese
- Salt
- Pepper
- Butter for greasing

Directions

1. Preheat the oven to 350° Fahrenheit.
2. With the butter, grease a muffin tin.
3. Chop the scallions and bacon and add in the bottom of each muffin tin.

4. In a bowl, whisk the eggs with salt and pepper.
5. Add in the cheese and blend.
6. Pour the egg mixture into the muffin tins on top of the onions and bacon.
7. Bake for twenty minutes and serve.

Nutrition:

Calories 336

Fat 26 g

Protein 23 g

Carbohydrates 2 g

Fiber 0 g

## 460. Strawberry & Lime Smoothie

Preparation time: 5 minutes

Cooking Time: 25 minutes

Serving: 2

Ingredients:

- 8 ounces of strawberries
- One can of coconut milk
- Two tablespoons of MCT oil
- ¼ cup of egg white protein powder
- One tablespoon of freshly squeezed lime juice
- ¼ teaspoon of sweetener
- One tablespoon of sunflower lecithin powder

Directions

Put all of the elements in a food processor and blend on high until creamy smooth. Serve and enjoy.

Nutrition:

Calories 480

Fat 46 g

Protein 8.1 g

Carbohydrates 21.2 g

Fiber 5 g

Sugar 11.8 g

## 461. Instant Pot Carrots Sweet And Spicy

Preparation time: 10 minutes

Cooking Time: 45 minutes

Serving: 1

Ingredients:

- One teaspoon Paprika
- 1 cup of water
- Two teaspoons Ground Mustard
- 1 lb. carrots
- ¼ cup Organic Blackstrap Molasses
- Two tablespoons Butter
- One teaspoon Cumin
- Two teaspoons minced Garlic

- Two tablespoons Stone Ground or Yellow Mustard
- Hot Sauce (to taste)
- Salt and Pepper (to taste)

Directions:

1. Cut your carrots the long way into quarters-and cut those down the middle.
2. Enhance one cup of water to the Instant Pot. Include the trivet or steam basket, and at that point, have your carrots. Put the lid on; ensure the valve is set to sealing.
3. Set the Instant Pot for Manual – High – 1 Minute. Release the pressure using the fast release technique.
4. Carefully put aside the carrots (which ought to be cooked through-you can test with a fork), and dump out the water.
5. Set the Instant Pot to Sauté.
6. Add in butter and molasses. At the point when the butter has softened, include the remaining ingredients and mix.
7. When everything is very much blended (should not take over a minute or something like that) off the Instant Pot and include the carrots once more into the pot.
8. Stir to coat the carrots with the sauce blend.

Nutrition:

Calories 552

Fat 44 g

Protein 26 g

Carbohydrates 10 g

Fiber 9 g

Sugar 2 g

## Cinnamon Sour Cream Coffee Cake

Preparation time: 10 minutes

Cooking Time: 45 minutes

Serving: 2

Ingredients:

- 1 cups of almond flour
- 1tablespoons of baking powder
- 1/8 teaspoon of baking soda
- cups of sugar substitute
- 1 egg
- 2teaspoons of cinnamon
- 1/8 teaspoon of salt
- 1/8 teaspoon of nutmeg
- 1/2 stick of butter (1/2 cup)
- 1/2 cup of sour cream

For the topping:

- 1/2 cup of almond flour
- 1/2 stick of butter
- 1/4 cup of coconut flour
- 1 teaspoon of cinnamon
- 1/4 cup of sugar substitute
- 1/4 cup of pecans
- 1/8 teaspoon of salt

Directions

1. Preheat your oven to 350° F.
2. Grease a 10-inch, spring-form cake pan with butter.
3. Begin by making the topping. In a bowl, mix the sugar substitute, coconut flour, almond flour, ground cinnamon, pecans, and salt.
4. Slice one butter stick into thin pieces. Add the details to the dry mixture. Mix to form crumbs and set aside.
5. In another bowl, mix the almond flour, baking powder, sugar substitute, spices, and salt.
6. Thaw a stick of butter and let it cool.
7. Now combine the melted butter with the eggs and sour cream, blending well.
8. Mixture the butter mixture into the dry mixture to create your cake batter. Mix well and spread in the cake pan.
9. Sprinkle the crumb topping over the batter.
10. Bake the cake for forty-five minutes to one hour. Allow the cake to cool and serve.

Nutrition:

Calories 283 Fat 28.5 g

Protein 5.9 g

Carbohydrates 7.1 g

Fiber 3.1. G

Sugar 1.9 g

## Cinnamon Chocolate Smoothie

Preparation time: 10 minutes

Cooking Time: 35 minutes

Serving: 1

Ingredients:

- ¾ cup of coconut milk
- Two teaspoons of cacao powder, unsweetened
- ½ ripe avocado
- One teaspoon of cinnamon powder
- sweetener to taste
- ¼ teaspoon of vanilla extract
- ½ teaspoon of coconut oil (optional)

Directions

Blend all of the ingredients in your blender or food processor and enjoy it.

Nutrition

Calories 300

Fat 30 g

Protein 3 g

Carbohydrates 14 g

Sugar 2 g

Fiber 10 g

## Cream Soda (Phase 1)

Preparation time: 10 minutes

Cooking Time: 5 minutes

Serving: 1

Ingredients:

- 1 cup diet vanilla soda
- 1 tbsp. heavy cream
- 2 tbsp. whipped cream cheese

Directions

1. Combine whipped cream cheese and heavy cream in a small bowl. Whip until combined and fluffy.
2. Spoon cream cheese and massive cream mixture into the bottom of a glass. Fill the rest of the glass with vanilla soda.

Nutrition:

150Cal., 36gCarbs

## Blackberry Yogurt Nuts (Phase 2)

Preparation time: 10 minutes

Cooking Time: 1hr minutes

Serving: 2

Ingredients:

- 1 cup plain, unsweetened Greek yogurt
- 10 Macadamia nuts
- 1/2 cup fresh blackberries

Directions

1. In a food processor, combine yogurt and nuts until paste forms.
2. Combine pasta and blackberries in a small bowl, mixing them gently until combined.
3. Lay coated blackberries out on a baking sheet in a single layer and refrigerate for 1 hour.

Nutrition:

Calories 43

Total Carbohydrate 10 g

Dietary fiber 5 g

Sugar 4.9 g

Protein 1.4 g

## Cherry Plum Bread Pudding (Phase 3)

Preparation time: 15 minutes

Cooking Time: 45 minutes

Serving: 2

Ingredients:

- 1 TBS. butter
- 6 slices whole-wheat bread, stale
- Three ripe plums, chopped
- 1 cup pitted cherries
- 2 cups unflavored almond milk

- Four eggs, beaten
- 1 tsp. cinnamon
- 4 TBS. cream cheese

Directions

1. Preheat oven to 350 degrees. Grease the bottom and sides of a 9"x13" pan with butter. Arrange torn chunks of bread over the bottom of the pan.
2. In a large mixing bowl, combine fruit, milk, eggs, cinnamon, and cream cheese. Whip together until well combined.
3. Pour mixture over bread, and bake for 45 minutes, or until the top is well browned.

Nutrition:

341 calories; total fat 11g; saturated fat 5g;

## Cream Cheese Energy Balls (Phase 4)

Preparation time: 2 hrs. and 20 minutes

Cooking Time: 0 minutes

Serving: 2

Ingredients:

- 1/2 cup cream cheese
- 12 Brazil nuts
- 1 cup shredded coconut
- Six fresh dates
- 4 TBS. oat bran

Directions

1. Combine cream cheese, nuts, dates, and oat bran in a food processor. Blend until completely incorporated.
2. Form into 1" balls, roll in coconut, and place on a cold baking sheet.
3. Refrigerate for 2 hours.

Nutrition:

Calories: 109.6

Dietary Fiber: 2.4 g

Protein: 2.5 g

Sugars: 7.1 g

## Classic Almond Flour Pound Cake

Preparation time: 30 minutes

Cooking Time: 50 to 55 minutes

Serving: 2

Ingredients:

- 1 cup Splenda
- 1 cup or two sticks butter, softened at room temperature
- 2 cups almond flour
- One teaspoon baking powder
- Five eggs, at room temperature
- One teaspoon vanilla extract
- One teaspoon lemon extract

Directions:

1. In a large bowl, cream one cup of Splenda and two sticks of softened butter well. After this, add five eggs one by one, beating well the mixture before adding in the egg.
2. Combine two cups of almond flour with one teaspoon of baking powder in a separate bowl.
3. Slowly mix the wet mixture into the dry one with continuous beating.
4. Add a teaspoon each of vanilla and lemon extracts. The same goes for the color of the cake; just add food color if desired.
5. Pour mixture into a greased nine-inch or ten-inch baking pan. A spring form pan or a round cake pan can be used. Bake for fifty to fifty-five minutes at 350°F.
6. Let it cool for about twenty to thirty minutes after baking. Top with cream cheese frosting if desired. Makes twelve servings.

Nutrition:

143Cal, 4gCarbs. 26gFat, 9gProtein

## Flourless Chocolate Pecan Torte

Preparation time: 20 minutes

Cooking Time: 30 minutes

Serving: 2

Ingredients:

- 2 cups unsalted pecans
- ⅓ cup of cocoa powder
- ¼ cup erythritol, if desired
- ½ cup or one stick melted butter
- ½ cup of water
- 1 cup sugar equivalent of artificial sweetener of choice
- Four eggs
- One teaspoon vanilla extract
- One teaspoon baking powder

Directions:

1. Preheat oven to 350°F.
2. Pulse two cups of unsalted pecans in a food processor until they are meal, but not as small as cornmeal.
3. Add one-third of cocoa powder, a cup of artificial sweeteners, and a teaspoon of baking powder into the food processor and pulse again. Also, add erythritol if desired.
4. After the dry ingredients, add half a cup of melted butter, another half cup of water, four eggs, and a teaspoon of vanilla extract and process until everything is combined well.
5. Grease an eight-inch or nine-inch spring form pan with cooking spray. Pour batter into the pan and bake at 350°F for about thirty minutes, or until a toothpick comes out clean when inserted in the middle of the cake. It is best to check if the cake is made twenty-five minutes after putting it in the oven.

6. Let it cook for another ten minutes. Serve with chocolate sauce if desired.

Nutrition:

340Cal. 28gCarbs. 25gFat. 4gProtein

## Chocolate Torte Cake

Preparation time: 20 minutes

Cooking Time: 25 minutes

Serving: 2

Ingredients:

For the torte: 1½ cups Splenda

- One teaspoon almond extract
- ½ teaspoon cream of tartar
- Six egg whites

For the chocolate cream filling:

- 1½ cups heavy cream
- ½ cup Splenda
- ¼ cup unsweetened cocoa powder
- ¼ cup Crème de Cacao
- ½ teaspoon vanilla extract
- ¼ cup slivered almonds, for topping, if desired
- Melted unsweetened chocolate or chocolate syrup, if desired

Directions:

1. Preheat oven to 300°F. For the chocolate cream filling, mix one and a half cups of heavy cream, one-half cup of Splenda, one-fourth cup of unsweetened cocoa powder, and one-half teaspoon vanilla extract in a medium bowl. Beat until the mixture is thick, and then add Crème de Cacao. Continue beating until stiff. Set aside.

2. For the torte, mix six egg whites with one teaspoon of almond extract and half a teaspoon of cream of tartar. Beat until soft peaks form. After this, slowly add a cup and a half of Splenda. Mix well.

3. Coat cookie sheets with cooking spray (or Pam). Put meringue on the cookie sheets, forming six-inch circles on each.

4. Put inside the preheated oven and bake at 300°F for twenty-five minutes or until meringue turns to light brown. Remove from cookie sheets immediately and let them cool for about ten to fifteen minutes.

5. On a plate, place one layer of meringue and top with a third of the chocolate cream filling. Repeat step until all meringues and chocolate cream filling are used.

6. Place inside the refrigerator overnight

7. Before serving, sprinkle slivered almonds and drizzle with melted unsweetened chocolate or chocolate syrup on top if desired. Makes ten servings.

Nutrition:

410Cal. 54gCarbs. 19gFat. Three %3gProtein

## Chocolate Angel Food Cake

Preparation time: 15 minutes

Cooking Time: 20 minutes

Serving: 2

Ingredients:

- 6 to 10 packets of Splenda
- Eight eggs, separated
- ¼ cup soy flour
- ¼ teaspoon cream of tartar
- 1tbsp. unsweetened cocoa powder
- One sachet of the fat-free cocoa mix (Swiss Miss Fat-Free with Splenda recommended)
- 1tbsp. chocolate-flavored protein powder

Directions:

1. Preheat oven to 350°F.
2. Beat eight egg whites in a medium bowl, slowly adding cream of tartar one-fourth teaspoon of cream of tartar. Add three packets of Splenda while beating the eggs and cream of tartar to a stiff but not dry consistency.
3. In another medium bowl, combine eight egg yolks with Splenda's remaining packets, the number of which depends on personal sweetness level preference. Add half of the fat-free cocoa mix sachet and half a teaspoon of the unsweetened cocoa powder. Mix well.
4. Combine one-fourth cup of soy flour with a tablespoon of chocolate-flavored protein powder and the remaining cocoa mix and unsweetened cocoa powder in a third bowl.
5. Take one tablespoon of the first mixture and combine it with the second. After mixing the combinations well, pour in the second mixture into the remainder of the first. Sift the dry mix over the combined yolk and white combination and fold them nicely. Coat a Bundt pan or a loaf pan with a cooking spray (or Pam). Pour the well-combined batter into the pan and bake it for twenty minutes at 350°F.
6. Let it cool for about twenty minutes. Top with peanut butter and chocolate frosting if desired.

Nutrition:

130Cal. 29gCarbs. 0 Fat. 3gProtein

## Cheesecake

Preparation time: 45 minutes

Cooking Time: 1hr to 40 minutes

Serving: 2

Ingredients:

For the crust:

- Two tablespoon sugar equivalent of artificial sweetener of choice

- Two tablespoons melted butter
- 1 cup almond meal

For the filling:

- Four eggs, at room temperature
- 1½ pounds cream cheese, at room temperature
- ¼ cup sour cream
- 1⅓ cups sugar equivalent of artificial sweetener of choice
- 1½ teaspoons lemon juice
- 1½ teaspoons vanilla extract

Directions:

1. Preheat oven to 375°F.
2. In a large bowl, combine two tablespoons of artificial sweetener, two tablespoons melted butter, and one-cup almond meal to form the crust.
3. Put mixture into a spring form pan and press to the bottom. Bake for eight to ten minutes, or until lightly browned and fragrant.
4. After baking the crust, decrease oven temperature to 350°F if using a water bath for baking, or increase to 400°F if not.
5. In another large bowl, beat one and a half pounds of cream cheese until fluffy.
6. Add four eggs, one-fourth cup of sour cream, one-third cups of artificial sweetener, one and a half teaspoons of lemon juice, and one and a half teaspoons of vanilla extract. Continue beating, scraping the bowl and beater's sides every time so that ingredients are fully incorporated.
7. After ingredients are well combined, scrape the bowl's sides and the beater more time and beat the mixture for another minute.
8. Pour mixture into the pan over the crust.
9. If using a water bath (at 350°F): Using foil, wrap the sides and the pan's bottom. Put the spring form pan in a bigger baking pan. Pour water into the baking pan, ensuring that water does not spill on the spring form pan where the cheesecake is. Bake for an hour to an hour and a half. When the center reaches 155°F or when the cake is firm, the center is slightly soft, removing the cheesecake from the oven.
10. If not using a water bath (at 400°F): Put the spring form pan on top of a sheet pan just in case the cream cheese filling drips. Put the cheesecake into the oven at 400°F, and immediately turn down the temperature to 200°F. Bake for an hour to an hour and a half. Check the temperature of the center after an hour. When it has reached 155°F or when the cheesecake is firm, the middle is slightly soft, removing the oven's cheesecake. (Note: An unglazed ceramic tile, brick, or a

pizza stone will help hold the heat in the range, ensuring an even temperature throughout the baking process. Put one of either three at the lower rack, if available, when not using a water bath in baking a cheesecake.)

11. Chill overnight in a refrigerator.
12. Top with chopped strawberries or raspberries if desired. Makes sixteen servings.

Nutrition:

Calories: 472 •Carbs: 54g •Fat: 18g •Protein: 20g

## 473. Pumpkin Cheesecake

Preparation time: 45 minutes

Cooking Time: 1hour and 40 minutes

Serving: 2

Ingredients:

For the crust:

- 1½ cups almond meal
- 4 tbsp. sugar equivalent of artificial sweetener of choice
- 4 tbsp... melted butter
- ½ teaspoon ginger, grated
- ½ teaspoon cinnamon

For the filling:

- Three 8-ounce packages of cream cheese, at room temperature
- One 15-ounce canned pumpkin
- Five eggs, at room temperature
- 1½ cups sugar equivalent of artificial sweetener of choice
- ½ cup heavy cream
- One tablespoon vanilla extract
- 2½ teaspoons cinnamon
- One teaspoon nutmeg
- ¾ teaspoon ginger, grated
- ½ teaspoon salt
- ¼ teaspoon cloves
- ¼ teaspoon allspice

Directions:

1. Preheat oven to 375°F. Put a parchment paper over the bottom of a spring form pan and tighten it around the sides. Butter the sides and the bottom of the pan with parchment paper. Wrap the outside of the pan with foil to avoid leaks.
2. In a large bowl, combine one and a half cups of almond meal, four tablespoons of artificial sweetener, four tablespoons of melted butter, half a teaspoon of ginger, and another half a teaspoon of cinnamon to form the crust. Pour the mixture into the spring form pan and press it to the bottom.
3. Bake the crust in the oven at 375°F for eight to ten minutes, or until

slightly brown and fragrant. After this, remove the crust from the oven and set aside. Lower oven temperature to 325°F.

4. In another bowl, beat one and a half pounds of cream cheese until fluffy, scraping the pan's sides and the beater while doing so.

5. Add one and a half cups of artificial sweetener into the mixture, along with two and a half teaspoons of cinnamon, a teaspoon of nutmeg, half a teaspoon of salt, a three-fourths teaspoon of ginger, one-fourth teaspoon of cloves, and another one-fourth teaspoon of allspice. Continue beating and scraping.

6. Add a can of pumpkin and a tablespoon of vanilla. Continue beating and scraping.

7. Add three eggs first and beat well for a minute, then scrape. Add the last two eggs and half a cup of heavy cream and beat for another minute. Set aside.

8. Put the spring form pan inside a slightly bigger baking pan. Fill the baking pan halfway with water to form a water bath.

9. Pour mixture over the crust in the pan and bake the cheesecake for about an hour at 325°F, or until the cheesecake is firm but slightly soft in the center.

10. Remove the cheesecake from the oven and let it cool for one to two hours at room temperature. Refrigerate overnight after cooling.

11. Remove the cheesecake from the oven and let it cool for about three hours at room temperature. Refrigerate for another three to four hours after cooling.

12. Makes sixteen servings

Nutrition:

Calories 321

Total Fat 23 g

Saturated fat 10 g

Sugar 22 g

Protein 6 g

## Strawberry Cocktail

Preparation time: 10 minutes

Cooking Time: 5 minutes

Serving: 2

Ingredients

- 4 – 5 overripe strawberries
- 1½ tablespoon full cream
- 1 cup pineapple juice
- Lime zest
- ½ cup vodka
- Lime – a few drops
- 1½ tablespoon sugar syrup (if needed)

Directions

1. In a mixer jar/blender, add strawberries, pineapple juice, and cream
2. Blend the mixture well to a juice consistency
3. Add vodka and lime drops to the cocktail
4. Serve with crushed ice in a salt rim glass decorated with strawberry and lime zest

Nutrition:

Calories 33 Total Fat 0.3 g

Saturated fat 0 g

Total Carbohydrate 8 g

Protein 0.7 g

## Frozen Coffee Slush

Preparation time: 15 minutes

Cooking Time: 0 minutes

Serving: 2

Ingredients

- 133 ml coffee brewed with water
- 1 Splenda (sweetener)
- 66 ml double cream
- 1/3 teaspoon vanilla extract

Directions

1. Pour the coffee and sweetener into ice cube trays and freeze hard.
2. Whip the cream and blend with other ingredients and refrigerate
3. Empty frozen coffee cubes into food processor and process into a chunky slush
4. Serve immediately

Nutrition:

Calories 0 Protein 0.1 g Caffeine 40 mg

## Vanilla Coconut Milkshake

Preparation time: 5 minutes

Cooking Time: 0 minutes

Serving: 1

Ingredients

- Vanilla Powder (sugar-free, about two tablespoons)
- 1 cup of coconut milk (225ml)
- Ice cubes

Directions

1. Place coconut milk, vanilla powder, and ice cubes in a blender
2. Blend it until it is smooth and creamy
3. Pour in a glass and serve it

Nutrition:

Calories 240. Total Fat 4.5g

Saturated Fat 3g Cholesterol 35mg

Sodium 85mg Total Carbohydrate 29g

## Carrot Juice / Carrot Milkshake

Preparation time: 5 minutes

Cooking Time: 0 minutes

Serving: 1

Ingredients Two big sized carrots

- Lemon juice from 1 lemon
- Sugar/sweetener – as per requirement

Directions

1. Wash and peel the carrot
2. Cut into small chunks
3. Put it in a blender with sugar/sweetener and milk (for a milkshake)
4. Blend it well with little water
5. Filter the carrot juice and add lemon juice to it. Mix it well. If you want to diluted juice, add more water

Nutrition: 60Cal. 3gCarbs. 1gFat. 8gProtein

Soups

## Mushroom Soup – Referred From Dr. Atkins Website

Preparation time: 30 minutes

Cooking Time: 30 minutes

Serving: 2

Ingredients:

- Two spring onions / green onions
- One diced onion
- 125g button mushrooms
- 3¾ cups chicken stalk
- 1 tbsp. sherry (Spain wine)
- Chili and soy sauce as required
- One-piece fresh and sliced ginger
- Chopped green chilies soaked in white vinegar, as required
- Salt as per taste
- Pepper powder, as required

Directions

1. Slice spring onions and mushrooms thinly
2. For stalk, boil the chicken in plenty of water (to which diced onions is added) till the chicken becomes soft
3. To the above stalk, add ginger and spring onion
4. Bring to boil and simmer for 20 minutes
5. Add mushrooms and simmer for 10 minutes. Remove the ginger from the soup, add sherry and seasoning to taste
6. Serve hot, along with chili and soy sauce and chilies soaked in vinegar

Nutrition:

Calories 39 Saturated fat 0.5 g

Total Carbohydrate 3.3 g Protein 0.7 g

## Spinach And Cucumber Soup – Author's Creation

Preparation time: 15 minutes

Cooking Time: 30 minutes

Serving: 2

Ingredients

- 3 cups spinach – washed and chopped
- 1 cup cucumber
- Water, as required
- 1 teaspoon butter
- ½ teaspoon black pepper
- ½ teaspoon cumin powder
- ¼ teaspoon ginger paste
- Lemon juice from one lemon
- Salt to taste

Directions

1. Put spinach and cucumber in a vessel and pressure cook it (for one whistle)
2. Remove the ship after the spinach and cucumber are cooked, and blend the contents
3. Heat butter in a pan, add black pepper powder, cumin powder, ginger paste, and salt
4. Add blended spinach, cucumber, and lemon juice to the pan
5. Cook on medium heat for 5 minutes
6. Serve hot

## Cheesy Omelet

Preparation time: 10 minutes

Cooking Time: 10 minutes

Serving: 1

Ingredients

- One finely chopped onions, medium size
- One finely chopped tomato, medium size
- Green chilies, optional
- 1 tbsp. virgin olive oil
- Two eggs, beaten
- ½ cup cheddar cheese
- Salt as per taste

Directions

1. Take a bowl and beat eggs in eat
2. Add a pinch of salt for taste
3. Add finely chopped onions and tomatoes to this
4. Heat a pan and pour the beaten eggs, onions, and tomatoes and spread it
5. Pour little olive oil on the sides
6. Sprinkle the cheddar cheese over the mixture and cook for a minute
7. Flip to the other side and also cook for a minute. Your omelet is ready to eat

Nutrition:

Carbs3 g. Dietary Fiber0 g. Sugar1 g. Fat16 g. Saturated30 g.

## B. Yellow Squash And Gruyere Frittata

Preparation time: 10 minutes

Cooking Time: 10 minutes

Serving: 2

Ingredients

- 2 tbsp. butter, divided
- Two medium yellow summer squash cut into ¼ inch rounds
- 1 tbsp. thinly sliced sage or basil leaves, tightly packed
- Ten large eggs
- ¼ cup of water
- ½ teaspoon salt, or according to taste
- ¾ cup shredded gruyere cheese

Directions

1. Melt one tablespoon butter in a 12-inch non-stick ovenproof skillet over medium heat.
2. Add squash and sauté for 8 minutes
3. Stir in sage/basil
4. Cook till the squash becomes tender with browned in spots or 1-2 minutes more
5. Meanwhile, arrange oven rack 6 inches from the heat source; heat broiler
6. Whisk eggs, water, and salt together in a bowl
7. Melt remaining tablespoon butter in a skillet and pour eggs on squash
8. Reduce heat to medium-low, cover, and cook until set on bottom and edges, but the top is still loose for about three minutes
9. Uncover and sprinkle cheese evenly on top
10. Broil frittata until just set, for about 1 minute. Cut in wedges to serve.

Nutrition: 22g Protein, 24.8g Fat, 0.1g Fiber, 319.6kcal Calorie

## Garden Fresh Salad

Preparation time: 10 minutes

Cooking Time: 50 minutes

Serving: 2

Ingredients

- 2 tbsp butter
- 1½ cup broccoli, cut into flowerets
- 1½ cup spring onion, cut into small pieces / diced
- 1 cup green pepper, cut into small cubes
- ½ cup tomato, cut into small cubes
- One small onion, cut into small pieces
- ½ teaspoon black pepper powder

- Salt as per taste
- Extra virgin olive oil
- Two eggs, optional
- 2 cup sour cream
- ½ cup cheddar cheese

Directions

1. Take a pan and heat butter
2. Sauté all vegetables and boil them for 5 – 7 minutes
3. Drain the extra water, which can be used for soups
4. Whip cream in a separate bowl and add beaten eggs (if required) with the cream
5. Pour the cream (with eggs) into the cooked vegetables
6. Add cheese and cook/bake for about 30 minutes, till it sets
7. Allow it to cool, cut, and serve

Nutrition:

Calories: 150 •Carbs: 11g •Fat: 10g •Protein: 2g.

## Sweet And Sour Broccoli Salad

Preparation time: 30 minutes

Cooking Time: 30 minutes

Serving: 2

Ingredients

- ½ cup sweet and sour sauce
- 1 cup broccoli flowerets, blanched
- 1 tbsp. sesame oil
- Black sesame seeds
- Handful roasted cashew
- Two stalks of scallions (spring onions)

Directions

1. Pour ¼ cup of sweet and sour sauce in a large bowl
2. Add broccoli and mix
3. Make sure the flowerets are evenly coated with sauce
4. Sprinkle with a tablespoon sesame oil and mix
5. Toss in a preferred amount of sesame seeds and some sweet and sour sauce if required
6. Add roasted cashew and mix thoroughly
7. Garnish with some scallions (spring onions) and one last stir

Ingredients:

- One tablespoon soy sauce
- One garlic clove (minced)
- Three tablespoon sugar
- One tablespoon rice wine / white vinegar
- One tablespoon ketchup
- ½ tablespoon sriracha (it is a sauce made of red chili pepper, garlic, vinegar, salt, and sugar)

Directions:

1. Take a bowl
2. Add soy sauce and add white vinegar
3. Add ketchup, sriracha mix, sugar, and minced garlic and mix well
4. Cover with clean wrap and microwave for two minutes, stirring at every 30-minute interval
5. After 2 minutes, remove from microwave and mix well

Nutrition:

One cup: 385 calories, 31g fat (4g saturated fat), 10mg cholesterol, 240mg sodium, 24g carbohydrate (17g sugars, 4g fiber), 7g protein.

## Lettuce And Grape Salad

Preparation time: 10-15 minutes

Cooking Time: 20 minutes

Serving: 2

Ingredients

- One head of lettuce chopped (of your choice)
- One cucumber, peeled and chopped
- 1 cup seedless white grapes
- ¼ cup of sweet, white onion
- 3-4 tablespoon of extra virgin olive oil
- One tablespoon fresh mustard, or more if you like it more flavorful
- Two teaspoons of honey (or to taste)
- Two teaspoons of fresh lime juice
- Salt to taste

Directions

1. Mix the ingredients for the dressing and keep for 10 minutes for the flavor to infuse
2. Mix the ingredients for the salad and toss with the dressing
3. Keep in a covered container in the fridge

Nutrition:

105Cal.

11gCarbs.

6gFat.

3gProtein

## Crustless Spinach, Onion And Feta Quiche

Preparation time: 20 minutes

Cooking Time: 25 minutes

Serving: 2

Ingredients

- 1/3 medium-sized onion, diced
- 2 ounces fresh express baby spinach (app. 200g)
- 1 large eggs
- 1/8 cup all-purpose flour
- 1/8 teaspoon baking powder

- Pinch of cayenne pepper (red chili powder)
- 1/2 cup non-fat milk
- 1/8 cup feta cheese (tofu can be used instead)

Directions

1. Preheat oven to 400 F
2. Lightly grease a 10-inch quiche or tart pan or a pie plate
3. In a medium frying pan, cook diced onion with a bit of vegetable oil or cooking spray over medium-high heat until translucent and tender
4. Add in fresh spinach and cook until just witted
5. Set aside to cool for a few minutes
6. In a large mixing bowl, whisk together eggs, flour, and baking powder
7. Whisk again by adding milk
8. Then, stir in spinach and onion mixture
9. Pour quiche base into prepared pan. Top with feta cheese
10. Bake for 25 minutes or until the center is set and the outer edge is golden brown
11. Let sit for 5 minutes, slice, and serve.

Nutrition:

Calories: 134.1

Protein: 10.3 g

Dietary Fiber: 2.2

## 3 Minute Chocolate Cakes Ingredients:

Preparation time: 10 minutes

Cooking Time: 1 minute

Serving: 2

Ingredients:

- 1/4 cup almond flour, 1 ounce
- One tablespoon cocoa
- 1/4 teaspoon baking powder
- Three tablespoons plus one teaspoon granulated Splenda or equivalent liquid Splenda
- Two tablespoons butter, melted
- One tablespoon water
- One egg

Directions

1. Mix the almond flour, cocoa, baking powder, and granulated Splenda, if using, in a 2-cup glass measuring cup.
2. Stir in the liquid Splenda, if using, butter, water, and egg. Mix well with a spoon or fork. Scrape batter down evenly with a rubber spatula. Cover with plastic wrap and vent by cutting a small slit in the middle.
3. Microwave it for 1 minute until set but still a little moist on top. Cool slightly and serve warm topped with whipped cream or cool completely and frost as desired.

## 3 Minute Wpi Chocolate Cake

Preparation time: 10 minutes

Cooking Time: 3 minutes

Serving: 2

Ingredients:

- 1/4 cup wheat protein isolate, 1 ounce
- Two tablespoons cocoa
- 1/4 teaspoon baking powder
- 1/4 cup granular Splenda or
- Equivalent liquid Splenda
- Two tablespoons butter, melted
- 1/4 teaspoon vanilla
- One tablespoon water
- One egg

Directions:

1. Mix the wheat protein isolate, cocoa, baking powder and cocoa, baking powder, and cup glass measuring cup.
2. Stir in the liquid Splenda, if using, butter, vanilla, water, and egg. Mix briskly with a spoon or fork. Scrape batter down evenly with a rubber spatula.
3. Cover with plastic wrap and vent by cutting a small slit in the middle. Microwave 1 minute until set, but still a little moist on top. Add a few seconds more if too wet. Cool slightly and serve warm topped with whipped cream or cool completely and frost as desired.
4. That has an entirely different texture than the original 3 Minute Chocolate Cake. It's more like a sponge cake. I added an extra tablespoon on cocoa to increase the chocolate flavor but didn't think to increase Splenda's amount. I believe the additional 1/8 teaspoon should be sufficient.

Nutrition:

225 •Carbs: 0g •Fat: 0g •Protein: 0g. 225

## Magically Moist Almond Cake

Preparation time: 10 minutes

Cooking Time: 35 minutes

Serving: 2

Ingredients:

- 3/4 cup butter, softened *
- 1 cup granular Splenda or
- equivalent liquid Splenda
- Four eggs
- 1/2 cup heavy cream
- One teaspoon vanilla
- 1 1/2 cups almond flour (5 ounces Honeyville brand)
- 1/2 cup coconut flour, sifted (2 1/2 ounces Aloha Nu brand)
- 1/4 teaspoon salt *
- Two teaspoons baking powder
- 1 cup water, optional (see my comments below)

Directions:

1. Put all of the ingredients in a medium to the large mixing bowl. Beat with

an electric mixer until well blended and creamy. If the batter is too stiff, you can beat in up to 1 cup of water to thin it a little.

2. Spread in a greased 9x13" pan. Bake at 350ē for 30-35 minutes until golden and firm to the touch.

3. Cool completely before serving. It's probably best to store this in the refrigerator because almond flour baked goods tend to get moldy quickly at room temperature.

Nutrition:

Calories181.6

Total Fat12.8 g

Saturated Fat5.1 g

Total Carbohydrate14.4 g

Sugars10.8 g

Protein3.9 g

## Simply Delicious Sugar-Free Cheesecake

Preparation time: 30 minutes

Cooking Time: 1hr and 30 minutes

Serving: 2

Ingredients:

For the Filling:

- Five 8-ounce packages of cream cheese softened
- 1-1/2 cups sugar equivalent
- substitute
- Three eggs
- ½ cup Fage Total Classic Plain Greek yogurt
- 1 Tbsp. lemon juice
- 1 ½ tsp. vanilla extract

For the crust:

- 1 cup almonds, whole
- 2 Tbsp. sugar equivalent substitute
- 4 Tbsp. butter, melted
- For the topping:
- 1 cup unsweetened, heavy
- whipping cream
- 2 Tbsp. sugar equivalent substitute Fresh fruit

Directions:

Making the crust:

1. Process nuts together until resembling coarsely crushed graham crackers. Mix almond meal, butter, and sweetener.

2. Press in bottom of a 9-10" spring form pan. Place in the fridge.

Making the Filling:

1. Heat oven to 325 degrees Fahrenheit.

2. In a mixer, beat cream cheese with sweetener on medium for about one minute. On low, add eggs, one at a time, until just blended. Finally, add Fage, lemon juice, and vanilla and beat until blended (10-30 seconds).

3. Pour into crust. Place a pan of water in the rack below the cheesecake. Bake until set, 1 hour 15 minutes-90 minutes. Cool on a rack for 15 minutes before moving to chill in the refrigerator.

Making the Topping:

1. Combine whipping cream with sweetener and beat in a mixer for 3-5 minutes, or until stiff peaks.
2. With a spatula, gently frost the top of the cheesecake with topping. Cover with fresh fruit.

Nutrition:

Calories325

Fat31g

Protein7g

Total Carbs6g

Net Carbs5g

Fiber1g

Sugar2g

## Walnut Brownies

Preparation time: 10 minutes

Cooking Time: 25 minutes

Serving: 8 brownies for 2 persons

Ingredients

- 1/2 cooking spray
- 2 Ounces sugar-free chocolate
- 1/2 cup unsalted butter
- 1 1/2 Tablespoons granular sugar substitute
- 2 large eggs
- 1/4 Cups soy flour
- 1/4 Cups water
- 1 1/2 Tablespoons chocolate extract (optional)
- Two teaspoons vanilla extract
- 1/2 cup chopped walnuts, toasted

Directions:

1. Line an 8x8 baking pan with foil and spray with cooking oil.
2. Preheat oven to 350 degrees.
3. Melt chocolate in the microwave and set aside.
4. Use a mixer set on high to blend butter and sugar until fluffy or about 4 minutes in a small bowl.
5. Turn mixer to low and beat in each egg.
6. Add in melted chocolate and mix well.
7. Add in soy flour, sugar, and extracts until smooth.
8. Use a wooden spoon or spatula to fold in nuts.
9. Pour mixture into the prepared pan and cook for 20 to 25 minutes.

Nutrition:

Net carbs per serving: 2.2 g

## Almond Cookies

Preparation time: 20 minutes

Cooking Time: 12 minutes

Serving: 2

Ingredients

- 1/2 cup butter, softened
- 4 1/2 ounces almond flour (1 cup plus two tablespoons)
- 1 cup granulated Splenda or equivalent liquid Splenda
- One egg
- 1/2 teaspoon vanilla
- 1/2 teaspoon almond extract
- 1/4 teaspoon baking soda
- 1/4 teaspoon cream of tartar
- About 32 sliced almond pieces

Directions:

1. Blend butter with a mixer on medium in a small bowl.
2. Add half the almond flour and the Splenda.
3. Add in remaining ingredients except for the almonds.
4. Beat in the rest of the almond flour.
5. Cover the bowl and place it in the refrigerator for 1 hour.
6. Roll the dough into 32 small balls and place them on a cookie sheet.
7. Top each ball with an almond slice.
8. Bake at 350 degrees for 10 to 12 minutes.

Nutrition:

Net carbs per cookie with granular Splenda: 2 g

Net carbs per cookies with liquid Splenda: 1 g

## Easy-Peasy Cheesecake

Preparation time: 10 minutes

Cooking Time: 4hrs minutes

Serving: 2

Ingredients

- 1/4 packet unflavored gelatin
- 1/4 cup of cold water
- 4 ounces cream cheese, softened
- 1/8 cup granular Splenda or equivalent liquid Splenda
- 1/4 teaspoon vanilla

Directions:

1. Place water in a microwave-safe bowl and sprinkle gelatin in.
2. Let sit for 5 minutes before putting in the microwave for 1 minute.
3. Stir until gelatin is completely dissolved.
4. In another bowl, beat together the cream cheese, Splenda, and vanilla.
5. Slowly blend in the gelatin.
6. Grease a pie pan.

7. Pour cream cheese mixture into pie pan and place in the refrigerator for 3 to 4 hours.

Nutrition:

Net carbs per serving with granular Splenda: 3 g

Net carbs per serving with liquid Splenda: 2 g

## Peanut Butter Cookies

Preparation time: 10 minutes

Cooking Time: 10-12 minutes

Serving: 2

Ingredients

- 1 cup creamy or crunchy peanut butter
- 1 1/3 cups granular Splenda or equivalent liquid Splenda
- One egg
- One teaspoon vanilla
- Extra granulated Splenda for fork

Directions:

1. Place a sheet of parchment paper on a baking sheet.
2. In a small mixing bowl, blend all ingredients.
3. Roll the dough into 20 balls and place them on the cookie sheet.
4. Dip the fork in the sugar and use it to press down the dough into a cookie shape.
5. Bake at 350 degrees for 10 to 12 minutes.

Nutrition:

Net carbs per cookies with granular Splenda: 3 g

Net carbs per cookie with liquid Splenda: 1.5 g

## Chocolate Frosty

Preparation time: 10 minutes

Cooking Time: 0 minutes

Serving: 2

Ingredients:

- 1/2 Cups water
- 2 Tablespoons heavy cream
- 2 Tablespoons sugar-free chocolate syrup

Directions:

1. Place ingredients in a blender and drop in 3 ice cubes.
2. Blend until smooth and frothy.

Nutrition:

Net carbs: 0.8g

## No-Bake Cookies

Preparation time: 20 minutes

Cooking Time: 0 minutes

Serving: 2

Ingredients:

- One tablespoon butter
- Three tablespoons heavy cream
- Two teaspoons cocoa
- Liquid Splenda equal to 2/3 cup sugar
- One tablespoon natural peanut butter
- Two tablespoons oats
- 1/4 cup unsweetened coconut
- 1/4 cup almond flour, 1 ounce
- 1/4 teaspoon vanilla

Directions:

1. In a small pot over medium heat, bring the butter, cream, Splenda, and cocoa to a boil.
2. Boil one minute and then add in peanut butter.
3. Mix in remaining ingredients.
4. Remove from heat.
5. Drop by spoonful's onto wax paper.
6. Shape into cookies if necessary.
7. Allow chilling in the refrigerator until firm.

Nutrition:

Net carbs per cookie: 1 g

## Raspberry Smoothie

Preparation time: 10 minutes

Cooking Time: 0 minutes

Serving: 2

Ingredients

- 1/2 Cups unsweetened coconut milk
- 4 Ounces silken tofu
- 1/2 Cups fresh raspberries, plus more for garnish
- 2 Teaspoons granular sugar substitute
- 1/8 Teaspoons coconut extract to taste

Directions

1. Put all ingredients into a blender.
2. Add an ice cube and blend.
3. Add two more ice cubes and blend until smooth.

Nutrition:

Net carbs: 3.5g

## Pecan Macaroons

Preparation time: 10 minutes

Cooking Time: 10 minutes

Serving: 2

Ingredients

- Two egg whites
- 1/4 cup granular Splenda or equivalent liquid Splenda
- 1/4 teaspoon vanilla
- Pinch salt
- 1 cup ground pecans, toasted

Directions

1. Beat egg whites until foaming.
2. Beat in salt, Splenda, and vanilla until stiff peaks form.
3. Use a spatula to fold in pecans.
4. Drop spoonful on a greased cookie sheet and cook 8 to 10 minutes at 375 degrees.

Nutrition:

Net carbs per cookie: 1g

## Chocolate Cake

Preparation time: 3 minutes

Cooking Time: 1 minute

Serving: 2

Ingredients:

- 1/4 C Soy Flour
- 1 T Cocoa Powder
- 1/four t Baking Powder
- 5 Packets Splenda
- 2 T Melted Butter
- 1 T Water
- 1 Egg

Directions:

1. Blend nicely left column in 2-Cup Pyrex baking dish (flour, cocoa, baking powder, Splenda).
2. Add water, melted butter, and egg. Blend thoroughly with a fork.
3. Cover with plastic wrap (To vent, reduce small slit in center of plastic wrap). Microwave on high for 1 minute or until
4. The knife comes out clean. Cool a bit; eat warm with whipped cream or cool absolutely to ice.

## Lemon Cream Pie

Preparation time: 10 minutes

Cooking Time: 30 minutes

Serving: 2

Ingredients:

Crust:

- half C floor nuts (macadamias or walnuts)
- Two packets Splenda
- 1/4 C bake mix

- 3 T melted butter

Filling:

- 1/2 Pint (eight FL oz.) heavy cream
- One package deal sugar-loose Lemon Jell-O
- 3/4 C water
- One packet Splenda

Directions:

Crust:

1. Chop nuts in a food processor or utilizing hand.
2. Try to get as best a grind as viable without turning them to butter.
3. Combine nuts, bake mix, and Splenda in a bowl.
4. Add in melted butter and blend till you have a crumbly aggregate that will hold its form if pressed collectively (you could not want the entire three T of butter).
5. Grease a pie dish (7-eight" works best), and pour in crust mixture.
6. Press firmly into the bottom and facets of the pan, developing the side about 2".
7. Bake this in a 300 F Degree preheated oven for approximately 10-14 minutes, until it merely slightly begins to darken (careful - do not over bake).
8. Remove from oven and cool.

Filling:

1. Heat 3/4 C water in a small saucepan. When boiling, upload the bundle of Jell-O.
2. Stir to dissolve completely, and then take off the heat.
3. Chill till the Jell-O liquid is cold but not beginning to set (about 20 minutes in the fridge).
4. Pour 3/4 C of heavy cream into a calming bowl (the alternative 1/4 C will be whipped for a topping. However, this is to be done merely before serving).
5. Beat until very stiff peaks form. Add the chilled Jell-O liquid to the whipped cream.
6. Beat for a few seconds, just sufficient to thoroughly blend.
7. Pour the filling into the cooled pie crust and unfold to shape an even pinnacle.
8. Place inside the fridge and relax for at least three hours.
9. Just before serving, beat the remaining 1/4 C of heavy cream, including Splenda, to taste.
10. Cut the pie into portions and serve with a dollop of whipped cream.

Nutrition:

Calories: 317.5

Saturated Fat: 8.2 g

Total Fat: 16.3 g

## Pumpkin Squares

Preparation time: 10 minutes

Cooking Time: 25 minutes

Serving: 2

Ingredients:

- 1 cup Atkins or Keto Pancake/Waffle Mix
- 1 cup Splenda
- One teaspoon baking powder
- 1/2 teaspoon baking soda
- Two teaspoon floor cinnamon
- half teaspoon floor ginger
- One teaspoon ground cloves
- If you do no longer have these
- Three spices, you could substitute
- Tablespoon of Pumpkin pie spice.
- 1/4 cup chopped nuts(non-obligatory)
- 1/2 vegetable oil
- 1 cup canned pumpkin
- Two massive eggs
- Optional Cream cheese topping
- four oz. Softened cream cheese
- 2 Tablespoons Splenda
- 1/2 teaspoon vanilla flavoring

Directions:

1. Preheat oven to 350 tiers.
2. Mix eggs, oil, and sugar collectively nicely.
3. Add pumpkin and stir again.
4. Add final elements and mix for approximately 1 minute.
5. This batter may be beaten through hand if preferred.
6. Pour into a lightly sprayed and dusted 9x9 rectangular pan.
7. Bake for 22 -25 minutes or till a toothpick inserted comes out easy.
8. Allow cooling! For the non-obligatory topping, mix cream cheese, Splenda, and vanilla. Spread onto cooled cake. Cut into 16 squares.

Nutrition: Calories 26 Total Fat 0.1 g

Saturated fat 0.1 g

Total Carbohydrate 7 g

Protein 1 g

## Chocolate Walnut Cake With Chocolate Fudge Frosting

Preparation time: 40 minutes

Cooking Time: 25 minutes

Serving: 2

Ingredients:

- ½ lb. Walnuts

- ½ c. Cake-Ability
- ½ c. Cocoa
- ¾ c. Splenda, granular shape
- 2 t. Vanilla extract½ c. + 3 T. Canola oil, divided
- 2 T. + 1 c. Water, divided
- three eggs
- three oz. Steels Gourmet Chocolate Fudge Sauce

Directions:

1. Preheat oven to 350°F. Grease an eight or 9-inch spherical baking pan.
2. Grind walnuts to quality in Vita-Mixer.
3. Pour into blending bowl and upload Cake-Ability, cocoa, Splenda, vanilla extract, ½ c. Canola oil and 2T. Water and blend till mixed.
4. In a bowl, combine eggs with ultimate water and canola oil and beat briefly.
5. Slowly pour into mixer bowl while it is on blending at medium speed.
6. Blend till clean.
7. Pour into organized baking pan and bake for 25 minutes, or until knife inserted in center of the cake comes out smooth.
8. Remove from the oven. Allow cake to cool entirely within the pan, and then put off and placed on a plate.
9. Frost pinnacle of cake with Steel's Gourmet Chocolate Fudge Sauce.

Nutrition:

190Cal. 45gCarbs

23gFat 10gProtein

## Fluffy Cream Cheese Frosting

Preparation time: 10 minutes

Cooking Time: 0 minutes

Serving: 2

Ingredients:

- 1 pound softened cream cheese
- 2 tbsp. xanthan gum
- 1/2 stick softened butter
- 1/2 tsp. liquid Splenda

Directions:

1. Beat cream cheese & butter together, sprinkle on xanthan gum very slowly as you are beating it.
2. Spread on cake...Especially my zucchini cake recipe.

## Yellow Angel Food Cake

Preparation time: 40 minutes

Cooking Time: 1hour and 30 minutes

Serving: 2

Ingredients:

- 1/4 cup soy flour
- 2/three cup synthetic sweetener
- 4 egg yolks

- 6 egg whites 1 teaspoon cream of tartar
- 1/4 teaspoon salt
- 1 teaspoon vanilla
- 3 tablespoons water

Directions:
1. Preheat oven to 300f.
2. Spray a Bundt pan with cooking spray very properly.
3. Whip egg whites with cream of tartar till stiff peaks shape.
4. In some other bowl mix the alternative substances with simply enough water to shape a batter.
5. Fold batter in the egg whites then pour into pan. Bake on 275 for 1 & half hours. Don't permit it get too brown.

## Suisse Buttercream Frosting

Preparation time: 10 minutes

Cooking Time: 0 minutes

Serving: 2

Ingredients:
- 1 cup egg replacement
- 3/4 cup synthetic sweetener
- 1/4 teaspoon cream of tartar
- 1 teaspoon vanilla extract
- 1 half of cups unsalted butter -- softened

Directions:
1. In a massive bowl, beat softened butter until creamy Beat the egg substitute and cream of tartar on high speed, regularly including Splenda as you beat, till you have soft peaks.
2. Add the meringue in huge dollops to the butter and beat until easy and creamy.
3. Add paste coloring for your liking.

## Sponge Cake /Lemony Cream Cheese Frosting

Preparation time: 40 minutes

Cooking Time: 30 minutes

Serving: 2

Ingredients:
- 2 jumbo eggs -- separated
- 1/2 dash cream of tartar
- 3 1/2 packets sweetener
- 1 tablespoons vanilla extract
- 1 teaspoon grated lemon peel
- 1 tablespoon lemon juice
- 2 tablespoons Atkins Bake Mix
- 2 tablespoons heavy cream Frosting
- 1 1/2 ounces cream cheese -- room temperature
- 1 1/2 tablespoons heavy cream
- 1/2 tablespoon butter -- room temperature
- 2 packets sweetener
- 1/4 teaspoon vanilla
- 1/2 tablespoon lemon juice

Directions:

1. Preheat oven to 325f.
2. Spray a 9" square cake pan with butter taste cooking spray.
3. Beat egg whites till stiff with cream of tartar.
4. In some other bowl, beat final cake elements till clean.
5. Pour over overwhelmed whites and gently
6. Fold in, being careful not to interrupt the whites down too much.
7. Bake in a 325f oven for approx. 30 minutes or till browned throughout on pinnacle and puffy. .
8. Remove from oven and allow cool to room temperature. (Cake will fall inside the middle).
9. To make frosting, beat room temp butter and cream cheese until easy.
10. Add closing substances and beat properly.
11. Spread over cooled cake.

## Spice & Nut Cake

Preparation time: 40 minutes

Cooking Time: 40 minutes

Serving: 6 slices of cakes for 2 persons

Ingredients:

- 1/2 cup 0 carb soy protein isolate
- 1/4 cup flax meal
- 1/8 cup wheat gluten
- 2 teaspoons baking soda
- 1/4 teaspoon salt
- 1 tablespoons cinnamon
- 1/2 tablespoon vanilla extract
- 1/4 cup oil
- 1 eggs -- unbeaten
- 1/4 cup chopped walnuts
- 1 tablespoons heavy cream
- 1/4 of cup synthetic sweetener
- 2 teaspoons liquid saccharin

Cream Cheese Frosting

- 4 oz. cream cheese -- softened
- 1/2 stick butter -- softened
- 1/4 cup artificial sweetener
- 2 teaspoons liquid saccharin
- 1 tablespoons vanilla extract
- 1/2 teaspoon cinnamon

Directions:

1. Preheat oven to 350.
2. Mix all cake components together by way of hand; this comes out very thick, gloppy & sticky.
3. In an extra-large cake pan (in case you don't have a huge pan use 2 or 3 smaller pans),
4. Location parchment paper and spray with Pam, positioned combination into pan and spread out so it is no extra than 1/3" thick (if it's miles too think it doesn't flavor proper) it's going to sing his own praises to over 1/2 thick.
5. Bake at 350¼ for 25-40 minutes. (Relying on altitude) till knife comes out smooth. Cut into 1" rectangular

pieces (this is very rich), makes approximately 25-30 servings.

6. Frost with Cream cheese frosting.

Frosting:

1. Cream all frosting ingredients together,
2. Add more sweetener or extract on your taste, and spread on top of warm cake and allow to cool.

## Quick Pie Crust

Preparation time: 20 minutes

Cooking Time:10 minutes

Serving: 2

Ingredients:

- 1/4 cup Atkins Bake Mix
- half cup pecan meal
- 1/4 cup unsweetened coconut meat
- 1/4 cup butter -- melted

Directions:

1. Combine elements and mix nicely.
2. Press into pie plate.
3. Bake at 350degrees F for 10 minutes.
4. Fill with your favored filling mine is sugar free lemon jells with 8 oz. Of cream cheese
5. Combined in NOTES: Counts for pecan meal no longer included in totals

## Raspberries Smoothie

Preparation time: 15 minutes

Cooking Time:0 minutes

Serving: 2

Ingredients

- 125 ml of full-fat coconut milk
- 250 ml of cold tea
- 100g of raspberries

Directions:

Place all the ingredients in a high speed blender and blend until smooth.

Nutritional values:

Fat 14 g, Carbohydrates 8 g, Proteins 2 g.

## Blueberry Smoothie

Preparation time: 15 minutes

Cooking Time:0 minutes

Serving: 2

Ingredients

- 125 ml of full-fat coconut milk
- 100 g frozen wild blueberries
- 1 scoop keto collagen powder
- 2 tablespoon almond butter

Directions:

Place all the ingredients in a high speed blender and blend until smooth.

Nutrition:

Fat 16 g, Carbohydrates 7 g,

Proteins 2 g.

## Strawberry Smoothie

Preparation time: 10 minutes

Cooking Time: 0 minutes

Serving: 2

Ingredients

- 400 g full-fat coconut milk
- 150 g fresh strawberries, sliced
- 1 tablespoon lime juice
- ½ teaspoon vanilla extract

Directions:

Place all the ingredients in a high speed blender and blend until smooth.

Nutrition:

Fat 42 g,

Carbohydrates 10 g,

Proteins 5 g.

## Raspberry Smoothie And Avocado

Preparation time: 20 minutes

Cooking Time: 0 minutes

Serving: 2

Ingredients

- 70 grams of frozen and unsweetened raspberries.
- 3 tablespoons lemon juice.
- 1 tablespoon of Truvia sweetener (if needed)
- 1/2 ripe avocado.
- 100 ml unsweetened almond milk

Directions:

Add all the ingredients in the blender and mix until you get a smooth texture.

Nutrition:

Net carbs per serving: 8 grams.

## Chocolate Smoothie

Preparation time: 20 minutes

Cooking Time: 0 minutes

Serving: 2

Ingredients

- 100 ml unsweetened almond milk
- 1 tablespoon coconut oil
- 1 tablespoon almond butter
- 1 scoop chocolate keto protein powder or -collagen protein plus 1 tablespoon MCT oil- or chocolate bone broth protein
- 5 to 8 ice cubes

Directions:

Place all the ingredients in a high speed blender and blend until smooth.

# Conclusion

The benefits of the diet are immeasurable. You can always use this diet to lose weight but also to keep your immune system more robust. You will avoid many of the diseases and infections that the people of our time are exposed to. You may wonder how you will stick to this diet when you live in such a fast-paced world. But do not worry. You will find a grocery list to help you finish shopping for the food in this diet in an hour!

These recipes cater to the needs of the diet. You will find that most of the food in this diet has low amounts of sugar and carbohydrates. That is because of the objective of the diet. These recipes leave your mouth watering

I hope you enjoyed reading it!

Made in the USA
Columbia, SC
30 December 2020